BECOMING
HOLYFIELD

ALSO BY LEE GRUENFELD

The Halls of Justice

The Street

The Expert

All Fall Down

Irreparable Harm

Confessions of a Master Jewel Thief

Writing as "Troon McAllister"

The Green

The Foursome

Scratch

Barranca

The Kid Who Batted 1.000

BECOMING HOLYFIELD

A Fighter's Journey

EVANDER HOLYFIELD

WITH LEE GRUENFELD

ATRIA BOOKS

New York • London • Toronto • Sydney

ATRIA BOOKS

A Division of Simon & Schuster, Inc.
1230 Avenue of the Americas
New York, NY 10020

First Atria Books hardcover edition February 2008

ATRIA BOOKS and colophon are trademarks of Simon & Schuster, Inc.

For information about special discounts for bulk purchases,
please contact Simon & Schuster Special Sales at 1-800-456-6798
or business@simonandschuster.com.

Designed by Dana Sloan

Manufactured in the United States of America

1   3   5   7   9   10   8   6   4   2

Library of Congress Cataloging-in-Publication Data

Holyfield, Evander.
Becoming holyfield : a fighter's journey / by Evander Holyfield
with Lee Gruenfeld.
p. cm.
"Atria non fiction original hardcover."
1. Holyfield, Evander. 2. Boxers (Sports)—United States—Biography.
I. Gruenfeld, Lee. II. Title.

GV1132.H69A3 2008
796.83092—dc22
[B]
2007017686

ISBN-13: 978-1-4165-3486-0 (alk. paper)
ISBN-10:   1-4165-3486-5 (alk. paper)

For Annie Laura Holyfield
and Carter Morgan

CONTENTS

CONTENTS

BECOMING HOLYFIELD

PART I

Amateur

Prologue

Atlanta, 1978

The kid's name was Stevie Kirwood, and he wasn't bad at all: a quick left hand, light on his feet and a couple of years of ring savvy so that the usual tricks you can play on a rookie wouldn't work.

Try as I might, I couldn't put Stevie down; his reflexes were too good and he was reading me too well. So even though I landed a lot of punches, not many were good solid hits. Stevie would see them coming, and while he couldn't get completely out of the way, he'd duck or twist or sidestep enough to keep himself from getting too hurt.

On the other hand, he was spending nearly all his time protecting himself and hardly laid a glove on me. I was getting a nice workout while racking up points with the judges and could coast to an easy victory, but that's not how I liked to do things. I threw everything I could against Stevie, but he was still standing when the bell signaled the end of the third round, which is as far as amateur fights go. Barely standing, anyway: He was completely exhausted and hardly had the strength to come to the middle of the ring for the decision.

With the ref between us, a hand on each of our arms, we waited for the official announcement. I knew the standard language and lip-synced it in my head along with the announcer: "The winner, by decision . . . Stevie Kirwood!"

Wait a minute. Who? Stevie Kirwood?

I turned to the ref, my eyes wide and my jaw hanging open. Was he kidding? Had he gotten our names mixed up? But there was Stevie, arms raised high, dancing away toward his smiling corner men. Someone who'd never seen a boxing match in his entire life and had watched this fight from half a mile away through dark glasses would know I'd won, and they gave it to Stevie?

I screamed at the judges and spat on them. I grabbed the ref, picked him up and threw him out of the ring and into the third row of chairs. I climbed up onto the ropes, raised my arms and yelled to the audience that I'd won the fight, and then I went on television and wrote letters to every sportswriter in Atlanta.

Actually, I didn't do any of those things. I just stood there for a second, fighting to keep the pain and humiliation from my face, and then walked back to my corner to get my gloves unlaced. I didn't do anything because Stevie Kirwood was white, and one thing a black fighter in the Deep South learns early on is that knockouts—clean knockouts—are the only way to guarantee a victory against a white kid. Anything else is a crapshoot. So when the decision went to Stevie I did what I'd done before on those rare occasions when I'd lost a decision to someone I was sure I'd beaten: I did nothing.

Later in my career sportswriters liked to talk about my polite manners and what a good sport I was in defeat, as well as in victory. I didn't get angry when unfair stuff happened, and I didn't prance around or go all show-offy when I won. But it's not because I'm such a saintly guy— Lord knows I'm not—it's just how I was brought up. I was taught to behave that way, and near as I'm able to figure, it was because of three things: my mama, a boxing coach named Carter Morgan, and old-fashioned southern racism.

4

Mama—and her mother as well—had some mighty strong beliefs about how kids were supposed to behave, and a lot of it came from the Bible, although Mama liked to frost that cake with a little of her own icing. Pride being a mortal sin wasn't just a slogan for Mama; it was God telling us how to live. Pridefulness to her wasn't just about bragging or showing off, it was about going nuts when things went sour, as though you were too good to suffer a little injustice once in a while. She thought it was a waste of energy to fight things you had no hope of changing, and that you were better off directing your efforts to making sure it didn't happen again, or at least being smart enough to avoid the same situation in the future altogether. One of the things she knew it was useless to fight was someone in authority who'd already made up his mind, especially if you were black and poor and living in the South. Arguing would only get you into more trouble, so the only reason left to argue was pride, and that was no kind of reason at all.

When I was about four I was playing in the front yard with my older brother Bernard and our beautiful collie, Lassie. That dog was an over-grown pussycat who'd never hurt anybody, but when a mean drunk wandered into the yard and began harassing her, throwing stuff at her and laughing when she got hit, she broke her chain and chased him away.

About an hour later the drunk showed up with the sheriff and pointed to Lassie. The sheriff came into the yard and said, "This guy filed a complaint so I gotta shoot your dog."

Me and Bernard figured he was just kidding, or putting on a show to calm the drunk down, but our older sister Annette saw what was going on, ran out and pulled us inside. Lassie scooted under the house, which she always did when we let her loose in the middle of the day because it was nice and cool down there.

We watched through the window as the sheriff pulled a shotgun out of the squad car and walked up to the house. He looked back at the drunk standing by the car, then leaned down where we couldn't see him anymore. A couple of seconds later the whole house shook as he fired off the shotgun. Then he stood up, rested the barrel on his shoulder and walked back to the car, like all he'd done was shoot a can off a fence or something. The drunk guy saw us looking through the window and laughed, then grabbed at the car door handle three or four times before he finally managed to get it open and fall into the car.

Annette wouldn't let us move while the sheriff was still there. "He din't do nothin'," Bernard said to me, and shook his head, hard. "Just makin' that drunk fool think he did." He was trying to convince himself as much as me.

When the car was finally out of sight my brother and I ran out the door. Usually when the front door opened Lassie would come flying out from under the house so fast she was at the bottom of the porch stairs before we were, but this time we didn't see her at all, and when we looked under the house there was blood and fur all over the place.

No hearing, no due process . . . a cop just up and killed our dog. "What're we gonna do?" I asked Bernard.

"Nothing," Annette said behind us.

Later that night when Mama got home she said the same thing as Annette. I asked her how that could happen, that some guy could shoot our dog and there was nothing we could do about it.

"Didn't say it was right," she answered. "Just said there's no use trying to do something about it because you can't. And that policeman, he knows you can't. That's why he done it." And she went on to tell us that if we tried to do something about it, things would only get worse, not better, so we shouldn't waste time on it. "You let it be."

I didn't do anything when treated unfairly by a teacher, either. All I had to do was watch other kids try to argue, the teacher getting madder and madder and the situation just getting worse for the kid. I learned to keep my public hurts private, and after I became better known in the larger world and had other people to go to bat for me, I knew better than to carry on like an overgrown brat.

I didn't get angry and make a scene the first time a bad decision went to a white kid, even though I was fixing to, because Carter Morgan saw me and caught my eye just in time. He stared at me with a frown and shook his head. Not a lot, just a little, but in a way that let me know that I was to settle down and get hold of myself.

When I ran up to him after leaving the ring, I hadn't gotten a word out before he pumped his hands at me, palm down, and said, "I know. I know."

"But I walloped that kid!" I said, nearly in tears. "I had him down in the first—"

"I *know!*" Carter said more forcefully. Then he took me into the locker room, sat me down and explained. "People around here, they don't like to see black kids beating white kids. A close decision can—"

"But it wasn't close!"

"Yeah." He scratched the back of his head. "And you can go back and argue it. But you want to fight again, don't you?"

I shot him a look: *Of course I do.*

"Then hush up and let it go. That's all there is to it."

"But it ain't right!" I insisted. How could that be all there was to it? "You tellin' me there's nothin' I can do about it?"

Carter shrugged. "There's one thing you can do . . ." he began.

"Yeah?" I jumped at the small bit of hope he held out. "What? What can I do?"

"You can knock guys out," he answered. "There's nothing they can do when you knock guys out. They don't like it, but there's nothing they can do. So if you want to win, what you gotta do, you gotta knock 'em out."

Which is what I spent the rest of my career trying to do. By the time my amateur career ended following the 1984 Olympics, I'd won by knockout seventy-five times. I don't want to brag, just make a point, but something Howard Cosell would later tell me during the Olympics was really true: In amateur fights, which only went three rounds back then (many are four now) and where safety is everything, knockouts are few and far between and going for them is risky. For an amateur to win by KO as many times as I did was awfully rare, and now you know why it was so important to me. Don't get me wrong—knockouts are important to every fighter—but to me they had special meaning. They're how I protected my wins.

But I didn't win all the time. Sometimes it was because I'd been outfought, and I could handle that. But sometimes it was a loss by unfair decision. When that happened, I did what I could, based on what was in the rules: file a protest, ask for a hearing, "proper channel" things like that. And if it didn't work and there was nothing else to be done, I dropped it.

Understand, this had nothing to do with meekly swallowing whatever was dished out to me. Far from it. When it was appropriate to fight, I fought. But I made good and sure there was a reason to fight other than foolish pride. I made sure there was something to be gained, because from the time I started boxing at the age of eight I always had my eye on a larger goal, and Mama and Carter helped me to see that sometimes you had to make sacrifices and grit your teeth without complaining if it meant getting closer to that bigger goal. And even if it didn't, there was no excuse in the world for behaving badly.

I hung around outside Carter's roped-off training area for months trying to get into the boxing program. Kids made fun of me, because of how small and scrawny I was, but I didn't make trouble and I didn't let them push me away. I took whatever they dished out because it wasn't important to defend my pride to them; it was important *to get into that program.* If I acted up and caused a fuss, Carter wouldn't have stood for it and I wouldn't have had a prayer of getting past the door. So I took the small hurts and the teasing because anything else would have moved me farther from my goal rather than closer.

Did it bother me standing there in silence while a bad decision was announced? Of course it did. It was awful being humiliated and robbed like that. But I wanted to keep fighting and Carter taught me to solve the problem a better way than storming around and complaining and feeling sorry for myself. I got stronger and more skillful so I could whup opponents to the point where it was impossible for anybody to rob me of victories.

Those lessons drummed into me by Mama and Carter Morgan paid off throughout my whole life, in more places than just the ring, and they continue to pay off today. My upbringing made me who I am, and I feel I have a calling to inspire people to be the very best that they can be. I wanted to write this book so that others can benefit from what I learned, and maybe avoid some of the mistakes I made along the way.

But just preaching about stuff isn't what I'm about, and I doubt it's anything you want to read. What I'd rather do is tell you some stories about my life. Even though they're stories you might already have read about in newspapers or magazines, you haven't heard my side yet, what really happened the way I lived it. And to me they're not just individual stories, even though some might be pretty interesting or exciting or funny. They're all part of how I got to be who I am, and I'm hoping that reading about them might touch you in a way that helps you put your own life in perspective and makes it just a little bit better. Or, if not your life, then maybe your children's.

CHAPTER 1

———

Childhood

I don't think there's a harder job than being a poor, black, single mom raising a large family in the rural Deep South. And I don't know anyone who did it better than my mother, Annie Laura Holyfield.

I was the last of nine kids, eight of them living. (A brother, Jimmy, died of pneumonia shortly after childbirth before I was born.) So Mama had a lot of practice before I came along. There wasn't a trick she hadn't seen or an excuse she hadn't heard. She'd also already seen how various ways of dealing with kids worked out later in their lives, so by the time she got to me, she had her philosophy pretty well worked out: Discipline, consistency and a lot of attention were things a parent owed a child. It was the responsibility you took on when you had children, and there was no choice involved. If you believed in God as strong as Mama did, raising your kids right wasn't just a promise you made to them; it was a promise you made to Him, too.

But those things were worthless if you didn't slather an ocean of love over all of it. No matter what you did to make your kid straighten up and fly right, the most important thing was to make sure he had no doubt that he was loved. That had to be at the foundation or the rest of the structure would rest on shaky ground, ready to collapse at the first of the many difficult tests that every life brings.

I saw a lot of tough parents in the neighborhoods where I grew up. I saw plenty of kids getting whupped upside the head all the time. But what I saw coming from many of those parents was anger and impatience. It wasn't discipline; it was punishment, for things those kids did to their parents, like distracting them from something they were doing or wasting their time or embarrassing them or just plain annoying them. That kind of thing only makes a kid fearful and resentful.

Mama whupped me plenty, probably more than the rest of my sisters and brothers put together. But it wasn't because she'd come to the end of her rope after bringing up the others; it was because I needed it. I was willful and rambunctious and had more energy than I knew what to do with. I got into trouble all the time, not because I was a bad kid but because I liked to push the boundaries and see what I could get away with.

But unlike a lot of the parents of those other kids I saw, Mama never disciplined me because she was annoyed or impatient. Every whupping came with an explanation. "When I say be home at five, you be home at five." If I asked her why I had to be home at five, she'd say something like, "You don't ask me that after you're already late. You gonna do that to people when you're all grown up, break your word and then try to talk your way out of it?" There was a lesson every time, and she was never unfair. Strict, for sure, but not unfair. She was predictable, too. I can't remember a time I got a whupping that I didn't know for sure it was coming. So I pretty much learned early on about making choices and controlling my own life. Don't want a whupping? Don't play in that abandoned house when she told you not to. Very simple.

But, as I said, most important of all was the love. Growing up I never once doubted that my mother loved me, not for a second, even if I was mad at her or she at me. I never once felt that I had to perform or accomplish anything to "earn" her love. It was just there, always. I might do things that made her angry or sad or proud or happy, but nothing I did could affect how much she loved me. It was that, more than anything, that shaped who I eventually became and how I try to treat my own kids.

I learned a lot of lessons from Mama, about perseverance and keeping your eye on the big picture, about letting go of resentment that could drown you if you let it, and about picking your battles carefully. I learned not to nurse grudges, but to just do what needed to get done and move on. Having goals and working to achieve them wasn't just some tired cliché Mama read in a magazine somewhere. It was a way of life. Nothing got her dander up worse than hearing excuses for not accomplishing something. That was a lesson that would go to the very heart of how I behaved when I became a boxer. I've had more than my fair share of bad calls and bad luck, like being denied an Olympic gold medal and having a piece of my ear bitten off during a fight, but I like to think that I didn't dwell on them, that I didn't go crazy and complain, that I figured out how to get past them and move on. It was pretty much always the right way to have done it.

Sometimes later in life I'd have cause to wonder if maybe I should have been more forthcoming about a setback, like the time I lost a fight because my shoulders were badly injured. But there would have been no way to do it without it sounding like an excuse, so I just let it go. That caused me a lot of problems, including having my boxing license taken away, but you know what? Eventually, it turned out that keeping it to myself was the exact right thing to do, even though it didn't seem that way at the time. Without Mama having driven all those lessons home, I probably would have given in to the temptation to rant and rave about the unfairness of it all, and not only not accomplished anything by it but made it harder to correct the situation.

I'll give you the best example of how strongly Mama stuck to her principles, even when it cost her something to do it. Like I said, I started boxing when I was eight, and she hated it right from the start. She didn't like the idea of people beating each other up, no matter how controlled and "legitimate" it was. In the environment she'd grown up in, fighting was never a good thing. And what mother can stand the idea of somebody else trying to beat up on her kid? But she didn't stop me from doing it.

I didn't lose a fight until I was eleven, but when I did, to a kid named Cecil Collins, it devastated me. I came home and told Mama I was quitting the sport.

Big mistake. "You go on back in that ring and beat that boy!" she said. This from a woman who didn't want me boxing to begin with. "You don't quit until you do what you set out to do!"

So I went back and fought Cecil again. And again I lost. "Go back and fight him again!" Mama said.

I did, and this time I beat him. It felt wonderful, like I'd just climbed Mt. Everest or hit the winning home run in the World Series.

"Well, there you go!" Mama said, beaming. *"Now* you can quit!"

I didn't quit—there were some things even my wise mama didn't understand—but you get the point. If I hadn't gone back in there and tried again and again, I probably would have spent a large part of my life regretting it. But Mama knew how I'd feel once I won, all proud and happy. Her attitude wasn't, "See? I was right." It was, "Don't you feel good having finished what you started?" It was that feeling that shaped my later approach to life, not the fact that I'd done what Mama asked, and that's why the lesson was so valuable. It really came from me; Mama just pushed me to get there.

She had more to do with who I am than any other single person. Carter Morgan ran a close second, but by the time he got to me, my mother had already gotten the train headed down the track.

Mama was born Annie Laura Riggen in July 1928 in Atlanta. Her grandmother had a very large family that stuck together through the years, so even though Mama only had one brother and no sisters, there were always a lot of kids of various ages running around. It wasn't until her grandmother passed that Annie Laura realized that one of her sisters was really her aunt. They were the same age and nobody had bothered to explain things.

Mama got married to Joseph Holyfield when she was fifteen. She took his last name, and after they split up in 1953, she kept it. Shortly after that she moved the family to Atmore, Alabama, to take care of her mother, who'd had a mild stroke. Atmore, a mill town about forty miles northeast of Mobile and two miles from the Florida border, is where she met Isom Coley, a lumberjack who was a gentle man despite being incredibly strong physically. He and Mama made plans to marry, but somehow never got around to it. So when they had me in 1962, her last name was still Holyfield, and that's the name she passed on to me. Isom and Mama had a falling out before I was born so I grew up without him around, but later on he would come to all my fights and never had a problem with me having a name different from his.

As for a first name, Mama hadn't given it much thought before I was born. A friend of hers suggested "Evander" because she'd just read something somewhere about a hero of that name in Roman mythology. He was the son of Mercury, born in Greece with the name Euandros, which means "good man." He went to what is now Italy and founded a new city on the site where Rome would eventually rise, and became its king, Evander.

I hated both my names when I was little. They were unusual, and other kids were always cracking wise about them. One of my mother's girlfriends was called "Chubby," which my siblings thought was pretty hysterical. Some of them started calling me that because I was as skinny as a pencil. You'd think that "Chubby" was about the rottenest name you could hang on a little kid, but I didn't mind it at all. It sure beat "Evander." When I got to school I even insisted the teachers call me Chubby, and most of them did. It still comes back to haunt me once in a while: When I fought my first title bout as a professional, someone scrawled "Nail him, Chubby" on a blackboard in my locker room, and when the ABC cameras showed me warming up, there it was on national television, big as life. I had to explain it during the postfight interview.

Later in life I came to appreciate my real names more and more, especially as I began to discover my spiritual side. Evander might be an unusual name in the United States, but when I went to the Olympics in Greece in 2004, people loved to open up baby name books and show it to me. I also once visited Evander Childs High School in the Bronx, which was named for a prominent New York educator.

Our house at 81 King Street in Atmore is still standing today. It amazes me now to see it. When I was very young it seemed huge and fine, but that just shows you how oblivious a kid can be to hardship, because it was a run-down little nothing of a bungalow. But all my memories of the place are fond ones, at least if you don't count my dog getting shot.

My brother Bernard and I were the babies of the family, so while everyone else was either in school or working, we got to roam around the quiet neighborhood playing with other kids. This came with a small measure of guilt, though, because our older brothers and sisters didn't have time for that. They all worked, and worked hard, even the ones in school. Mama didn't plan for us to live in a shack forever and just accept whatever life handed us. She was a devout Christian who tried to live by the teachings of the Bible, and what that meant to her was that you had a duty to work hard and try to better yourself. It didn't matter what you did—Mama cooked in a restaurant—but as long as you were doing it, you had to do it well and with an eye toward making things better and better.

Grandma Pearlie Beatrice Hatton was confined to a wheelchair and wasn't able to work, but she had plenty of energy and found ways to burn it off. Most of the ways usually had something to do with disciplining Bernard and me, which she did often and with a lot of enthusiasm. She also did it with a lot of old-time religion. I didn't mind the whuppings so much; hardly a day went by that I didn't get scratched and bruised playing sports in empty lots so I got used to dealing with pain pretty early, and Grandma's idea of a "whupping" was usually just a sharp pinch on the arm. It was the religious lectures that drove me nuts, because while she was quoting from the Bible, I could hear other kids outside laughing and having a great time. Once in a while, without thinking, I'd say, "Couldn't you just go ahead and pinch me already so I can go back outside?" That usually backfired, because she'd say, "No!" and realize I really wasn't paying attention, which only brought on more fire and brimstone and sometimes the switch, which that "frail" little lady used like she'd trained for it. It got even worse after Bernard and I saw someone in the house late at night and Grandma decided that it was an angel come to bestow God's blessing on us. Once that happened, she got even more zealous about making sure we turned out right. But, just as with Mama, we knew Grandma loved us, and we loved her right back. Later in life I'd come to think a lot about those Bible lessons, too. I wonder if Grandma knew at the time that, even though a lot of what she tried to teach us had no immediate effect, it would pay great dividends later.

Mama moved all of us, including Grandma, back to Atlanta when I was four. We stayed with my eldest sister JoAnn for the first few months. She lived in her mother-in-law's house, and when all of us were added in, there were fourteen of us under one roof, but I don't have a recollection of anyone minding very much. By the time I went to kindergarten at E. P. Johnson Elementary School, we'd moved into our own place.

Bernard and I figured to pretty much pick up where we'd left off in Atmore and roam around the new neighborhood looking for any kind of games we could get into. But Grandma got real protective now that we were in the "big city" and subject to all kinds of new dangers and bad influences. The reins were on pretty tight and that meant even more disciplining from her, because when the choice came down to sticking to the front yard or risking getting our arms pinched if we wandered off, it was a pretty easy decision. Adding disobedience to our list of sins made Grandma even more zealous, which made her more protective and tightened the apron strings even further, which made Bernard and me even bigger sinners when we disobeyed her, and . . . you get the picture.

Before any of this could get out of hand, something happened, a little thing, that would change my life forever. It was one of those incidents that really gets you to wondering about things like destiny and fate and whether anything that happens to you can truly be called an accident.

Bernard and I were playing ball with a new friend in the neighborhood when he suddenly said he had to leave. We hadn't heard his mother call him, and it wasn't getting dark. Who leaves in the middle of playing ball? So I asked him where he was going.

"Boys Club," he said, and ran off down the street. Bernard figured that it was probably one of those clubs that kids form that has a grand total of four guys in it and a life span of about a week. But the next day when we met up with him again, he said, No, this was a real club, with a building and everything.

"What do you do there?" I asked him.

"Just stuff," he answered.

"What kind of stuff?"

"You know, like baseball, football, basketball, swimming, Ping Pong, handball . . ."

My eyes must have been popping out of my head, because he stopped after a while and asked if we'd want to go there.

Would I want to go to Disneyland and Heaven all rolled into one?

But it cost money. I don't remember the exact amount but it was only something like twenty-five cents a year. Still, as hard as everybody in the family was working and trying to save, it might not make for an easy sell at home.

It didn't, but not for the reason I thought. "Club?" Mama said, all suspicious. "What kind of club? I don't like the sound of that."

"It's where kids play ball," I insisted.

"Where is it?"

"I don't know."

"How do you get there?"

"Bus comes and picks you up."

"Who's watching?" Grandma wanted to know. "Who's making sure you little troublemakers aren't tempted by the devil?"

Good question. I had no idea, so I just started making stuff up. All the kids in the neighborhood belonged, it was the safest place in the whole country, there were ten adults in charge for every kid who walked through the door . . . if they'd let me go on I probably would have said that Jesus Christ himself had started the organization two thousand years ago. But I didn't get that far, because Mama and Grandma must have planted a chip in my brain when I was born that sent "He's lying" signals right to their radar. I'd barely gotten into my speech when I knew the jig was up.

Strangely, neither Mama or Grandma went off on me for making up such a load of trash, maybe because they thought there was something worth having a look at here or just because I was being so outrageous that nobody could take me seriously. Either way, Mama said she'd check around and see what's what.

I didn't wait for her to get around to it. I got the phone number of the Warren Memorial Boys Club, I brought our friend home to tell her about it, and I even got his mother on the phone and handed the receiver to Mama. She asked a lot of questions but still wasn't convinced, and neither was Grandma. This was turning into a major catastrophe, and a really cruel one, too. What was God thinking? How could he dangle something like that in front of two sports-crazy kids and then snatch it away like that? We maybe got into a lot of trouble, but come on: We weren't *that* bad.

The same day Mama talked to our friend's mother on the phone, he came by the house to see if we were going to the club with him that afternoon. Our faces must have told the whole story. He sat down on the porch and got glum with us, and then Grandma rolled up to the door in her wheelchair.

"What do you kids really do in that place?" she demanded, trying to give our friend a hard time.

"Depends on which days," he said.

"Yeah? Like what?"

"Well," he said, "on Saturdays we have Bible classes."

Man, you'd have thought Grandma had just seen the Burning Bush right there on the porch. Her jaw dropped open, her eyes went wide and she stayed that way so long I thought maybe she was having another stroke.

Then she found her voice. "Annie Laura!" she rasped, calling my mother. "Annie Laura!"

Mama came running. "What's the matter?"

Grandma pointed to our friend with a rolled-up magazine that shook in her hand. "This boy here, he says they got *Bible classes* down at that club!"

"Bible classes!" Mama exclaimed.

After making good and sure the startled kid wasn't just making it up, Mama told us we could give it a try. That afternoon Bernard and I went to the corner an hour before the bus was supposed to come and hopped around impatiently until it finally arrived.

You know how a lot of times in life you build something up in your mind so big and for so long it can't help but be a disappointment when it actually arrives? Well, this was just the opposite. When that bus pulled up in front of the Boys Club, it was all Bernard and I could do not to jump out the windows before it came to a stop. There were kids all over the place doing just what our friend had told us. There was football and baseball underway outside, and when we went through the front door there were more activities going on than our eyes could drink in: shuffleboard, pinball, pool, boys playing musical instruments, working on woodcraft projects . . . and none of it was cut-down kiddie stuff, either. The indoor swimming pool was a full twenty-five-meter job and the baseball diamond outside was also regulation and so was the football field. The basketball court was, too, but I noticed that one whole end of the gym was fenced off. At first I didn't pay much attention to it, but that would change later.

Bernard and I were so over the moon at all this stuff we didn't know where to start, so we signed up for everything. But before we were allowed to do anything, we got read the riot act. The Boys Club wasn't just a recreational free-for-all; it had rules. Hundreds of them, and the adults running the place were serious about all of them. Step out of line and there were a couple of ladies standing by who were ready to explain things to you all over again, in ways you couldn't help but understand. It was kind of like living with Grandma, except with much better toys.

My brother and I tried it all, but it didn't take me long to find myself getting drawn to football more and more. It was not only fun to play; I seemed to have a knack for it. I was very small for my age but, despite my size, I would win a bunch of MVP trophies over the next few years.

It wasn't just natural. I worked harder at the game than the other kids. There were men there who knew football inside and out, and knew how to teach it, too. Once they realized how eager I was to learn, they spent a lot of time with me, on things like fundamental skills and playmaking. I got double- and triple-covered by the opposing teams a lot so I often had to fight my way through bigger kids and try to be creative in how I was going to get the ball down the field. I didn't always win the MVP award, but I always got the "Most Hustle" trophy.

There were two reasons I was willing to work that hard. The first had to do with growing up without a father. The few times I asked Mama about my father, all she would say was, "You don't need to know. Just pray for him." So I did, every time I said my prayers.

Being the last of eight kids with no father and only one mother to go around, I must not have gotten as much attention as I needed because I found myself doing things to win approval from other dads. I always worked hard at whatever I did, and those other dads liked that. They used to say to their own sons, "How come you don't work as hard as Evander?" And the more they approved of me, the harder I worked. I liked that kind of attention. I thought that a lot of those fathers wished I was their son and that made me feel pretty good. As I got older, though, and started to accomplish some things that weren't dependent on anyone else's approval, I stopped going after it and I also pretty much forgot about my father, too.

The other reason for all that hard work was that I'd decided that I wanted to be a professional football player. Not just for any team, either, but the Atlanta Falcons. Mama was real big on having long-term goals and working to achieve them. She wasn't much impressed by hard work if all it did was get you through the day. You had to be headed somewhere, and I was. I took a lot of ribbing about my size at first—I only weighed sixty-five pounds when I joined the Boys Club—but that stopped pretty quick. Even young kids have enough street smarts to know that it's not very cool making fun of someone who just ran over you on the way to a touchdown. I was the club leader in sacks and solo tackles and was averaging over three hundred yards and four touchdowns a game. I had plenty of time to grow and put on weight.

One of the interesting things about the Boys Club is that a lot of the kids were black and poor, and nearly all of the adults who ran the place and put time and money into it were white and middle class. I didn't take much notice of that while I was there, but I'd have occasion to think about it later. There was a lot of racism in the South in the late 1960s, and a rising wave of black self-assertion as well. So there were white southerners who thought it shameful that other white people were investing so much in black kids, and there were black southerners who thought that black kids shouldn't be getting so much direction from whites. But because the club was such a sheltered, self-contained environment, I didn't have any interaction with people who were critical of its racial mix. I probably wouldn't have cared much anyway—I was just a kid having too much fun.

Thing is, white people have helped me all my life. A lot of black people have, too, of course, but because of how Mama raised me and because of the Boys Club, I never learned to make those distinctions, or religious ones, either. I've had a manager named Finkel, a promoter named Muhammad, a trainer named Duva, and everything in between. Makes no difference to me. All I want to know about somebody is, can he do the job and can I trust him. I've gotten some flak about that philosophy, which I'll tell you about later, but I ignored it all.

CHAPTER 2

———

The Ring

The people who ran the Boys Club were very demanding. It wasn't enough for them that what we now call "at risk" kids were simply off the streets and out of trouble for a few hours a day. They cared deeply about the boys, and about their futures, and what mattered was that the kids came out of the place better than when they went in. Preparing boys to be men wasn't some empty piety to those people; it was very important in their lives.

There was no running in the hallways, no swearing and no fighting. You called the adults "sir" and "ma'am" and you never gave them back-talk. Those were all important things, but the most important, the first commandment, was good sportsmanship. When you won, you didn't razz the other team; you gave them a cheer. When you lost, you didn't complain about the referees. You showed respect to everybody on the field, even the scrawniest, weakest kid who couldn't catch a ball if you handed it to him. There were no second stringers. Everybody played. If there were too many kids for one team, another team was formed.

The worst punishment possible for a transgression was sitting out a game. I would rather have been beaten to a pulp than not be able to play. I literally dreamed about upcoming games. I'd visualize every play over and over, trying to imagine what the opposition might do and what I'd do to counter it, and what they'd do in return and what I'd do to answer it. After all of that, not to play on game day was the worst torture imaginable, so I learned, fast, never to let that happen. I had a lot of smart aleck in me and the temptation to give the ref or an opponent some sass was strong. But it wasn't as strong as wanting to play, so I got into the habit of holding my tongue. That was part of how I learned to focus on the big picture and not get distracted by the small stuff.

As long as you followed the rules, you pretty much had the run of the Boys Club. Anybody could sign up for anything, so you were free to try it all until you found something that really grabbed you. There were always new kids roaming around watching what was going on, because you could wander wherever you felt like.

Except for one place: that fenced-off end of the gym I'd noticed on the first day. It was off-limits to anybody who didn't have business there. There were small round bags hooked underneath circles of wood, big leather bags like brown oil drums hanging from the ceiling, a huge mirror mounted along one wall and, in the center of it all, a square platform raised up off the ground and enclosed by ropes.

It was the boxing area, and very little talking was going on in there. Everywhere else in the club, at least in those places where sports were played, it was pure bedlam, kids laughing and yelling and generally carrying on. At the far end of the gym, though, it was quieter, almost solemn. All I could hear was the sound of leather hitting leather, some grunting here and there, the soft swishing of somebody jumping rope. Somehow all that quiet made the activity seem more intense. More important.

I was fascinated by the place. That probably had more to do with its being forbidden than anything else, but the more I watched, the more drawn to it I got. The rest of the gym was available to everybody, so nobody stopped me from watching, but once in a while when I'd wander too close, some kid on his way in or out would startle me by yelling, "Hey!" Then he'd jerk a thumb or nod his head toward the other end of the gym and say, "Git on outta here!" Not mean, necessarily, but hard. Confident, too, like he had the right and didn't need to overdo it to make his point. Who were these guys? What made them so special?

They sure were serious, and they worked harder than I'd ever seen kids working, including me. The whole operation seemed to be run by one guy, Carter Morgan, a white man about fifty years old with a deeply lined face that made him look like he'd seen his share of the world. Mr. Morgan didn't say much, but when he did, those kids listened. And once in a while when he'd nod in approval or pat one of them on the back, the effect was electric, like the kid had just scored a touchdown in the final game of the season.

For about a week, whenever football was over for the day, I went over to the gym and watched, without getting too close to the fence. When I went home I tried to duplicate the moves I'd seen, but had no way of knowing if I was doing them right.

One day when Mr. Morgan was on his way in, I pointed to the fenced-off area, and said, "Can I go in there?"

"No," he said without stopping.

I watched some more, and learned a few more moves. Or thought I did. After about another week I went up to Mr. Morgan again. "How come I can't go in there!" I demanded.

This time he stopped. "Young 'un," he said, looking at me but pointing toward the boxing area, "that there is for serious boys. Boys who're willing to work hard. You know anything about hard work?"

"Yeah," I told him.

"Uh-huh." He looked me over, all sixty-five pounds and eight years old of me, shook his head, and then walked away.

Now I was mad. I went back, but this time I pressed my face right up against the metal meshwork of the fence. I'd watch for a while, then hit the air while the other kids hit the bags, then watch some more. After a few days of that I marched into the fenced-off area after the last kid had left for the day. Before Mr. Morgan could throw me out, I said, "Let me hit the bag!"

"No!"

"Just once! Let me hit it once!"

He looked at me for a long moment, then held up a finger. "Once," he said.

I ran over to one of those little round bags hanging up in the air before he could change his mind, but before I got there I heard him yell, "Hey!" and stopped. When I turned he said, "Not the speed bag," and pointed toward one of those big drumlike things. So I went over there, hauled off and punched it as hard as I could.

I don't know what I was expecting—maybe that I was going to knock it right off its chain and into the wall—but that bag didn't go anywhere. I'm not even sure I started it rocking. It was like hitting a brick wall, and for a few seconds of shocking pain, I thought I'd broken my wrist.

I heard Mr. Morgan sigh behind me, then the sound of his footsteps as he walked over. I didn't turn around. My one shot to show him I was worthy of joining his exclusive little club within a club and I'd blown it completely. I tried not to rub my wrist.

"Young 'un," he said—he was to call me that until the day he died—"you wanna be a fighter, you gotta be tough." Then he turned around and walked off.

But he didn't throw me out.

I kept bugging the heck out of that poor man. I guess he got really annoyed seeing me hanging on that fence all day, because eventually he let me come inside and fool around on the speed bag. They had to put a stool under it so I could reach the thing, and some of the other boys snickered at me, but one stern look from Coach Morgan put a stop to that. It must have been painful for him to watch how badly I hit the bag, so when he had time he'd show me a few things: how to position my hands, how to anticipate the way the bag was going to bounce so I'd be ready to hit it again at the exact right moment.

Pretty soon he let me at the heavy bag again, this time showing me the right way to hit it so that I wouldn't hurt myself. After a few days of that we got into how to hit it harder, and how to stay balanced while doing it. We got into conditioning, too. I began doing calisthenics, skipping rope and running.

I discovered early on how those kids felt when they'd nudged a little approval out of Coach Carter. He wasn't one of those self-esteem dispensers bent on making you feel good even when you haven't accomplished anything. When he gave you a compliment, it meant you'd earned it. Maybe that's why those kids were working so hard, because it sure had an effect on me. I thought I was putting in a lot of effort on football, but it was nothing compared to what I was doing here. No matter what I did in the boxing area, I did it to the point of exhaustion. It paid off, too. When the coach let me start sparring, I was astonished at how quickly it could tire you out. It didn't look that hard when I'd watched other kids do it. Many years later a young woman would say the same thing to me at a charity function. So I bet her a hundred bucks to ten she couldn't punch the air hard and nonstop for one minute. She got going and when she was good and sweated up she gasped, "How long so far?" and I said, "Fifteen seconds." I won the bet.

The more attention I paid to conditioning, the longer I was able to last in the ring. As it happened, after I started fighting real matches, that wasn't very long, because I ended most of my bouts early. Once I got the taste of victory, my arm held high in the air, it was a sweeter feeling than even an approving nod from Coach Morgan. I won my very first match. The next one, too, and the next. I started boxing when I was eight and didn't lose a fight for three years.

There were a lot of lessons to be learned other than technique and fitness. In the beginning I felt sorry for my opponents, because some of them cried when they lost or got hit too hard. So I tended to ease up on them. Coach Morgan saw me doing that, and asked me what was going on, so I told him. He didn't say anything at first, just waited until a fight in which he knew I wasn't giving my all. In between rounds he knelt in front of me and said, "Why aren't you finishing him off?"

I said, "I don't want him to cry."

Coach stepped aside and pointed to the other corner. I leaned over to see around the opposing coach and there was my opponent, looking at me and laughing. It was a perfect setup, like that scene in *The Color of Money* where Paul Newman shows Tom Cruise what happens when you make the mistake of feeling sorry for the other guy. It wasn't like someone had twisted my opponent's arm to get him into the ring, and he wasn't about to ease up on me. The point was to win, and that was your job.

Once I started participating in matches against other clubs, there was no longer any need to worry about making my opponents cry. At that early age you get matched up according to how old you are, not what you weigh. Because I was so small for my age, I found myself fighting kids who were a whole lot taller and heavier and didn't cry. I still beat them, but it took a lot more effort.

About the time I entered high school we moved into the Jonesboro North Projects. Even though it was government-subsidized housing, it wasn't free, so we had some new financial pressures on us. Everybody old enough to work found whatever jobs they could, everything from waitressing to warehouse stocking, factory work and cleaning. Bernard and I wanted to do our bit, too, so we fixed up a little wagon and spent hours scrounging in vacant lots and construction sites for empty bottles to turn in for the deposits. Like most kids who were dirt poor, though, we didn't really know it. We never went hungry, always had clean clothes, and slept in the same beds every night, even if those beds had to be shared.

The move put us into a different school district, too, and because of a new set of antisegregation laws, Bernard and I had to go to a school where white kids were being bused in from outlying locations. We were warned to expect trouble, because a lot of white people weren't happy about that, but I didn't get it at first. Down at the Boys Club we had every kind of color and ethnicity playing sports together, and I had a hard time understanding why it would be any different at this new school. Well, it was. Kids tended to stick with their own kind, and maybe that's why we never had any trouble there. The law could tell you where to go to school but it couldn't do much about who you hung around with once you got there.

In any event, school wasn't the center of my life. The Boys Club was. Very gradually, Coach Morgan was beginning to play a fatherly role in my life. That was fine with me, because I'd never even met my real father. It was also fine with Mama. She looked pretty skeptically on this boxing business, and didn't like it at all, but she liked Carter Morgan and the influence he was having on me. My relationship with Morgan became even more important later, when I got into high school. I went out for football, and was so small I almost didn't make it, but my tenacity and willingness to work hard squeaked me through. Still, I didn't get to play, just warm a bench. I wanted to quit, because what was the point of staying on the team if I didn't get to play? But Mama wouldn't let me. She told me to keep working hard, so I'd be ready if I ever got the chance.

It didn't come all season. Finally, during the last game I begged the coach to put me in, and he did. I weighed all of 110 pounds but proceeded to stop every opposing player who came near me, even if he weighed 190. Nobody got past me, and pretty soon they quit coming my way and I had to go chase them down. The crowd roared its approval and the coach looked at me with renewed interest, but it was the end of the season. I'd spent the whole year working hard, and for what?

I wasn't actually all that concerned about high school football. My real ambition was to play for the Atlanta Falcons. But it was starting to become obvious that I was just too small, and no amount of heart or will or determination was going to convince anybody to give me a shot at playing pro ball. I believed in myself, but there's no virtue in being unrealistic.

Fortunately, I had boxing to fall back on. I didn't have to convince anybody to let me into the ring. I only had to be convincing once I got there. But I needed a big, giant ambition to keep me motivated, just as the thought of wearing a Falcons jersey had kept me going in football. I got just such an ambition, at the exact right time, and it came courtesy of Coach Carter.

It happened during a junior division event. It was one of the toughest matches I'd had since I started in the sport. My opponent was a big, strong, talented fighter who had every move in the book, including some I'd never seen before. It seemed like I was making a new adjustment every twenty seconds just to try to stay even with him. Eventually I fell into a smoother rhythm and started figuring out how to draw him into my game instead of getting sucked into his, and I ended up winning the match.

All the other Warren Memorial fighters poured into the ring to congratulate me, and the spectators gave me a standing ovation. It was a great moment, except . . . Coach Morgan was sitting quietly out of the ring, just staring. That was unusual. He was always the first guy to get to me, tell me well done and review the bout round by round. But there he was, looking across the room and tapping at his lower lip.

When all the brouhaha finally died down and my gloves were unlaced, I went over to him. Maybe he thought I'd fought a lousy fight, even though I'd won? No, that couldn't be it. By then I knew him well enough to be able to anticipate all his critiques. I knew when I fought well and when I didn't, and this was one of my best ever.

As I approached, he looked up at me, still not saying anything. I sat down next to him and waited.

"Young 'un," he said, taking his hand away from his face and turning to me, "one'a these days you're gonna be the champion of the world."

You hear that kind of thing all the time when you're a young boxer and winning a lot. The guys yell it out to each other, people call it from the stands. But I'd never heard it from Coach Carter before. I searched his face for some kind of sign that he was just being glib or kidding around, but it wasn't there. He was deadly serious. I remember the moment to this day, just like I remember the day men walked on the moon. It was the moment my ambition to be a pro football player began to give way to a different dream.

Carter suffered from emphysema and was in very poor health. He'd have these wracking fits of coughing that were so bad I wasn't sure he'd live through them. Sometimes it happened when he was driving some of us to fights and we thought for sure we were going to go right off the road and into a tree. But as bad off as he was, he worked with me right up to the day he died, when I was sixteen. I would have felt lost after that but his son, Ted, took over and trained me until it was time for me to leave home and take the next big step in my career.

CHAPTER 3

─────

Childhood's End

The Boys Club was essentially zero cost and somebody was always paying my way to events, so I sort of always just assumed that boxing was free. After I graduated high school, though, I was too old for the Boys Club. Not only that, the cost of fighting was going up. Getting on a bus to nearby towns and cities was one thing. Traveling to places like Venezuela for the PanAm Games or Las Vegas for the Olympic trials was going to be a lot more costly, and amateurs didn't get paid to box. If I wanted to keep fighting, I was going to need a way to pay for it. The best way was to find a sponsor, because then I'd be able to train and fight full time instead of work at a job.

Getting that kind of help wasn't too difficult for a figure skater or a gymnast. Most of the athletes in high-visibility sports like those came from middle-class backgrounds with money of their own had good connections. But when you're poor and black and competing in a controversial sport that's perceived as "violent," it's a different matter. There are people who don't even think boxing belongs in the Olympics. Mostly that's people who don't understand the sport, but that doesn't stop them from speaking out about it.

My high school math teacher, John Smith, understood the pickle I was in. He was convinced I had a future as a boxer and wanted to help out. He picked me up one day and drove me all over town introducing me to local businessmen, trying to get them to consider sponsoring me. We visited restaurants, plumbing companies, pharmacies, construction outfits, you name it. Everybody was very nice and friendly, but Atlanta just wasn't much of a boxing town. Those people who did know a little something about boxing thought I was too small, too quiet, and too "unassertive" to be a successful fighter. They thought it took an out-sized personality like Ali's to make it in that game. John tried as hard as he could, but we got nowhere, so I needed to find a job.

Once again the Boys Club helped me out. They had a program to get jobs for the older kids who were leaving the club. They hooked me up with Epps Aviation, an outfit at the airport that provided services for private airplanes. I started off as a gofer ("Go fer this, go fer that . . ."), running errands, doing janitorial work and stuff like that. After about a year, I got moved up to the line crew where I refueled airplanes and towed them to and from hangars and parking areas. Some of the guys I worked with said I should be a pilot, but even then I knew I didn't want to spend my life flying other people around. I wanted to be the guy who got flown around by other people. My ticket to that goal was boxing, not flying, and I wasn't willing to devote time to anything that would distract me from it.

On the other hand, without a sponsor I had to support myself. My salary at Epps when I started was $2.65 an hour, which wasn't enough, so I also worked as a lifeguard at a public pool and sold peanuts and pop-corn at the stadium in Atlanta during Braves and Falcons games. With three jobs, it seemed like all I did was work, and it was hard to get any training in. I fought a lot of bouts bone tired and on little sleep, but I was still winning nearly all of them.

With everything that was going on, I had no time for girls. But sometimes things demand your attention whether you have time or not. One day when I was working at the pool a beautiful girl I'd never seen before walked in. You could tell right away that she wasn't from the projects like just about everyone else at the pool. My first thought was that she was way out of my league. All the lifeguards were angling and maneuvering to get near her and draw her attention, but I hung back. I didn't have the budget for girls like that, and most of them wouldn't even talk to "ghetto boys" like me.

A buddy of mine named Red couldn't take his eyes off her. Then he noticed that a friend of ours, a girl named Jackie who was also a lifeguard, seemed to know her. Red had enough assertiveness for both of us and came up with an idea. "I'm gonna go tell Jackie to ask her which one of us she likes best," he said.

"Which one of who?"

"You and me," he answered, and was off before I could stop him.

A few minutes later Jackie came over. "She said she likes the dark one." That was me!

Just then I heard some kids yell, "Mr. Holyfield! Mr. Holyfield! That girl's on the board!" I turned to see the new girl standing on the diving board and all these guys telling her to jump in. I blew my whistle at her, because she wasn't supposed to be on the board until she demonstrated to the lifeguards that she knew how to swim.

When she looked over at me I yelled, "Hey, you! Get off the board!"

She shrugged, said, "Okay," and jumped in. I went to get a rescue hook and kept an eye on her as she kind of splashed her way over to the side of the pool, just managing to keep her head above water.

When I got back she was climbing out. "You can't use the diving board until you prove you can swim," I informed her in my best official voice.

"Prove it to who?" she wanted to know.

"Me. You gotta take a swim test."

"When?"

"Right now, if you want." I told her to swim along the side of the pool and I'd follow her with the hook.

She shrugged again, then jumped back into the water and started swimming. Like a dolphin. I couldn't believe how good she swam. All that splashing around under the dive board had been a gag.

Her name was Paulette Bowens and I was right: She wasn't from the projects. Her family had their own house in a nice neighborhood, but we started seeing each other anyway. It started off slowly, because I had no experience with girls and it was all new to me. To both of us, really. It wasn't a normal kind of dating experience because of all the hours I was working while still trying to get all my training in. We found ourselves grabbing precious moments whenever they became available. Sometimes I'd only be able to see her at two or three in the morning, and afterward I'd sleep in my car until it was time to go to work. I also didn't have two nickels to rub together after meeting fight expenses, so we usually shared one cheeseburger and a soda, but I don't recall either of us ever minding or even commenting on it.

In 1983 the U.S. Olympic Committee staged its Sports Festival event in Colorado Springs, where they'd built a new sports center with six gyms and seating for three thousand. I won my division and became the number-one-ranked amateur in the United States. I'll tell you about that a little later, but the important thing for now is, it got me a slot in the PanAm Games and I was invited to train with the U.S. Olympic team in Colorado. That meant even more time away from Paulette, so when I did manage to get home for a day or two, those were pretty frantic hours.

Late in the summer of that year, I got a call from Paulette telling me she was pregnant. I was so shocked I could hardly speak. When I finally found my voice I heard myself uttering the classic idiot line, "How did that happen?" and got the standard joke in response: "The usual way." But I was serious; neither of us was stupid or frivolous and Paulette had been taking precautions. We'd talked about it on many occasions.

35

It's kind of interesting that one of the first things I worried about was how to tell Mama. It wasn't like her sensibilities were going to be offended. She'd had kids out of wedlock herself, so that wasn't it. The problem was that Mama had been determined to break what she called the "generational curse." By that she meant that each generation repeats the mistakes of the previous one, and she wanted to end that vicious cycle. Having kids out of wedlock was one of those mistakes, and here it was all over again. I was so concerned over how disappointed she was going to be that I called my sister Eloise and said, "You tell Mama. I can't."

Mama called me after they spoke. "How can she be pregnant!" she fumed. "You don't even have sex yet!"

Oh boy. Could my wise mother really be that naïve? "Sure I have," I told her, then quickly added, "but never in your house."

That was important to her, and it was true, but she was still pretty upset. As I said before, she'd had kids out of wedlock herself, including me, so you wouldn't think it was that big a deal, but she'd wanted to break that generational curse and I'd disappointed her. "You were supposed to be better!" she said at one point, and that hit me pretty hard.

Paulette and I didn't talk seriously about getting married yet. My own thing is, I *wanted* to be married. It's something I've always felt strongly about. I wanted to take care of somebody, to have a soulmate, to have a bunch of kids that I could bring up right, the way I was brought up. But I was at the Olympic Training Center in Colorado and Paulette was living at home in Atlanta with her parents. She didn't get along with them very well and wanted to move out as soon as she could, but once the baby came she'd have no choice because she'd need help taking care of the baby and wouldn't be working. I'd given up my apartment in the projects when I went to Colorado, and we couldn't set up our own house on what I was making. I wouldn't have any real money until I turned pro, and even then nothing was certain: I had all the confidence in the world, but I was also a realist. A lot could happen between

36

now and then, like getting hurt with a career-ending injury before I even had my first pro fight.

Evander Jr. was born on April 3, 1984. This was a critical time for me, as I was about to try to earn entry into the Olympics. I'd found a job loading trucks at a Budweiser plant near the training center, and the people at Epps Aviation let me work a few hours here and there whenever I came home, but money was still tight. Now I had a new baby to support as well. A blessing came in the form of a gift from Texas oil heiress Josephine Abercrombie, who wanted to get into the fight promotion business and was also trying to revive interest in boxing by creating the Houston Boxing Association. She knew I was going to turn professional someday and was hoping I'd consider signing with her, so after I won the Golden Gloves in St. Louis she gave me two thousand dollars without any strings other than "Remember me when the time comes." She had interests in oil, real estate, cattle and thoroughbred horses, so when she decided to get into boxing, she had the money and influence to back it up.

Just as I was thinking how best to use the money, Paulette called to tell me that my old 1968 Dodge Dart was wheezing its last. It ran so bad and needed so much work, she didn't want to put the baby in it to go to the doctor. I had to do something before the thing decided to just blow up and leave her stranded somewhere. On my next trip home I went looking to see what two thousand dollars would buy. I found a 1982 Buick that seemed to be a perfect fit for us, but the price was twice what I had. A salesman saw me looking at it and swooped right in on me, then started to swoop away when I told him I'd put two thousand down and give him the rest in a couple of months. I told him to go check my credit.

He came back and said, "You don't have any credit."

I said, "Well, I don't have any *bad* credit," but that didn't seem to matter. He looked like he was through with me, so before he walked away I asked to speak to the man in charge. I had no idea what I was going to say to him, but that's what you do when things aren't going your way: You speak to the top guy.

A few minutes later the salesman pointed me toward an inside doorway that led to an office. As I walked in, the man behind the desk said, "So what can I do for you?"

I read the name plate on his desk. "Mr. Sanders, I'd like to buy that Buick. I'll pay for half the car now, and the rest later."

"Later when?" he asked.

"When I get back from the Olympics."

Up until that point he'd been polite. Now he was interested. I was to learn that Ken Sanders was a big sports fan. He said, "You're going to the Olympics?" I said yeah, and he said, "In what?"

"Boxing."

"Who are you?" I told him, and he said, "I've heard of Michael Grogan. Never heard of you." Grogan was the number-one champ for four straight years in the 165-pound division, and also an Atlanta native.

"Promise me you won't sell that car in the next hour," I said to him. Then I went home, got my book of clippings and brought it back to the dealership.

I opened it to a picture of Grogan and me together at the Sports Festival holding up our medals. "See?" I said to Sanders. "I won gold, too."

Sanders looked at the picture, looked at me, looked at the picture again, and then said, "Okay. I'm going to cosign the loan for you." He also told me he was going to give me a monthly stipend to help with expenses.

"Just like that?" I asked him. "What do you get out of it?"

"Bragging rights. I just want to be able to tell people I put you in a Buick and I'm supporting you."

Ken was a Georgia Bulldogs supporter and was used to being around jocks. He would help out scholarship athletes, get them cars and things like that. He loved sports and athletes and didn't ask for anything for himself other than to be a part of things. He was just a good-hearted, sincere guy, and we got along real well. In addition to cosigning the auto loan, he gave me three hundred dollars a month to help get me through the trials and the Olympics, and he was smart enough to do that through the Georgia Amateur Boxing Association so it wouldn't hurt my amateur standing.

CHAPTER 4

___

Trials

By 1983, I'd compiled an amateur record of 160 wins and 14 losses, with 75 of my wins coming by way of knockout. That's an awful lot of knockouts in a three-round sport where wins usually come on points, yet few people outside Atlanta had even heard of me. (Just so you know: When compiling a fighter's statistics, technical knockouts are counted the same as knockouts.)

Part of the problem was that I'd graduated high school weighing 147 pounds. and had kept growing steadily afterward. That meant I was forever changing weight divisions. So as soon as I began making my mark as a welterweight, I shifted up to junior middleweight and started all over again. At just about the time I made it to the top of that division, I became a middleweight. All of that jumping around made it difficult to establish a reputation. Atlanta at that time was not known as a breeding ground for boxers, so there wasn't enough public interest for anybody to keep track of somebody like me.

But there was a lot of interest among people who were in the sport. The governing organization for amateur boxing in the United States is the USA Amateur Boxing Federation, which is part of the U.S. Olympic

Committee, and luckily for me the president, Loring Baker, and two of its referees were from Georgia. With an added assist from Buddy and Bo Davis of the Georgia Amateur Boxing Association, they tried to get me a slot in a series of matches against Cuba. The Davises had known me since I was eight and thought that if they could just get the U.S. national officials to have a look at me, they'd give me a shot. That's the kind of dedicated people they are. Buddy is still the president of GABA today and has been for about forty years, and he and Bo have devoted their entire lives to the sport of boxing. GABA was to be one of the first organizations I started supporting financially after I turned pro, and I still do.

The plan worked. Even though I lost by decision in a tough, close bout, I made enough of an impression on the U.S. officials, including U.S. boxing team coaches Roosevelt Sanders and Pat Nappy, to get myself invited to train for a tryout for the Pan-American Games. The trials were held as part of Sports Festival in Colorado Springs.

My first two opponents at the trials had beaten me before, but this time I beat them both. It wasn't easy, though; the fights were long and grueling and took a lot out of me, and then I had to go back into the ring the next day to face Rickey Womack.

There's no hard evidence, just a feeling on my part and some other people's, but there's a case to be made that U.S. boxing officials were anxious to have someone other than Rickey Womack represent America in the Olympic light heavyweight division. They were afraid he'd end up embarrassing the whole country. Despite his success in the ring, Womack was a deeply troubled man: emotional, volatile, and occasionally displaying signs of even more serious mental difficulties. He had a physically abusive father who was once accused of murdering Rickey's two-year-old brother. After social services took Rickey and his seven brothers and sisters away from his mother, Rickey went into foster care. He started boxing at the age of thirteen at the fabled Kronk Gym, which was run by Emanuel Steward, one of the all-time great trainers. Four years later he was convicted of armed robbery, and when he got out in

1981, Steward and his wife took him into their own home and treated him like a son while he trained at Kronk.

Despite the Stewards' love and attention, Rickey couldn't seem to break out of his old ways. Kronk boxers began reporting missing items after his return from prison, and when the team went to Tokyo for a tournament, Rickey stole a watch from a store while the manager was watching him. Mark Breland was with him at the time, and was detained until Steward managed to get him released.

When the Pan-Am trials came around, Rickey was the number-one-ranked amateur in the country and the odds-on favorite to go to the Olympic Games. He was tough, street-hardened and very experienced and was being handled by a professional team including one of the best trainers in the business, while I was basically a nobody from a nothing gym and my trainer hadn't even come with me.

I beat him anyway, which nobody expected, but because of the way the trials were set up, all that did was get us into a box-off a few weeks later in another city. This time we had to fight twice. Early in the first match my arm got hurt. I kept going anyway and fought as hard as I could, but it wasn't enough. The officials and coaches knew I was injured and heaped praise on me for hanging in there, but I was upset about losing. I thought seriously about giving up and going home before the second match.

But I decided that facing Womack in the ring a second time would probably be a lot easier than facing Mama in the kitchen and telling her I'd quit, so I stuck around and fought him again the next day. This time I beat him, and that's how I became the number-one-ranked amateur in the United States and got a spot at the Pan-American Games.

The PanAms were held in Caracas, and it's the first time I'd ever been out of the United States. I fought a Cuban and thought I'd won, but the decision went the other way. Howard Cosell asked for an interview with me. Just before the taping he told me he thought the decision was correct, and we debated it a little. It was a nice conversation, very friendly, no big deal, but once the cameras got rolling, Cosell reached deep into his legendary vocabulary and started hurling twenty-dollars words at me. I had no idea what he was asking me. Rather than look silly by answering questions he wasn't asking, I just shook my head. Cosell paused, because he hadn't asked a Yes-No question and didn't understand what I was doing, then he asked another one. That one I understood even less, so I shook my head again. He tried one more; same thing. Finally the director broke it off, and as I walked away he said, "What's the matter with you?"

I pointed at Cosell. "He's using all of these big old words," I explained, "and I don't know what he's talking about." It left Cosell and me feeling less than warm about each other, and the interview was never shown on television.

My next stop was the Golden Gloves in St. Louis, and that's where I met Mike Tyson for the first time. Although we weren't going to fight each other—Mike was in a higher weight class—we were the top candidates for the "Most Outstanding Boxer" title and badly wanted to outperform each other. The title went to the fighter who scored the most convincing wins. Mike won all five of his bouts, four by knockout. I won all five of mine as well, but knocked out every opponent. This didn't sit well with Mike, even though he was awarded the "Most Outstanding Boxer" title anyway.

Then in June the Olympic trials were held in Fort Worth, Texas. This time it was Rickey Womack's turn to beat me, but I wasn't out of the Olympics yet. I'd beaten Sherman Griffin earlier so I still had a chance, but I'd need to win a box-off just to get another shot at Rickey. The box-off was to be against Bennie Heard in Colorado, but he dropped out for some reason, and so it was down to Rickey and me for the top spot. To decide which of us would get to go to the Olympics, there would be yet another box-off a month later, July 7 and 8, at Caesars Palace in Las Vegas.

The box-off was a tense competition for me because by that time

Womack was ranked number one in the world, so in order for me to get the Olympic spot, I had to fight him twice, on consecutive days, and win both bouts. I did just that, making my next stop Gonzales, Texas, to train with the rest of the U.S. Olympic team. But the toughest part of the Olympics—getting there—was already over for me. No fighter I would go up against during the Games was as good a fighter as Womack.

But I wasn't ready to leave Las Vegas just yet. Mike Tyson was there for his own box-off, against Henry Tillman, and still hadn't forgotten my five knockouts at the Golden Gloves versus his four. As we were sitting together after the day's formal bouts were over, somebody said, "Hey, wouldn't it be cool to see Mike and Evander go at it!" This despite the fact that Mike was in the heavyweight division and I was two categories smaller. But with a lot of urging from the other guys, Mike and I got into the ring together. It probably didn't help Mike's mood any that his Olympic Trials roommate, Rickey Womack, had just lost the Olympic spot to me. What was supposed to be "a little friendly sparring" turned into such an all-out slugfest that an official ran over to call it off and warned us not to "spar" with each other again.

Sadly, Mike lost two controversial decisions to Henry Tillman and didn't go to the Olympics.

After the trials, Howard Cosell wanted to interview me again, and promised that he wouldn't make me look bad. He was true to his word. We quickly became friends and he remained a supporter of mine for the remainder of his career.

When I arrived in Los Angeles for the Games, I might as well have landed in Antarctica for all the attention that was paid to me. My teammates were some of the best-known names in amateur boxing and nobody had any idea who I was. A lot of people, including reporters, pronounced my name "Holly-field." Sports journalists from all over the world buzzed around the other fighters and interviewed them every chance they got, but not a single reporter even said hello to me, not even the ones from Atlanta. Believe it or not, though, I was fine with that. I'd made the U.S. Olympic team and was happy to be a part of it.

After I knocked out my first opponent, people started to pay some attention. When I knocked out my second opponent, they started asking questions about me. When I knocked out the third one, Howard Cosell held me up for the world to see and my life changed forever.

But I still had to get through the semifinals . . .

CHAPTER 5

Olympiad

Memorial Sports Arena—Los Angeles Olympic Games
August 10, 1984

Down in the locker room with U.S. Olympic boxing coach Pat Nappy before the fight I tried to focus, but the sounds of the crowd upstairs were coming right through the heavy concrete walls and it was hard not to let some of that excitement get to me. Not to mention that I already had at least a bronze medal in hand.

Most Olympic sports that have head-to-head matches, like volleyball and basketball, have a "playoff" for the two individuals or teams that lose their semifinal events, to determine who gets the bronze medal. It used to be that way in boxing, too, but in 1952 it was changed so that the two fighters who lose their semifinal bouts both get a bronze. Since I was already in the semifinals, a medal of some kind was a done deal. The idea that I was an Olympic medalist was so crazy wonderful that I had a tough time wrapping my mind around it and tried not to think about it now. I had work to do and needed to concentrate.

"Not gonna be as tough as Okello," Nappy was saying, referring to yesterday's quarterfinal bout against Sylvanu Okello of Kenya, "but nobody who gets this far in the Olympics is a pushover."

I knew that, and wasn't taking Kevin Barry, my next opponent, for granted. I never took anybody for granted, because I'd seen enough people get surprised when they took *me* for granted and I wasn't about to make that mistake myself.

But it was hard not to feel pretty confident, especially after my match against Okello. Howard Cosell interviewed me before the fight and I told him I was going to go hard at the Kenyan. Howard didn't seem to like that. He thought Okello was hard to hurt and that trying to knock him out could backfire on me. He reminded me that the Kenyan had knocked his last opponent out. If I wasn't super careful he could do the same to me.

But I'd studied Okello's fighting style. I told Cosell that I thought he was a really good counterpuncher, a guy who lets you take the first punch and then quickly comes back at you while you're a little off balance. I left it at that—for all I knew Okello was watching me on television—but what I was thinking was, if he was going to let me keep getting the first punches in, I'd hit him so hard he wouldn't be able to come back. By the time he figured out that his strategy wasn't going to work with me, I'd have the advantage in the fight.

Howard had taken a liking to me following our little misunderstanding at the PanAms, and after the official interview he pulled me off to the side. "You're the sixth American in the quarterfinals today," he said. "All the others won their bouts." It was his way of telling me I had to hold up my end.

He leaned toward me. "Now, listen," he said with great seriousness. "This Okello is good. He's better than the two guys you already fought and he's better than whoever you'll be meeting in the semis or the finals. He's tough and he can take a punch. Are you listening, Evander?"

I guess I must have been smiling. It was hard not to, listening to that famous voice. His mouth was only a foot away from my head but he still sounded like he was delivering a lecture to about nine million people instead of just me. *This . . . O-kel-lo . . . is good!* I loved the way he said my name, too: *E . . . Van . . . Derholy . . . FIELD!* He made it sound like a whole sentence, or a piece of a song. I assured him that I was listening.

"All right, then. Go for points. Don't try to knock him out; it's too risky. Box the man and get the points!" I nodded politely, kind of thrilled to have such a famous and experienced guy give me advice even though I didn't plan on taking it.

The U.S. coaches taped the ABC telecast of the Okello bout and a bunch of us on the team watched it that night. Tell you the truth, we watched it about twenty times, with a lot of whooping and hollering, because two minutes into the first round Howard said on the air, "Only thing that troubled me about what Holyfield said in the pre-fight interview was that he was looking to put him out early. I've stated repeatedly in this competition, in an Olympic boxing tournament you go in to box. You don't look to load up and knock the opponent out."

Twenty-two seconds later I loaded up and knocked the opponent out.

Howard loved it, and couldn't stop grinning afterward. I think he actually got a kick out of having been proven wrong. We spoke on the air ringside a few minutes after the fight ended and he said, "I must say, my young friend, you had the opponent absolutely cased, just as you described it in the prefight interview. You went to him and you got him." I had to bite back my own smile in order to get a response out, and it was caught on camera.

Cosell had the last few seconds of the fight replayed on the air as we talked and asked me to take him through it. I'd set Okello up with a left jab that pushed his right hand out of the way, then caught him flush in the face with a right. That got him up against the ropes. I threw a quick left jab to keep him off balance, then a hard right to the body and a full-out uppercut to the jaw that sent him sprawling through the ropes.

Okello was plenty tough, though: After a few seconds of being in a kind of daze, he untangled himself from the ropes and managed to get to his feet, but by then the count had ended and it was over.

Howard was right about one thing: Okello was a better fighter than Kevin Barry, my semifinal opponent. I wanted to KO my way to the gold, and was three for three so far, so I was determined to knock Kevin out and very confident that I could.

It was only too bad Mike Tyson wasn't there. As much as I liked Henry Tillman personally, I was sorry when Mike lost to him at the trials because it would have been fun to keep our private little competition going. I would have been up on him by one KO when the Olympics began and knew that Mike would have killed himself, not to mention the competition, to even the score.

Someone came into the locker room and handed Nappy a piece of paper. He looked at it, growled and crumpled it into his pocket.

"What?"

"Nothin'." He reached for some tape. "Gimme your hand."

I moved my arm away. "Nappy . . ."

He blew out a noisy breath and wiggled his fingers toward my arm. As I held out my hand, he said, "Ref's Yugoslavian."

I shrugged. "So what? I'm fighting a guy from New Zealand."

"Yeah, but after you beat him, you fight a Yugoslavian for the gold."

Now I understood. There wasn't a Yugoslavian fight fan alive who wasn't praying that I'd lose to Kevin Barry today so I wouldn't fight Anton Josipovic for the gold. Josipovic was a really good fighter, but after my knockout of Okello everybody knew that the only way I'd lose to him was if I got kidnapped by Martians. And that's why Nappy thought a Yugoslavian ref could be bad news for me.

All the scoring in a boxing match is done by judges sitting ringside, but the ref has more clout than all of them put together. He can instruct the judges to take deductions for violations, and he has the absolute power to stop the fight and declare a winner no matter where the points stand. If the ref favored a guy or had something against him, there was plenty he could do about it.

On the other hand, this was the Olympics, not some backwater gym. If anything, Olympic referees and judges go out of their way not to show favoritism because any mistakes they make are going to be seen by about half a billion people and get analyzed to death forever. I don't know why anyone would even want the job. My guess is that most Olympic event officials probably think more about not messing up than doing a great job.

But it was Nappy's job to worry so that's what he was doing. "I'll knock Barry out," I promised him, "and that way we won't have to worry about who's the ref."

When I climbed into the ring a few minutes later, the crowd of nearly twelve thousand was shouting my name, only this time they were pronouncing it correctly.

Unless you've been there, you can't imagine what it's like to compete in an Olympic arena. There are flags all over the place, dozens of television cameras pointing at the ring, the fans are totally nuts before anything's even happened, and there's a kind of feeling in the air that tells you that this is *important*. Reporters wearing special press passes seem to be everywhere, interviewing anybody who'll sit still for a minute, including security guards, spectators and even each other.

I moved around my corner a little to try to stay loose. I didn't know it at the time, of course, but Bob Lee, one of the ABC announcers doing the live broadcast, was telling the television audience and his partner, Al Bernstein, that I had to be a leading contender for the Val Barker Cup, which is awarded to the outstanding boxer of the Games. I was in the best shape of my life, I understood the strengths and weaknesses of both Barry and Josipovic, none of my fights so far had made it to the end of the third round, and I had absolutely no idea that in about eight minutes I was going to be the central figure in what sportswriters would come to call one of the cruelest moments in Olympic boxing history.

Think there's no arguing with a knockout?

So did I.

For the first few seconds of the fight I tried to feel Kevin out a little, testing to see if I'd nailed his style down right. He had quickness and was light on his feet, and he wasted no time before throwing a bunch of good left jabs. But I was so jazzed and ready, it felt like I knew what he was going to do even before he did, and I swatted his punches away easily. I flicked out a couple of little jabs myself and saw that his reflexes were good, then hit him with a few hooks. His reaction was to grab hold of me, a very common tactic to stop a flurry of punches, but not something I was used to seeing so early in a fight. Kevin threw some shots as we separated, just as he should have, like Magic Johnson always throwing the ball up at the basket when he gets fouled: You never know when one is going to connect. What he shouldn't have done was throw punches *while* holding me, which he was to do repeatedly, earning him cautions and warnings.

Less than a minute into the round Kevin started to figure out that he was in trouble, and that I was racking up points and he wasn't. I kept stepping into him and he kept stepping back as I began throwing harder and harder punches, and he couldn't seem to get off a shot of his own without grabbing me at the same time. At about the 1:15 mark of the round I caught him with a solid left and he wrapped his arms around me yet again. The referee, Gligorije Novicic, ordered us to stop and gave him a caution.

After that I was all over Kevin, and the crowd knew it. The noise began to grow and people were yelling my name again. Kevin looked like he was just trying to survive, covering up a lot and throwing only half-hearted punches. Novicic cautioned him again at the 2:30 mark, and when I waded in once more, Kevin wrapped his arm *backward* around me, his left forearm over my left shoulder. That left my entire right arm free and his whole back exposed, so I whacked him a good one to the back of the head. That started him swinging around and while he was busy trying to stay upright, I cocked my left arm and launched a left to his jaw. At that exact instant the ref yelled "Stop!" but it was too late: The punch was already on its way.

This time the ref gave *me* a caution. I thought it was going to be for a late hit, but Novicic tapped the back of his head, telling me it was for the punch I'd delivered to Kevin's head before the one to his jaw. The crowd began booing loudly, but it was a good call. Novicic knew I couldn't stop the jaw shot once I'd started it, but he was right to give me grief for the behind-the-head hit.

I wasn't interested in dancing cheek to cheek for the rest of the match hoping to get in a few punches here and there and gain points. Even though it was pretty obvious that I was dominating this fight, a bout decided by judges is like a trial decided by a jury: You may think you've won, but you just plain never know until the verdict comes in, and that was too big a risk for me. When I was a kid I'd lost too many decisions in fights I'd really won, and while I'd had to wordlessly swallow those defeats in order to keep on fighting, no way was I going to let that happen at the Olympics. I'd wanted to win by a knockout anyway and this sorry samba only made me want it more.

So far Novicic was doing a great job of controlling the fight, making it clear that he wasn't going to let either of us get away with anything. This was good for me, because I was about to go into overdrive and was pretty sure he wouldn't allow any cheap shots or tricks to trip me up. A few seconds after I got my caution I threw a light left jab at Kevin that barely touched him, but he covered up and backed off anyway, without hitting back. I threw another jab and another and he kept backing up until he was against the ropes, and still he hadn't thrown a punch of his own. By now the crowd knew that something was brewing and I knew that there were only a few seconds left in the round. I tapped him with a right and when his head turned in response I came back with a hard left hook. Kevin fell back against the ropes and started to fall, but he used the ropes to keep himself upright and instinctively went into a crouch. I threw a left that glanced off his headgear and then a right that missed and went behind his neck, but I came back with another left hook that knocked him sideways. I thought he might go down but he caught himself again, and that set him up for a right cross that buckled his knees and sent him stumbling.

Somehow, he stayed on his feet once again, and I could hardly believe it. The guy was really showing me some heart. He hadn't thrown a single punch since the last clinch but he'd taken an awful lot from me, and the man just refused to lay down.

But heart isn't enough to win fights. Kevin was clearly unable to either throw punches or defend himself and Novicic knew it, so as I got ready to lay into him again, the ref dove between us and waved us apart. He motioned me to a neutral corner, then turned to Kevin and started a standing eight count, watching him closely to see whether he could continue to fight. Kevin moved around and adjusted his gloves, trying to look casual, showing Novicic that he was okay so that the fight wouldn't be stopped. He was getting a little rest during the count, but two more of those standing eights and he'd lose the fight by technical knockout.

Novicic decided Kevin was okay and held out his hand palm up, the sign that we should continue. Kevin threw one punch and then wrapped his arms around me again. He wouldn't let go, and this was getting real old, real fast, so I spun him around and threw him through the ropes, causing a rope separator to come loose. Again he popped back up, and again got a chance to rest as the clock was stopped, this time so that the ref could repair the separator. I rocked Kevin a few more times after that but the round ended before I could do anything more serious.

Back in my corner Nappy sat me down quickly. "Be patient!" he ordered as he wiped sweat from my brow. He knew I was frustrated with Kevin's style. "Just keep doing what you're doing and we're in the finals."

"Can't shake him off me," I groused.

"Don't worry about it," assistant coach Roosevelt Sanders said. "He keeps that up, ref's gonna warn him right out of the match."

"How come he hasn't already?"

"'Cuz it's a lousy way to lose a fight," Nappy answered. "Ref won't end it that way unless he has to."

"You got it won," Sanders insisted, and then repeated what Nappy had said. "Be patient!"

Nappy telling me to be patient . . . that was funny. Kind of reminded me of Carter Morgan telling me to keep control of myself. Both of those great coaches could go off like land mines when something didn't go right, but insisted that I behave myself. "Just trying to stop you from making the same mistakes I did," Morgan always said to me.

There's this thing antelopes in Africa do when they're being chased by a lion. Every few seconds one of them will take a huge leap into the air. It's the antelope's way of saying to the lion, "Look how strong and fast I am," so the lion will leave it alone and go after one of the weaker members of the herd.

When we came out for Round Two, Kevin was acting like an antelope for the judges, bouncing all over the place, showing that he had plenty of energy and fight left in him. As soon as the bell rang he threw a few enthusiastic lefts, but covered up immediately when I came right back to him, then started holding me again. Novicic gave him a caution, and a few seconds after that Kevin held me again and this time Novicic had us move away and wait while he made a few hand signals. The last one was a thumb pointed upward, which told the judges that he was issuing a warning and that they should deduct a point from Kevin on each of the five scorecards. You can only cut a guy so much slack, I guess, and then points start coming off. Assuming Kevin had any points to begin with, which was unlikely. Warnings are serious: Three of them and you're disqualified.

When we started up again I caught Kevin with a hard left hook and then threw another just as the ref yelled "Stop." There was no way I could halt the punch in midflight, but Novicic gave me a caution anyway. The crowd started booing immediately but it wasn't that big a deal and I didn't think much about it. I got Kevin up against the ropes; he grabbed hold of me, as usual, then hit me in back of the head, and the ref yelled "Stop" again. Kevin hit me anyway, and the ref gave him a caution, but I couldn't tell if it was for hitting me in the back of the head or for hitting late. Cautions don't affect the scorecards; they're the ref's way of letting you know he saw a violation and that if you did it again there would be stiffer penalties.

Despite yet another caution, this time for a near-headlock, Kevin kept on holding me. But for some reason Novicic was giving him only cautions, not warnings or deductions. I saw Nappy and Sanders jumping up and down a little and figured they were raising some kind of fuss aimed at the ref, urging him to do what he was supposed to do and issue a warning. Sometimes coaches do that to let their fighter know they're supporting him, like a baseball coach going toe-to-toe with the ump even though there's no chance of getting a call changed. It also lets the fighter know that he shouldn't kick up a fuss himself, because somebody's already doing it for him and he should just stay focused on fighting. It worked, too, because even though no decent ref would ever pay attention to stuff like that, it was nice to know that somebody besides me was noticing.

At just about that point Kevin must have figured out that he was a goner unless he showed some fight, and he came up with a few decent punches. But he also got another caution, and the next time he held on to me Novicic had no choice but to order the judges to deduct another point. One more of those and Kevin was out.

This was starting to get silly. I could have gone out for a cheeseburger and still won on points. But that's the last thing in the world I wanted. I wanted to knock him out and now there was a real problem: If Kevin got another warning he'd be disqualified. I'd win all right, but by TKO, and that wasn't good enough for me.

It was time for me to let it all hang out. We were almost at the end of the second round and I didn't want it to go to a third. I needed to put Kevin down for good, and do it right now.

When the ref was finished issuing the warning and we started up again, I went after Kevin hard and, what do you know, he grabbed me again. This was like the opposite of that leaping antelope, Kevin practically shouting to the ref that he couldn't fight back. He had his arm clamped down tight over the ear hole on the right side of my headgear. I couldn't hear anything on that side and it was a little eerie, but I didn't have time to think about that and I also wasn't about to wait for Novicic to break us up for the thousandth time. This time I let Kevin hold me without trying to shove him away, but I kept my hands free and slammed him in the ribs with a right hook. The crowd saw it and also saw Kevin start to fall away. They started yelling, thinking maybe this was it, but Kevin managed to stay upright by hanging on to my neck. I pulled my body away and hauled off with another hook to the midsection, and this time Kevin surprised me by launching an uppercut at the exact same instant. Neither of us connected solidly but while he'd just thrown the one punch, mine was the first of a one-two combination. I'd been taught to always follow up a right with a left, and hardly ever threw just one punch. When I finished up the combination with a roundhouse left that caught him square on the jaw, it snapped his head to the side and his whole body went limp. No way was he coming back from that.

Just as I was throwing that last punch Kevin's arm finally left my head and uncovered my ear hole for the first time since he'd grabbed me some seconds before. I heard Novicic say something over the frenzied screaming coming from the crowd. It sounded like "Break!" and small wonder: Kevin had been hanging on to me like a bear cub to its mother. If he hadn't crumpled to the canvas after that last punch there would have been another points deduction. The guy was defenseless by then, and the knockdown was a mercy.

Novicic quickly jumped in between us and motioned me to a neutral corner. As I began walking away he started the count. Kevin sat up, looked around for a second and then got to his feet like a wobbly newborn deer and stumbled over to the other corner. I couldn't believe he was able to get up, and gave him credit for it, God bless his heart. He veered drunkenly but somehow managed to face the ref, as if to say "I'm not finished yet." Novicic was holding up fingers to indicate the count, and when he was done he grabbed Kevin and moved him back to the corner. The New Zealander was done for and the crowd was in near-hysterics. I'd just made a contribution to the American boxing effort with a semifinal win, and a gold medal in the finals was all but assured.

It's not my style to celebrate openly. I don't do victory dances and I don't gloat, especially not when another guy is feeling like his whole world just caved in, and I didn't do it then. Celebration would come later, in private with my teammates, after I took care of the Yugoslavian in the finals and had that gold medal around my neck.

But there was another thought that I have to confess was running through my head, a very selfish one. I was thinking, "Don't stop the fight! Let him continue, don't stop the fight!" Because Kevin had gotten up before the end of the count, it wouldn't be scored as a knockout. It was the ref's decision to stop the fight because of Kevin's condition, so it would only be a TKO. I thought, "The guy's been hanging on to me practically nonstop and you didn't give him a third and final warning, so don't stop us now! Let me knock him out!"

But I saw that it was hopeless. As Kevin hung his head and headed back to the corner, Novicic held his hand toward the judges, palm down, telling them not to bother with any more scoring. Then he turned around and came toward me. As he got closer he waved his fingers at me and I started forward to meet him in the middle of the ring, expecting him to send me back to my own corner.

But he didn't do that. He started making hand signals at me, and said, "When I say stop, you stop," or something close to that, like a schoolteacher scolding a child. What was the point of that? I just scored a decisive victory and I needed a shower, not a lecture. I had trouble catching all of it, especially with the crowd still screaming and clapping, and Novicic's English wasn't that good to begin with, but I did understand his last word before he turned away: "Disqualified!"

Disqualified? He couldn't possibly be serious. Had he actually expected me to reel back in a punch that was already on its way?

I remember exactly what I was thinking: "This is America. He can't do this. We'll get it straightened out."

As I went back to my corner Novicic went ahead of me, leaned over the ropes and said something to the judges. Before he'd even gotten two words out, Coach Nappy realized what was going on and took off along the ropes like a ballistic missile, screaming at the ref all the way. Sanders had to go after him and pull him back, which was about the time I realized that we weren't going to get it straightened out, and it's also when the crowd caught on to what was happening. The cheers began turning to boos, and very soon the booing got ugly.

There are a lot of clichés for a moment like that—the wind going out of your sails, a pin popping your balloon, the rug getting pulled out from under you—and you know what? Every one of them is dead-on accurate. That's exactly what it feels like, all rolled into one. I felt physically ill, dizzy, and so blown away I couldn't think straight. The only thought I could hang on to was the same one I'd had earlier: "This is America. He can't do this."

All those months of training and dreaming crashed into me like a multicar pileup. If somebody stronger, more talented and better conditioned had whupped me, all right then, I could live with that. I might not like it but at least it would make sense. I'd go back home, train harder and do better next time.

But what would I do now? I'd dominated this fight from the opening bell, knocked Kevin down, been ahead on all five cards and then dropped him altogether. How could I go back and do better next time?

Could this get any worse?

"It gets worse," Nappy said as Sanders undid my helmet.

I looked at Nappy but he wouldn't meet my eyes. He looked down at my gloves instead. "You're not going to get your bronze medal," he said without looking up.

I turned to Sanders.

"On account of you being disqualified," the assistant coach explained. "It's in the rules."

Buddy Davis was sitting ringside and had tears streaming down his cheeks. He knew the rules and had already figured out I wasn't going to get a medal. I had to look away to stop from crying myself, because as awful as I felt, I still had to go back to the center of the ring for the official announcement. I had to keep it together.

In the middle of the ring, Novicic took both our hands and the announcer said, "The winner, by disqualification . . . Kevin Barry!" The ref lifted Kevin's hand high into the air, turned us both around to face the other way, then walked away, leaving the two of us alone. Kevin immediately raised my arm and said "You won" into my ear, then walked me back to my corner and said the same thing to Nappy and Sanders.

The enraged crowd was on its feet, people yelling insults and profanities and shaking their fists and flashing thumbs down with both hands. Nappy raised his head slightly, pointing toward something behind me with his chin. "This doesn't look good," he said. I turned and saw that Novicic was being escorted out of the arena by guards who surrounded him to stop anyone from getting their hands on him. A crumpled paper cup came flying into the ring, then a few with soda in them and then a couple with ice cubes.

With the crowd on the edge of a riot, I was one of the few people in the whole place who was staying calm, something that was noted in nearly every one of the hundreds of newspaper articles and television features that would follow in the next few days and months. Writers and commentators talked about my "grace under pressure" and what a level-headed guy I was and how my behavior should make all Americans proud. It was all very nice, and sure made my mother feel good, and also made the whole thing a better story—I was a more sympathetic character than if I'd gone off the deep end and carried on for the cameras—but there was more to it than just good manners.

It was me being catapulted back in time to 1978, to my bout with Stevie Kirwood. It was me standing in the middle of a boxing ring, a place I'd come to think of as home, but once again finding myself a stranger. I'd overcome poverty and racism in the most poverty-stricken and racist corner of the country, convinced that I'd left injustice far behind, but in less time than it takes to walk across a ring I'd somehow fallen down a mountain and back into the pit. When you get rocked that hard and disoriented that badly, you don't sit around and plan your response. Conditioning kicks in, like an autopilot, and my conditioning said *Behave yourself!* I didn't know what else to do anyway, because in my limited experience there was no precedent for this. I was center stage in what was supposed to be the most honorable, unsoiled arena on earth, an Olympic boxing ring. There were hundreds of pages of detailed rules to ensure fairness, dozens of officials charged with enforcing them and the whole world watching it all. Something like this wasn't supposed to happen. It *couldn't* happen.

But it had, and in all my mental preparation, all my endless visualizations of every possible outcome, nothing like this had ever entered my imagination. So after nearly two weeks of Olympic excitement and ceremony and speeches and endless talk about high ideals and the glory of pure competition, I found myself in just another smelly little gym in another smelly little city, and me just another fighter who got too close to the sun and was brought crashing back to earth. So I reacted just the way I had when the ref raised Stevie Kirwood's hand instead of mine: I stood there and I took it and I behaved myself.

Why? It wasn't because I was a wimp or a house slave who didn't want to stir up trouble.

It was because everything I'd come to believe about life, everything I'd learned from Mama and Carter Morgan about how to be a man, told me that there was absolutely nothing to be gained by making a public spectacle of myself. They could take my victory and my medal but nobody on earth could rob me of my dignity unless I let them, and I wasn't about to let them. That's the way Mama wanted me to behave and that's the way Carter Morgan insisted it be, and it had worked pretty good up until then, so that's the way I was.

But it wasn't like I was going to quietly drift away without a fight. It was just that I would fight according to the rules, same as I would inside the ring. There were procedures for handling a grievance, and I had plenty of people to fight right along with me, people with brains and clout who appreciated my situation and didn't like it any better than I did.

My approach to that setback would eventually pay off, in more ways than I could have imagined at the time.

Well after the fight ended, the crowd in the Olympic arena had still not finished venting its outrage, although they'd at least stopped throwing stuff and the ring had been cleared of junk. Olympic officials decided to get the next bout started, probably thinking that the fans would settle down out of respect for the two guys fighting for a medal. It worked.

Jim Fox, executive director of USA Boxing, wasn't around to see it, though, because he was already off filing a formal complaint on my behalf. He was so anxious to get the process started he didn't bother having it typed or even put on an official form. He just scribbled it down on a piece of paper right there at ringside and personally handed it to Anwar Chowdhry, secretary general of the International Amateur Boxing Association, along with the hundred-dollar filing fee Jim had taken out of his own wallet.

Meanwhile, I got marched out of the ring and straight to an interview with Howard Cosell. I'd never seen him that angry, before or since. "Never in my career have I seen a decision this bad," he said on camera, practically sputtering into his microphone. "This is so bizarre!" He explained to the audience that a protest was under way—I have no idea how he'd gotten that information so fast—but after the cameras finally clicked off and the lights were lowered in the studio, he put his hand on my arm and said, real sadlike, "Don't get your hopes up, Evander. I've never seen a ref's decision reversed." He looked like he felt as bad as I did.

Back at the Olympic Village it seemed like everybody knew what had happened. A few people avoided me, like you avoid someone with a fatal disease because you don't know the right thing to say. Some athletes who hadn't completed their competitions yet also stayed away, like they didn't want any bad vibes or jinxes from hanging around a guy who'd just lost.

But most people went out of their way to be nice. "Hey, now you can load up on ice cream!" a few said to me. "You don't have to get up at five in the morning for a workout," some others said, pretending to be jealous. "You can stay out after ten!"

They just didn't get it. I *wanted* someone jabbing me in the ribs at dawn to go to practice. I *wanted* Coach Nappy yelling at me to stay the heck away from the dessert line and keep off my feet. I *wanted* somebody warning me to be back in the dorm by curfew. I wanted all those things, desperately, and a dozen other annoying restrictions and rules. Instead, I was completely free to have anything I wanted and to do whatever I wanted and I didn't want to have or do anything.

What was kind of interesting was that there was still a formal hearing pending, and if the protest was upheld, I'd be fighting Anton Josipovic the following day. Just in case, shouldn't people still have been all over me to keep following the rules and stay sharp? Was this their way of telling me that we were going to lose the appeal, just like Cosell said?

Those were the kinds of things that were rattling around in my mind, and the more athletes I ran into—some of them wearing fresh gold medals around their necks—the worse it got. By the next day I couldn't stand it anymore and went to the beach in Santa Monica to walk around on the sand.

On the other side of town in a meeting room at the Sports Arena, Jim Fox and Loring Baker, president of USA Boxing, presented our side of the argument to the protest committee. They didn't press hard on whether I'd heard Novicic's command to stop. Instead, they argued that the ref was incompetent and had lost control of the fight, and that the bout would never have gotten that far if he'd been doing his job right because he would have disqualified Kevin earlier in the round on account of all of his fouls. Kevin had already received points deductions twice along with a bunch of cautions, so it wasn't like this was new news, and Baker argued that Novicic should have deducted points again, which would have resulted in a DQ for Kevin.

The committee reviewed videotape of the fight, and Jim and Loring agreed that both Kevin and I had hit after the command to stop. But they were harshly critical of Novicic and insisted that it was his failure to enforce the rules that allowed such an unfair conclusion.

Jim and Loring are a savvy couple of guys, and they figured out early in the meeting that the committee would never go so far as to declare me the winner of the bout. They also knew it was useless to try to argue for a rematch—all else aside, the rules were clear that Kevin couldn't fight for another four weeks because he'd gone down after a head shot—so they decided to put all their marbles into a single plea: Let Holyfield at least keep his bronze medal.

Neither Kevin nor I were called in to be interviewed and, even more disturbing to Jim and Loring, neither was the ref. The committee felt it had everything it needed to reach a fair judgment.

I was still walking on the beach when the scheduled time for the decision got near, so I found a restaurant with a television going and walked in. A couple of people recognized me, so when I asked for them to change the station, nobody argued. But they didn't know the details of what was going on or even that there was a hearing underway.

Cosell's face came on the screen. Howard looked hangdog even when he was happy but now he looked just awful. "There's good news and bad news for Evander Holyfield," he said. I felt a catch in my throat: What could that possibly mean? "The good news is, his bronze medal won't be taken away. The bad news is, he won't be allowed to fight for the gold."

I hardly remember hearing that first part, because the second part floored me so bad. Even though I'd prepared myself for that moment by imagining it over and over, it didn't help. Until then there had been hope, however slim, and now there was none at all. Somebody in the restaurant said, "Hey, you won an Olympic medal!" Somebody else offered to buy me a beer. Nobody understood, and I got out of there as fast as I could.

On my way back to the village, I got over the shock and started thinking. If the committee upheld the ref's decision that I'd made a late hit and therefore deserved to be disqualified, why on earth would they award me a bronze medal? How could Cosell's "good news and bad news" both be true at the same time? It made no sense to me at all.

Nor to a lot of other people. The decision had been announced in the Sports Arena, but none of the committee members attended the news conference and nobody could reach them for comment afterward. So the press concentrated all their attention on me and I got interview requests from just about everybody at the Games who had a press pass.

The only people happy with the decision were the Yugoslavians who'd been worried about Anton Josipovic facing me in the finals. They got an early Christmas present: Their man was going to get the gold without having to fight me in the finals, or Kevin Barry, either, because of the four-week rule, so there were no finals at all. Kevin got the silver medal, Josipovic got the gold in a "walkover," and that was it for the light heavyweight division at the '84 Olympics.

In the days, weeks and months that followed, thousands of articles were written about this incident, and I doubt that there's been much written about me since that didn't at least mention it. A couple of writers tried to set the episode in the context of the political situation at the time. The Soviet Union, America's traditional fierce rival, wasn't at the Games. The Russians said it was because of poor security, but it was really them getting back at us for President Carter's boycott of the 1980 Moscow Games in protest of the Soviet invasion of Afghanistan. There was talk that, with the Games on U.S. soil and no Russians or East Germans to contend with, American athletes were getting preferential treatment on their way to vacuuming up every medal in sight. So after the American boxing team had steamrollered its way through most of its matches to the point where it looked like we were going to capture all twelve gold medals, people started wondering whether the decision against me was some kind of backlash against Yankee arrogance, a signal that America wouldn't be allowed to throw its weight around.

But it wasn't bias that tilted the competition toward the Americans. Not only were the Soviets and East Germans absent from the Games because of the boycott, so were the Cubans, and they were among the best fighters in the world (as I knew only too well: One of them had beaten me at the PanAms). It would be like the Japanese not showing up for judo and everybody wondering why South Korea got all the medals. Of course we were the heavy favorites.

* * *

I thought at the time that getting the bronze was worse than getting no medal at all, because it said to me that I deserved the gold but couldn't have it. As if to drive the point home, at the award ceremony Anton Josipovic, the gold medalist, pulled me up onto the highest tier and raised my arm into the air. It seemed like every time I turned around there was another reminder that an injustice had been done.

Now, however, I feel very differently about that bronze. Having an Olympic medal of any kind is an extraordinary honor. I cherish it and I've made my peace with what happened. It also helped that there are no villains in this tale, nobody to get mad at. And to top it all off, from a career point of view it's possible that I got a much more visible send-off into the professional boxing world than if I'd won a gold like ten other Americans.

But the important lesson here is this: I think that the single biggest factor in that committee awarding me the bronze medal was that I hadn't given them any reason not to. If I had carried on about how unfair it all was and accused the ref of bias and gotten on Kevin's case about how he'd fought me, if I'd refused to leave the ring after the decision or harassed the officials or leaped up onto the ropes and tried to incite a riot, I'm absolutely certain that the hearing would have lasted five minutes at the most and I'd have been sent home with nothing to show for my participation in the Olympics.

The best part of the whole thing wasn't the medal, either. The best part was when Mama said, "Son, I'm proud of how you handled yourself."

After the Games the American gold medalists went on a nationwide tour. I hadn't won a gold but was invited to tour with them anyway, and I did. It was an incredible experience, and one of the best parts was that I kept getting seated next to Mary Lou Retton at various dinners. She's every bit as wonderful in person as she is on television and I enjoyed talking to her.

Years later I ran into Gligorije Novicic at a European competition in which he was officiating. We were friendly to each other and talked a bit, and when the conversation got around to the Olympic semifinal bout, he said, "I'm sorry."

I couldn't tell if he was apologizing for making a mistake or just saying he was sorry that the whole thing happened, but it didn't much matter. I bore him no ill will then and I don't now.

It's just not my style.

The point of telling that story, and the one about my loss to Stevie Kirwood, is not to tell you about all these bad things that happened to me. Bad things happen to everyone. What's important is learning from them, and becoming better for them. You can spend your life being bitter or looking for revenge, or you can do what you can—or do nothing if there's nothing to be done—and move on and be stronger and not dwell on it. A lot more good things happened to me in life than bad, so there was no reason to get hung up on the bad. Everything was another lesson to absorb, or a mistake to be understood and corrected, not an insult or a grudge to be nursed, turning me into a bitter and resentful person.

What happened at the Olympics was terrible. It was as bad as I remember feeling about almost anything. But raising a public stink and acting like a spoiled brat wasn't going to help anything. I had good people going to bat for me and I had to trust that they knew what they were doing. And if they couldn't straighten it out, so be it. I had a whole professional career ahead of me and wasn't about to kick it off by being just another whiny athlete who got a raw deal. It wasn't the end of the world. It was just a rotten thing that happened, and I wouldn't let it overwhelm me, and I wouldn't allow it to make me behave in public in a way that would have brought shame to Mama, to Carter Morgan, or to any of the other people who had faith in the kind of person they believed I was.

My point in talking about bad things that happened to me isn't to make people feel sorry for poor Evander. I want them to learn from how I handled adversity. Try to think of a single athlete or any other well-known person who complained loud and long about something that went wrong and still had people think good things about them. I don't think you can do it. Everybody loves a winner, but nobody likes a whiner, even if the whiner has a good point. What people get excited about isn't how awful it was that something bad happened to you. What they care about is how you handled it. Did you stew in your own self-pity and blame others for your failures? Or did you pick yourself up and get on with it?

I remember a few years ago when Lance Armstrong was sent crashing to the ground in the Tour de France by some fan who'd gotten too close and tangled a bag he was carrying in Lance's handlebars. What impressed me was that Lance barely looked back to see what had happened. He didn't take out after the guy or complain about it later to reporters and moan about how unfair it was. He got back on that bicycle as quickly as he could and pedaled his heart out to get back to his place in the pack. Lance didn't want to make sure he had a good excuse for losing! He wanted to *win*, and he kept his eye on the prize and did win.

Somebody once said that no captain ever proved himself on calm seas, and it's true. A great champion isn't one who wins all the time and nails every shot and never messes up. A great champion is one who doesn't let setbacks defeat him. He's at his very best when things are at their very worst. Watching Tiger Woods hit the green from the middle of the fairway is nice. Watching him hit it from deep rough behind a tree after totally messing up his tee shot is mind-boggling. Guys like Armstrong and Woods don't have time to feel sorry for themselves when things go wrong. They don't want to be footnotes in the record with great excuses. They want to be at the top of the list, and you don't get to be the very best by taking your eye off the ball and letting things distract you, no matter how unjust they might be. Champions know how to capitalize on the good stuff and put the bad stuff aside quickly. There's just no other way to be the very best.

I don't spend a lot of time thinking when things go wrong. I don't sit there running through options and making conscious decisions about how I'm going to act, because how to act has been baked into me so deeply that there's no real choice.

And now you know why I behaved like I did when I got DQ'd at the Olympics. There was no point in coming unglued. I wasn't going to change the ref's mind. I wasn't going to get Olympic officials to overturn the decision right there in the ring. There was absolutely nothing I could do about the situation while standing there so I didn't try.

More important, it didn't mean my world had come to an end, although people watching on television might have thought it did. But they didn't know me. They saw a guy in a boxing ring at the most prestigious competitive arena in the world and assumed that my entire life had been focused on winning an Olympic medal and that nothing else mattered.

That wasn't close to being true. The Olympics were important to me. I wanted to win. People were counting on me and had gone to great lengths to get me there. But it wasn't my whole life. I was disappointed and frustrated and upset, but I wasn't crushed, like it was so awful I could never recover and I'd regret it for the rest of my life.

It was a defeat, and a lousy one. I'd had them before; I'd have them again. I'd do what I could to get it straightened out and, either way, I'd move on. What I wouldn't do is make a fool of myself. It's not the way I was brought up.

A note about Rickey Womack:

After he lost his chance at the Olympics to me, Rickey turned pro, signing a deal with Emanuel Steward and ESPN. Over the next year and a half he performed wonderfully in the ring, racking up an impressive 9-0 record.

Sometime during Christmas of 1985 he walked into a video store in the Detroit suburb of Redford carrying a nine-millimeter handgun that he used to beat the female clerk in the course of stealing money from the till and a handful of tapes. Two weeks later he tried to rob another video store in the same neighborhood, but a customer walked in while it was going on. Rickey shot him and then ran off, but he left behind the car Steward had given him. His wallet was inside and the police eventually tracked him down. The customer lived, but Rickey still had to do fifteen years in prison.

What kept him going while he was inside was the thought that he might return to boxing and become a champion. After his release, a former world champion heavyweight tracked him down and helped him get back into the ring. He had four successful fights, then won a unanimous decision against Willie Chapman. Despite the important victory, the crowd booed him loudly because they thought he hadn't fought well. Rickey apparently thought so, too, and in the car driving away from the arena with his manager, he was inconsolable.

It was the last psychological straw for Rickey, and he couldn't get past it. Two months later, after an all-night fight with his wife, he threatened her with a borrowed gun, then turned it on himself and took his own life in front of her.

The former world champ who tracked Rickey down after his release from prison and tried to help him get his life back was Mike Tyson, his roommate from the Olympic Trials.

CHAPTER 6

———

Isom Coley

When I got back from the Olympic Games, my mother announced that she was taking me to Atmore to see my father. I was surprised because by that time I'd just assumed he was dead. I told her I didn't want to go. What did I need a daddy for? I was twenty-one, I had just signed a big contract, I was on my own and didn't need anyone telling me what to do, especially a father I'd never met. I told Mama all I needed was her, because she was the one who'd been there for me before all of this stuff started to happen for me, when I didn't have a thing. "Why do I have to go see him?"

"Because I said so," was all she would tell me. I had a pretty good idea what it was really about: She wanted to kind of stick it to him a little, show him the kind of boy she was able to raise all on her own.

We drove the whole way, and I spent most of the trip wondering what I was going to say to this man who was supposed to be my father. We went to his brother Sam's house first because Mama knew where he lived but not where my father lived. When Sam came out, the first thing he said was, "He sure looks like Isom." And Mama said, "Well, it's his son, so why don't you tell us where he lives."

He did, and when we got there, Isom Coley was out in the back chopping wood and his son Mike answered the door of their trailer. As soon as he opened it his eyes grew wide and he yelled back into the trailer. "Hey! It's Holyfield!" I wondered how he knew that, and I soon found out: They knew who Evander Holyfield was and that he was from Atmore because they'd watched the Olympics, but it was only when Mike said, "What're you doing here?" that I realized they didn't know we were related.

"I'm your brother," I told him and the two other boys who'd shown up by then. They couldn't believe it but about that time Isom heard the commotion and came around the front. Seeing me there with Mama he knew right away who I was, and the strong physical resemblance between the two of us convinced his other sons as well.

It was an awkward moment. Isom was a very quiet and reserved man and wasn't much given to a lot of talking, and I hadn't come up with anything to say to him. But it ended quickly, because my step-brothers, who actually lived with their mother but were visiting Isom for the day, were so anxious to take me around town and show me off that I was out of there a few minutes later, leaving Mama behind to catch up with Isom.

I'd left Atmore when I was only about four so nobody remembered knowing me, but they all knew who I was from the Olympics. My brothers took me all over the place introducing me to everybody and exercising their newfound bragging rights. This wasn't the first time for them, though, because their older brother, Ray, played football for the St. Louis Rams. But I guess there was something extra special about an Olympic medalist, especially soon after the Games, because they sure made a big deal of it.

Everybody we met remarked on how much I looked like Isom, and then they'd launch into all of these stories about him. He couldn't read or write but he was about the strongest man they'd ever met. He used to make money taking bets on whether he could lift the front end of a car clear off the ground, and he never lost. He was a lumberjack by trade and had the reputation of being the hardest-working one around. I started to see that he was a highly respected man in Atmore. Everybody praised him to the heavens and I felt good about that, because I saw that I'd come from pretty solid stock. I knew I got a lot of my spirit from Mama, but now I saw that my work ethic and physical attributes, and maybe some of my reserve, came from Isom.

I didn't ever sit down and talk with him on that trip but it was Father's Day when we left so I called my sister Eloise and said, "I want to buy Isom a truck" and would she do that for me. She asked me why I just didn't do it myself and I said I didn't want Mama to know about it. I knew it would make her mad, that she would say he didn't deserve it because he wasn't around for me. Four years later—on Father's Day again—I had a house built for him in place of that trailer on his property. Again I had Eloise arrange it but this time Mama found out because of all of Isom's bragging about his son building him a house. Just like I thought, she got all upset. "He doesn't deserve it!" she insisted. "He never did anything for you!" But it wasn't a question of deserving it or not. My own thing is, who was to say that I deserved all that I now had? God just saw fit to give it to me, and I saw fit to give Isom a new truck and a new house and that's what I did.

I also reminded her that she'd told me to pray for him. As much as I loved her I knew she had her bad points so I assumed Isom had his good ones. As far as him not being with us, it may have been for the best, because I don't think he and Mama would have lasted if they'd lived together. Mama was high-spirited and strong-minded and Isom was easygoing and serene, the kind of man who was tough as nails but never got into trouble. They would have been like gasoline and matches.

Over the years, Isom and I found some common ground. The Bible teaches that a good tree can't bear bad fruit, and I assumed Isom was a good person because I felt that I was a good person. We started talking, a little at first and then more and more. My kids got to know him, too, and slowly grew to love him. I started bringing him to my fights around the time I became undisputed world champion and he came to every one right up until he passed in January 2007.

PART II

The Pro Ranks

CHAPTER 7

———

Going Pro

If I thought things were busy before the Olympics, it was nothing compared to afterward. Winning a bronze instead of a gold didn't seem to put much of a dent in my commercial appeal, probably because the people who really knew boxing understood that coming in third had nothing to do with my skills. It wasn't the medal they cared about. All they wanted to know was if I had championship potential.

I had a lot of offers, but the decision about who to sign up with eventually boiled down to two possibilities. The first was Josephine Abercrombie, the lady who gave me the $2,000 I used to buy that Buick from Ken Sanders. Ken was with me when she sat me down and said, "If you sign with me, I'll write you a check for half a million dollars before the ink even dries on your signature. For your first fight you'll get another $400,000."

While I tried to keep from falling over, Ken just nodded thoughtfully and said, "That's a very generous offer."

Generous? That $2,000 she'd given me after the Golden Gloves was the most money I'd every seen at one time in my whole life. I was making $8,000 *a year* working forty hours a week at Epps Aviation. Here she was telling me I'd have $900,000 after my first fight, so it wasn't generous, it was colossal, and I only hoped I could hold the pen steady when I signed the contract.

But I couldn't sign, because before the meeting Ken made me swear that I wouldn't jump at an offer even if a truck full of money was sitting in the driveway with my name on it. "Listen to all the offers first," he said, "and then make a decision, because it isn't going to be about just dollars."

So I told Mrs. Abercrombie how much I appreciated her faith in me, but I couldn't make a big decision like that without having all the facts in my hand. Her face kind of clouded over a little and she said, "I'm not negotiating, Evander. Those are the numbers I'm offering, and they won't change."

That surprised me a little. I wasn't maneuvering, I was just stating a fact. It was pretty much how I would handle all my negotiations in the coming years, without all the usual posturing and mind games. Once people figured that out about me, it saved a lot of time and made things go much smoother. On several occasions I had to walk away from huge deals because I'd already gone on record saying I wouldn't accept them as offered, but in the long run it worked in my favor. Of course, most of the time there were people who negotiated on my behalf, but the final decision was always mine.

Right now, Mrs. Abercrombie didn't know any of that about me— neither did I, yet—so she saw my hesitation as some kind of ploy. I assured her it wasn't, and she seemed to believe me. She wasn't happy, but she believed me.

The other key player was Main Events, which was owned by Lou Duva and his son Dan. Lou was one of the all-time legendary trainers and managers. He'd begun instructing fighters while stationed at Camp Hood in Texas during World War II. He kept doing it after he was discharged, but had a number of other businesses besides. In 1978 he started staging fights in New Jersey, and he'd do all kinds of crazy things to build some buzz for his events, like getting a truck driver friend of his to pose as a prince from Zaire. Three years later Main Events promoted the first bout between Sugar Ray Leonard and Thomas Hearns, which set a record of $40 million for the largest gross for a nonheavyweight bout.

Nineteen-eighty-four was a good year for Lou. He'd already signed my Olympic teammates Mark Breland, Pernell Whitaker, Meldrick Taylor and Tyrell Biggs, although I was hearing rumors that Mark had switched to Josephine Abercrombie's Houston Boxing Association. Middleweight gold medalist Frank Tate had gone with her as well.

Lou only offered me $250,000 to sign, and said I'd probably make $1.2 million over the next two years, which was less than what I could make with Abercrombie. To me that was the end of the decision-making process, but Ken said I should give it some more thought. I asked him why.

"Because you need to take a hard look at what's important to you," he said. "I want you to understand that there's more to this decision than you might think."

I asked him what he meant.

"If what you want is to get as much money as you can up front," he said, "then go with Mrs. Abercrombie. But if you believe that you could be the champion, and if that's what's important to you, then go with the Duvas. Because Mrs. Abercrombie can dump a lot of money on you, but she doesn't have any champions and never has. She's too new in the business."

He went on to tell me that it was kind of a crapshoot. If it turned out I didn't really have championship potential, I'd be better off going for the early big bucks. Nobody could really say either way, so I had to roll those dice myself, based on my own feelings about how good I could be. "If you do become champion, you'll make more money than you ever dreamed of," he said, "but if you don't . . ."

There was something else, too. Abercrombie wanted to both manage and promote me, which meant Ken would be out of the picture if I signed with her. "So what I'm going to do," he said, "I'm going to get as much for you out of her as I possibly can up front." He thought he should go to her right away and find out what that deal might look like, because until we did, I wouldn't have all the information I needed to make a good decision. I reminded him that Mrs. Abercrombie had said her first offer was her final offer, but it didn't concern him. "I'm not going to ask her for more," he said. "Just different."

Ken went back and suggested to her that she offer me a seven-year, $7 million deal. She thought that was reasonable, but Bob Spagnola, assistant director of her Houston Boxing Association, was there advising her and started shaking his head. "Don't do it!" he warned. "That kid'll be like just like the rest of them. You'll see. As soon as he gets that money he won't work hard anymore, he'll get lazy," and things like that. He wouldn't let it go, and eventually talked her out of it.

Ken wasn't disappointed. He thought I'd make so much money with Main Events that all of this I was thinking about now would be chicken feed. It would just take some time. "The Duvas make champions," he said, "and champions make money."

There was another problem with Abercrombie being both my promoter and my manager. There's a built-in conflict of interest in that arrangement, because as my manager she was supposed to try to get as much money for me as possible, but as a promoter she'd want to pay me as little as she could get away with. It would be like a baseball player whose agent was also the owner of the ball club he played for. It didn't make sense, even though in the boxing world it was surprisingly common. Don King spent his whole career promoting fights for the same guys he managed.

I trusted Ken and believed that he was thinking only of me. I believe it still. One of the first things he did when I decided to turn pro was get some help, because while he was a good businessman, he didn't know enough about the fight game and wasn't willing to risk making mistakes that could hurt me. So he sought out one of the best managers in the business, Shelly Finkel, and brought him on as co-manager even though it meant cutting his own commissions in half.

I took Ken's advice and went with Main Events, which of course turned out to be a great decision. As soon as I signed the contract, my amateur career was over. In the years following I'd see Josephine Abercrombie often at fights all over Houston, and we stayed good friends. She'd always come up to me and pretend to cry over having lost me. She did go on to produce three champions, including Frank Tate, but she could have had four.

I made my professional debut at a special "Night of Gold" at Madison Square Garden. They called it that because every fighter on the card had won Olympic gold in the 1984 Games just three months before. Everyone except me, anyway, but Lou Duva was running the show and he put me on the ticket. Just before the first fight of the night, Lou outdid Yogi Berra when he told a reporter, "Tonight is a new day."

A manager has to strike a careful balance when setting up a fighter's first professional bout. On the one hand, he doesn't want his guy walking into a buzzsaw and having his confidence so badly shaken that he's ruined forever. On the other, he doesn't want to face him off against a pushover so that everybody thinks the new guy can't hack it with a real fighter. What he wants is a serious fight with plenty of challenge so that when his guy wins—and he's supposed to win—the world sits up and takes notice. It's a tricky proposition, and when the manager can't find the perfect opponent, he errs on the side of going easy on his guy.

Mine was the first bout of the night, and Lou must have worn himself out setting up all of the other matchups by the time he got around to arranging my fight. The guy facing me from the opposite corner was Lionel Byarm, light heavyweight champion of Pennsylvania, and he wasn't about to let himself become a bit player in the story of my career. Before we were two minutes into the first round the crowd knew that something unusual was going on. I'd knocked out everybody I'd faced since hitting the national scene as an amateur, but as hard as I was pounding Lionel, he wasn't hitting the deck. He stunned me with a thunderous right, too, and what was supposed to be my coming-out party was turning into a very serious brawl.

We were scheduled for six rounds, twice the amateur duration, so when the sixth round started I was deep into brand-new territory. I'd never gone anywhere near that long before, and Lionel knew it. He'd been hitting me hard and fast since the start of the fight, but hadn't really gone for the big knockout punch. He was biding his time until I was worn down and vulnerable, thinking he could then pick his moment and put me away for good.

He couldn't, but that last round was as ferocious a battle as I'd ever been in. All my trademark finesse and dancing was out the window as we went toe-to-toe punching furiously. I'd never thrown that many hard punches in one fight, but I couldn't put Lionel away. I'd never eaten that many punches, either, and I have to believe Lionel was just as surprised that *I* wasn't going down. Part of the reason for all that intensity was that neither of us was confident that we had a decision in the bag, so we needed to either score a knockout or rack up a lot of points trying.

There was no knockout, but I won the decision and my pro career was officially underway.

Paulette became pregnant again early in 1985. I won my second fight at about the same time, and then two more in quick succession. That put some real money in my pocket so it seemed like the right time to get married. We'd have a place to live, too. The first thing I did when I got all that signing money from the Duvas was put myself right into debt by buying a condo for Paulette and me and a house for Mama. But the money from my first four pro fights made those mortgages a lot less painful than they were at first.

I had a few misgivings about getting married because there were one or two things that made me wonder whether Paulette and I were really compatible. But it was tough to figure out how important they were because we hadn't had a lot of experience sharing a household. That's not all that unusual, but a lot of times when I'd mention things and want to talk about them, Paulette would snap, "We're not married and you're not my father, so you can't tell me what to do!" Reminding me that I wasn't her father was something I should have paid more attention to, because Paulette didn't always get along well with her folks, and I wondered how that would affect our relationship with our own kids. I wanted to make sure we set good examples, starting with how Paulette and I behaved and treated each other. But, again, any time I tried to suggest something, she reminded me that I didn't have the right because we weren't married.

I let it pass, and took her at her word that, once we were married, she'd change in ways I thought would be good for our family. I wanted to believe her because I wanted to be married. It meant a lot to me. I couldn't imagine my kids calling anybody else "Daddy" and I wanted the chance to bring them up the way Mama had brought me up. I was well aware of the "absentee dad" problem—I grew up without a father myself—and I was fully committed to breaking that particular curse. I also worried about how I'd look in God's eyes, already having had one child out of wedlock. I didn't want to do that anymore, and the clock was ticking because our second child was already on the way. So, despite the uncertainties that nagged at me, Paulette and I tied the knot on May 17, 1985. I'd have cause later to look back on how I'd arrived at that decision and, while I'd like to be able to tell you that I learned a hard lesson and learned it well, I guess I should have paid more attention in class.

It didn't take me long to realize how naïve I'd been. Three days after the wedding we had an argument about how some financial matters were being handled. When we'd both said what we had to say and started winding down, Paulette suddenly said. "I want an annulment."

She didn't use the word "divorce." There's a difference. I said, "You mean, make it like the marriage never happened?" Yes, that's exactly what she meant.

That cut me right to the core. I'd wanted to marry Paulette, and I badly wanted for it to work, and now she was telling me she wished we'd never gotten married at all.

I was too devastated to think straight and felt like my whole world had just tilted to one side. I'd looked forward to getting married and getting our lives kicked off right, and just like that it had all gone south. There was nothing left to say, so I left the house.

Although I felt betrayed and angry, that wasn't the biggest thing on my mind. It was my kids I couldn't stop thinking about. After all, the main reason I'd gotten married despite my misgivings was for their sake. I wanted them to have both a mother and a father, which I felt was an important part of making sure they had every opportunity to be whatever it is they were meant to be. And, just like that, it was falling apart even before one of them was born.

It didn't take me long to make the decision that, no matter what, I wasn't going to let my children end up in a negative situation. I had money now, and had kind of felt that I could buy my way out of a lot of problems, but this was about more than money. This was about me putting aside my hurt feelings and doing what was right for the kids.

Paulette could be very emotional and maybe she'd only blurted that out in the heat of the moment. It sure sounded like she'd meant it but I promised myself to give her the benefit of the doubt and try to make the best of it so that the kids could have a normal family life. None of this was their fault and they deserved my best shot. I also reminded myself that I wasn't a quitter, and not just in the ring. I wasn't going to quit on my marriage, either. I would do the very best I could despite whatever sense of betrayal I was feeling.

After about an hour I wandered into a club where I knew some of my friends would probably be. There was a woman with them named Sheryl whom I'd never seen before. She didn't know who I was, which I kind of liked, and we started talking. She was very easy to talk to, and before I knew it several hours had passed. When I told her I had to go she nodded, then said, "Listen . . . uh . . . ." She was so well spoken it surprised me when she stammered, and for a second I thought she was about to ask me to go home with her. I wasn't going to do that but before I could work up a gentlemanly explanation, she said, "Would you like to come to church with me tomorrow?"

I could hardly believe it. Sheryl went to church, and not because she had to, either, but because she wanted to. I would learn later that she got along well with her parents, too, and that made a deep impression on me.

We weren't doing anything shady. Sheryl was just a nice person and there was nothing at all between us except for a few hours of conversation. That would eventually change, but it was a long ways off. Sheryl and I became good friends, but it was only when my marriage seemed beyond repair that it became something more serious.

At home I had some practical problems to attend to regardless of what else was going on. One of them was that bills were getting paid late, which bothered me a lot, but there was no way for me to stay on top of them myself because of all my traveling and training. Ken Sanders offered to have it all handled for me out of his office, but I was hesitant because I thought things like that should stay within the family. Ken assured me that it was standard operating procedure to have tedious details like that handled by a manager. Eventually I turned it all over to him. He had done everything so well for me, I knew this would get done right, too. It did, but I was more than a little embarrassed at how it had come about.

CHAPTER 8

Life in the Big Leagues

My introduction to Ken Sanders was one of many coincidences in my life that got me to thinking about whether there really is such a thing as a "coincidence" in the universe. He did so much for me, in ways both small and big, that there had to be more than chance behind our meeting.

Among the small things was the interest he took in how I dressed. He thought it was time I started looking like the professional I'd become instead of the amateur I'd been. Don King always used to say that you had to walk like you were already there in order to get somewhere, and Ken also believed that your appearance had a lot to do with how you were treated. There were things out there that people with money could do that I didn't even know about. As an example, I was broad in the shoulders and chest and very narrow in the waist and hips, so all my off-the-rack shirts were tight on the arms and chest and blousy around the waist. Ken told me that I could take shirts to the tailor and get them tapered. A small thing, I know, but wearing stuff that fit right made be feel better. He also hooked me up with his own accountant, who was very helpful in ways I wouldn't have known about on my own.

Then there were the big things. I was supposed to fight Tyrone Booze on ABC television in July 1985. I was twenty-two years old but still growing. I'd graduated high school weighing 147 pounds and now weighed 180. The problem was that I was fighting in the light heavyweight division and the upper limit was 177. I tried like crazy to make the weight—I ate next to nothing, drank water by the spoonful and ran myself half to death. I couldn't get the weight down because I was already as lean and dehydrated as I could possibly be. I wasn't fat; I was just growing. And the harder I tried to shave a few ounces, the worse I felt, to the point where I was practically in tears half the time.

I burbled it all out to Ken one day, and he said, "Leave it to me." While I was standing there he called up Dan Duva and told him he had to move the weight up. When Dan asked him what he was talking about, Ken said, "Change the classification. Make it 180 pounds."

Lou was on the phone by then and he and Dan both told Ken he was nuts. "You want Holyfield in this fight?" Ken asked them. "Then you'd better do something because there's no way he can make the weight unless he dies."

The Duvas called ABC and had pretty much the same conversation, but Lou had an idea. "Why doesn't he move up to the cruiserweight division?"

The problem was, the fight with Tyrone Booze had already been set. The ABC rep said, "How's Tyrone supposed to feel about that?"

The Duvas reported that back to Ken. "How's Tyrone supposed to feel about that?" Dan repeated to him.

Ken replied, "Well, how should I know? Why don't you call him and ask him?"

After some more arguing, somebody finally did just that, and what do you know: Tyrone was thrilled, because he was having the same problem as me. He didn't want to fight weak and dehydrated either. So he and I both moved into the cruiserweight division, also known as junior heavyweight.

I beat him in eight rounds, and even though everything worked out, Main Events didn't like getting pushed around by Ken. A number of things happened like that, Ken going to bat on my behalf, which he was supposed to do, and Dan and Lou not liking it. When I was in training camp with Pernell Whitaker, Meldrick Taylor and a few other fighters, I compared notes with them and found out that there were some inconsistencies in how we were being charged certain expenses. I told Ken it wasn't fair, and he took it to the Duvas and made them change some accounting policies. They were unhappy with me, and thought I was a troublemaker, and they got angry at Ken, too. What they were really unhappy about was having anybody take a close look at the accounts. The thing is, they weren't consciously trying to put one over on us. They were just using "accepted business practices" like everybody else and hadn't ever given them any thought.

But that got me thinking about whether I ought to just sit back on other things as well. There are so many funny ways of doing business that a lot of them are simply accepted over time, and if you look too closely, people think you're cheap or distrustful or you "just don't get it." I learned very quickly that if somebody tries to make you feel bad about asking perfectly innocent questions, there's usually one of two reason why: Either they don't understand it themselves and don't want to admit it, or they don't want you to know the answer. One thing I've come to believe is that people with nothing to hide rarely mind getting asked questions.

Main Events had me in camp at Grossinger's in New York. I didn't question it at first, because they had all their fighters at Grossinger's, and we all thought that's just the way it was. But one day when I was in kind of a grumpy mood I got to wondering and said to Ken, "Why do they have me all the way out here in the woods?" Ken asked the Duvas, and they said it was because a lot of their fighters were too tempted by things in the city.

Ken was laughing when he reported that back to me, and I had to laugh, too. The fighters in camp had enough money to bring in whatever they wanted, and not just from New York City, which was all of ninety minutes away, but from wherever they felt like it. But more to the point for me personally, I didn't smoke, didn't drink, didn't gamble, didn't see other women . . . why did I need to be kept apart from things I didn't want in the first place, just because of what some other guys might do?

But the Duvas didn't want me moving, because what if all the other guys wanted to do the same thing? It was a good point. Problem was, it had nothing to do with me.

By the way, the reason I was grumpy that day had to do with Grossinger's itself. It wasn't because of the facilities, which were beautiful, and they took great care of us. It had to do with the food. They kept a strictly kosher kitchen, and while they cooked up some wonderful stuff, once in a while I felt like having a pork chop or something else nonkosher and they couldn't do that. Five grand a month and I couldn't get a cheeseburger?

Ken backed me up, because he felt I was right, but it cost him. Main Events got all upset and argued with him. "Everybody does it this way!" the Duvas argued, and Ken argued right back, "That doesn't mean it's right, and by the way, I don't like you taking advantage of my guy." Whether or not, in a calmer moment later, Lou or Dan Duva thought I had a reasonable point, right then and there it was more bad blood between them and Ken. But it wasn't really personal, it was mostly a matter of economics. I was the golden goose, and the people around me felt they needed to establish control in order to protect their interests.

That was one of the first hints I got that having a bunch of money carried with it its own class of problems. I'd always thought that more money gave you more options, so how could it be bad? But that was incredibly naïve. Now when I hear stories about people who won the lottery and then had their lives fall apart, I have a pretty good notion of how that can happen.

After I became a heavyweight, Ken was spending nearly all his time on my behalf and decided to sell his car dealership. I'd already started thinking about securing a future for my family when I eventually quit boxing, and the dealership seemed like a good investment, so I offered to buy it from him. I didn't know how to run it, and didn't have the time anyway, so Ken set me up to meet some people he thought might be interested in partnering up with me. They'd run the business, and Ken promised to supervise things for me. The deal was sealed when I told them they'd be able to put my name out front.

It was a good business, and once my name went up in huge letters on a new sign, as well as on the license plate frames supplied with each car, it got even better. Pretty soon it was the number-one GM dealership in the region, even to the point where I heard some rumors that other dealers were complaining that we were being unfair to them. I was awfully impressed with the selling power of my name.

Until I got back from knocking out Buster Douglas in Las Vegas. As soon as I hit town, I got a call from one of my partners who told me that the dealership was about to go under and I needed to pony up $3 million to keep it going.

I couldn't believe what I was hearing. How was it possible for such a thriving business to go south like that, and how come I didn't hear about it until it became a $3 million problem?

Before I met with my partners, I made an even more bizarre discovery. It turned out that all of those complaints I'd been hearing about were coming exclusively from black-owned dealerships. It didn't take me long to find out why.

Hartsfield, Atlanta's big airport, had a policy of trying to support minority-owned businesses. One of the ways they did that was to require car rental companies operating on airport property to buy a certain percentage of their fleets from local minority-owned businesses. As soon as my partners had their hands on the dealership, they applied to the city of Atlanta for recognition as a minority-owned business, based on the fact that I was black. According to the city's own rules, they had to grant it.

But it was ridiculous. Those policies were designed to give a leg up to black business people who might have had some tough going because of racial discrimination. For a multimillionaire pro boxer to exploit those good intentions was not only cynical and greedy, it was embarrassing. The dealership had been large and well entrenched to begin with. Once my partners had an open door to start selling fleet cars to Alamo and other rental companies under the Holyfield name, those other dealers didn't have a chance. No wonder they were put out with me. I didn't mind my partners exploiting my name. That was part of the deal. But I never told them they could exploit my race.

As annoyed as I was with what they'd done, I didn't have time to dwell on it because it left me even more confused about the state of the business. We were outselling every other dealership in the region on the retail side and placing fleet cars by the dozens, so how could we be on the verge of bankruptcy?

When I finally met with my partners, there was a lot of hemming and hawing and "It's kind of complicated" and "You have to understand the business to appreciate the predicament," but their bottom line was clear: What difference did it make how we got there? I had to put the $3 million in or the business would go belly up. Why me? "Because you're the only one of us who has it."

I told them I wouldn't do it. They said that my reputation would suffer because it was my name on the big sign out front. They were also being threatened with lawsuits for not paying money they owed, and for alleged shady business practices, and how would that look for a famous guy like me?

That same night a television reporter cornered Ken and asked him about the allegations that Evander Holyfield was involved in corrupt business dealings. Was it true that I was giving away free cars to women left and right and hiding it on the books? Finally! Ken would clear up the rumors about me and we could go about resolving the situation like rational people. I hadn't gone anywhere near the business, hadn't touched the books and I sure didn't give away any cars.

Ken said "No comment" and walked away.

I called him up. "What's going on?" I asked him. " 'No comment' is the same as telling them I'm guilty!"

He said something about how you never comment when there's pending litigation. I pressed a little and found out that he'd been threatened with a lawsuit himself and was afraid to say anything for fear he'd jeopardize his own case. I gave Ken the benefit of the doubt and let it go.

I didn't know if someone was cooking the books or stealing outright and it didn't matter. They must have thought I was the biggest knucklehead in the world, some kind of cash machine who would automatically agree to buy the dealership's way out of any problems in order to protect my image. They thought they knew me real well, that I liked things neat, that I never paid bills late, that I hated to be in debt, that I tried not to let myself get distracted by problems that could be solved with money. So they kept up their shenanigans, assuming I'd take out my checkbook and straighten it all out. A lot of very savvy business people stepped in to help me resolve the situation. Most of their advice consisted of figuring out exactly how much it was going to cost me to make the problem go away.

There were a lot of surprised people when I refused to be pressured into bailing anybody out. I stuck to my guns and didn't pay out a single dime. Not only would it have been be a major rip-off, but if I paid money to settle the dealership's debts, I'd practically be admitting that I shared some blame. I assumed that my reputation wouldn't suffer when I hadn't done anything wrong except let myself get suckered, and if I was wrong, then fine, I'd live with my bad decisions. But I still wouldn't pay for theirs. And if they wanted to start involving me in lawsuits that had nothing to do with me, I'd fight them tooth and nail in the courts even if I had to go broke doing it.

It was a good decision. Once they saw that I was serious, they somehow managed to figure out on their own how to get everything resolved, and there was no damage to my reputation.

It wasn't a happy situation, and I lost most of my up-front investment, but fortunately I'd followed a rule of mine when I went into the deal, and that is never to gamble more than I can afford to lose. Sounds absurdly simple, I know, but it always amazes me how few people follow it. "I put it all into Acme Whatever and lost everything when it went bankrupt." Why would you risk everything you have on one thing? I think it's because people allow their greed to get the better of them. If you think Acme is going to double in value, you tend to think so much about the upside, and how much you're going to "lose" if it does double up and you left something on the table, that you dive in without thinking about what's going to happen if it goes bad. That's a gambler's attitude, not an investor's. Instead of being satisfied with a reasonable return in exchange for a reasonable investment, "hitting it big" is so tempting that people will roll the dice with their entire life savings. It's a bad idea. Even if it works, it is still a bad idea.

I've learned a lot of painful lessons about money, and about people, and about trusting my instincts. I cosigned a car loan for a singing group and got stuck with a $10,000 tab when they couldn't make the payments. Then I found out they'd sold the car for $10,000. These weren't bad guys (I'm still friends with three of them). The leader just thought that I was so rich that a few thousand here and there wouldn't mean anything to me. I loaned $23,000 to a friend to pay his taxes so the IRS wouldn't come after him. Instead of paying it back, he asked me for more money a few months later, and when I wouldn't give him any more, he got mad at me! After all, he reasoned, how could it possibly make any difference to me whether he paid it back or not?

One year when I asked Mama what she wanted for Christmas, she laughed and said, "Fifty thousand dollars!" I knew she was just kidding but I asked her why anyway. "Because the most money I've ever seen in one place is about five hundred," she answered. "I just want to see what it looks like!"

On Christmas morning Mama opened a present under her tree and found $50,000 in cash. I made her keep it. A year later when I asked her what she wanted for Christmas, she stuck a finger in my face and said, "What I *don't* want is any more money!" She told me a string of stories about what had happened when people found out she had that kind of money. Old relatives she'd never even heard of showed up at her door. Close family she *thought* she knew began arguing about who should get what, and Mama wasn't even in those discussions. People all over the neighborhood lined up for some. If she'd honored all those requests it would have taken about $20 million, so even though she didn't mind giving most of it away, she had to say "No" an awful lot. And when she did, you would've thought she was snatching food out of their mouths or kidnapping their children. They got mad, they called her names, they refused to look at her in the grocery store . . . all because she wouldn't give them all this "extra" money that they seemed to feel she was obligated to parcel out for the asking.

After the car dealership matter faded away, I decided to buy a radio station from a guy who had built it up and was looking to cash out. He knew I wanted to make some investments and came to me with a proposition. "I'll sell it to you outright for $5 million," he said. "Take a few weeks to find out for yourself if it's a bargain price, and let me know." I asked him why he was willing to let it go below its likely market value, and he said, "Because I don't want to spend a year of my life running around and marketing the station, negotiating, paying people commissions to do things I don't need to get done, and I don't want my staff getting all nervous about who's going to buy the place and what's going to happen to their jobs. Then they start leaving and the value goes down and who needs that? If it's done right, the business will grow and whoever buys it will be happy with me."

Sounded fair, so I did a little research and he was right. It was a nice price, and if he sold it without fanfare, the whole staff would still be in place when I took over. There was also great potential for growth. I was getting ready to fight Bert Cooper and told my lawyer to handle the details and make the deal while I concentrated on training.

When I got back, the station had been sold to someone else. I called my lawyer to find out what had gone wrong, and he said, "I decided it wasn't right for you. You don't know anything about running a radio station and it's a very complex business."

I said, "What are you talking about! I spoke with the whole staff and they were all going to stay if I bought it. The place practically runs itself!"

"I know," he replied. "But I still thought there was too much risk."

That he was so concerned about me was touching. That he didn't trust me to make my own decisions was galling. The owner sold it to someone else for $7 million. They turned right around and sold it for $18 million, and a few years after that it went for $100 million.

I learned two very important things from that incident and a few others. One is that I make pretty good business decisions. I may not know all the details all the time, but when it comes to figuring out the big picture, I have good instincts, and they're often better than those of the people advising me.

The other is that, when you have people advising you, you have to be very sensitive to whatever personal motivations they bring to the party. If somebody is in line for a commission, they're going to be hot to make the deal happen. But if it's a lawyer who's supposed to be protecting you, "Don't do it" is much safer advice than "Go for it." Lawyers suffer few consequences when they tell you to turn something down, but open themselves up to all kinds of grief if they approve of a deal and it goes sour.

I never ding anybody for advice that was right at the time it was given, even if it happens not to work out later. I also don't credit people for things that happen that they couldn't foresee. As a novelist friend of mine once had one of his characters say, "If a man tells you a coin is going to come up heads, and it does, it doesn't necessarily mean he knew what he was talking about."

So the bottom line is to always remember that an adviser's job is to advise, not decide. His value is in helping you to see all sides of the matter at hand, not making the decision for you. I've learned not to ask, "Should I or shouldn't I?" but, "Tell me the advantages and disadvantages." That also helps to make sure that an adviser doesn't get insulted if you go the other way. I also expect advisers to support a decision once it's made, even if they're unhappy with it. There's no sense sowing doubt by second-guessing, and if you think I made such a rotten decision that you just can't live with it, disappear for a while instead of hanging around telling me I'm wrong.

Sheryl, the girl I met the night Paulette told me she wanted an annulment, didn't know that I was married. It hadn't mattered when we were just friends, and when it became clear that Paulette and I weren't going to make it, I didn't know how to tell Sheryl without it looking like I'd been hiding something from her. Since I was going to get divorced anyway, I didn't think it made a difference.

I was wrong. Sheryl had put a photograph of me in the front parlor of her parents' house, where she lived. One day a relative of her mother's came into the house, saw the photo and said, "Hey! That's Evander Holyfield!" Turns out she was friends with Paulette's mother, and that's how Sheryl discovered I was married.

I apologized, not just to Sheryl but to her parents, whom I'd grown to like very much. I explained that I was going to get a divorce, and that seemed to satisfy everybody. They liked me as much as I liked them, and they understood that I'd been in a tight spot about explaining things to Sheryl before this. Since I'd been planning to dissolve my marriage, they figured I'd acted reasonably honorably.

I went home and told Paulette that I was ready to move ahead and end the marriage.

"No," was all she said.

"What do you mean, no?"

"I mean, I changed my mind," she said. "I don't want a divorce."

I didn't get it. We'd both agreed to this months before, and nothing had changed. Paulette wasn't clear about why she'd changed her mind, but it didn't matter. I now had to go back to Sheryl and tell her there was a problem. She was upset, of course; so was I. I upset her even more when I told her that I couldn't abandon my kids. If Paulette didn't give me a divorce, I wouldn't have any choice but to stay with her while I figured out what my next step would be. A formal divorce would give me certain rights to be with my children. If I simply left, I'd have no rights at all, and I couldn't take that chance.

Sheryl went to her mother to ask her what she should do. Her mother said, "If you feel this is your man, just be patient and see how it works itself out." Sheryl and I had a lot of long talks about how we'd handle this new situation, and while neither of us was happy about the whole thing, at least it was all out in the open and we were headed somewhere.

It was a tough time for me. I had no bad feelings toward Paulette and in many ways still loved her, but I didn't want to be married to her anymore. I loved Sheryl, too, and trying to keep both of them happy was a high-wire act, especially with everything that was going on with my career. I had to go to Paris to fight Mike Brothers, then Henry Tillman in Las Vegas. It was all part of my goal to become the first cruiserweight ever to become undisputed champion of the world, and it took a tremendous amount of energy and focus.

Shortly after I fought Tillman and was getting ready to face Ricky Parker, Sheryl told me she was pregnant. It wasn't at all planned, and it threw us both for a serious loop. For one thing, I had promised myself never to have another child out of wedlock. For another, it brought home how bitter Sheryl had been about finding out I was married and that I was going to have a problem getting a divorce.

I was in a practical quandary now. I wouldn't leave my two kids to go with a new one, even though Sheryl wanted me to, but there was also no thought on my part of breaking off with her. However it had come about, she was right about one thing she'd said, which was that the child she was going to have was mine, and therefore so was the responsibility. As far as I was concerned, I was going to be a part of Sheryl's life for at least the next twenty-one years.

CHAPTER 9

———

Champion

The Omni—Atlanta
July 12, 1986

One of the questions boxers get asked most often is, "What was your best fight?" It's not an easy question, and is a little like asking a mother who her favorite child is. People expect me to answer with one of the "big" ones, like when I became undisputed heavyweight champ of the world or when I knocked Mike Tyson out. And if I'm in a hurry or the person asking the question isn't really interested in a thoughtful answer, I might mention one of those and be on my way. But the truth is, it kind of depends on what you mean by the "best" fight, and there are a lot of ways to look at that. A boxing expert or television commentator might answer it one way, an historian of the sport another, a coach or trainer still another.

From my point of view, my greatest fight wasn't against Mike Tyson, Buster Douglas, George Foreman, Riddick Bowe or any of the other legendary champions I've fought. It was against a fellow named Dwight Muhammad Qawi.

The fight had historical significance. It occurred two years after the L.A. Olympics and was the first time one of the American boxers from those Games was fighting for a world title as a professional. A lot of my teammates from that "Class of '84" were there to cheer me on, like celebrated gold medalists Pernell Whitaker, Tyrell Biggs, Mark Breland and Meldrick Taylor. They were as excited as I was and marched with me to the ring, but instead of using my name, they kept calling me "Real Deal," something they'd started doing at the Olympics. After I got disqualified in the Kevin Barry fight, somebody said that I'd gotten a raw deal. I replied, "Doesn't matter. I'm still the real deal," and my teammates began calling me that. When they started doing it in public, it stuck and became my pro nickname.

I was only 186 pounds at the time and was fighting as a cruiserweight. I'd already fought eleven times as a professional and was undefeated, earning eight of those wins by knockout. So I had reason to feel confident, and I did, but I wasn't kidding myself that this was going to be easy, for a couple of reasons.

The first was Qawi (pronounced kah-WEE) himself. Known as the "Camden Buzzsaw," he was the WBA world champion, and this fight was in defense of that title. World champions defending their titles are like grizzly bears defending their young: They'd sooner die than lose.

Qawi was a very tough guy from a very tough background. His original name was Dwight Braxton, and when he was nineteen he was sent to Rahway State Prison for armed robbery and served nearly six years. Rahway had a great boxing program—one of the inmates in it was James Scott, a middleweight title contender—and Qawi joined up and learned the right way to use his fists. A month after he was released, and with no amateur boxing experience outside prison, he turned pro. He started off 1-1-1 but then reeled off a string of fourteen straight victories, which put him well up into the world rankings. The last of those fights was back at Rahway—as a pro fighter this time, not an inmate—where he went ten rounds against James Scott and won a unanimous decision. Three months later he fought the great Matthew Saad Muhammad, won by TKO in the tenth and became world champion. He then converted to Islam and changed his name to Muhammad Qawi.

At the time of our fight, Qawi's brother Stanley was himself incarcerated at Rahway as a repeat offender, so Qawi was probably pretty angry at the world when he stepped into the ring. It didn't help his mood any that we were fighting in Atlanta, my hometown, and while the crowd cheered for me, they booed him right from the start. He brought his Muslim minister into the ring to pray with him. My Christian beliefs were pretty well known among Atlanta fight fans by then, so it might have looked to some people like there was some kind of religious war going on. Even though there wasn't, it probably added to the tension in the arena.

There was a lot riding on this fight, and a lot of people counting on both of us, but that's not why I consider it to be my greatest. There was something else going on that night.

Even though I was undefeated in my professional career, only one of my fights had reached the eighth round, and only two others had reached the sixth. That's generally a good thing, because it means you dominated your opponents. The problem was, because I'd never gone the distance, nobody really knew whether I could. The rap on me from observers of the boxing scene when I was an amateur was that I ran out of gas early, and if any opponent ever took me into the late rounds, I'd never make it. I thought I would, but I didn't really know for sure.

Lou Duva, canny veteran that he was, had a strong feeling that my endurance was going to get tested in this bout. Qawi was incredibly strong and durable, and if he thought he was getting outboxed, there was a good chance he'd try to hang back a little and let me wear myself out. The fight was scheduled for fifteen rounds, an eternity in boxing, and if we went all the way, it would be almost twice as long as my longest pro fight up to then.

So Lou hooked me up with a fellow name Tim Hallmark, who owned a gym in Houston. Tim came up with a punishing, six-week conditioning program to get me ready, including stationary biking, running up and down steps, using a Versaclimber . . . more like getting ready for an Ironman than a prize fight. It was the hardest training I've ever done, and all of it was on top of my regular boxing training, which I did with Duva later in the day.

Part of that kind of conditioning is obviously to try to improve your stamina, but the other part, and just as important, is to get you familiar with being exhausted so you learn in advance how to deal with it and it doesn't surprise and shock you when it happens. I think I ran enough miles and turned enough pedals to go halfway to the moon in those six weeks, and my lungs felt like they were on fire all the time, but Tim was relentless and kept pushing me to do more. I couldn't complain, though, because Tim trained right alongside me, doing every single thing that I did, so I had no call to tell him he was being too tough. When the big night arrived, I felt like I was in the best shape of my life.

Once in the ring, I sneaked a few glances at Qawi when his robe came off. He looked to be in pretty good shape, too. This was a world-class brawler who'd won twenty-six fights, fifteen of them by knockout, and was never happier than when an aggressive opponent was willing to trade punches with him. At that very moment I realized there was no way he would ever lay back and let me wear myself out. He was going to be in my face every second.

That was fine with me. As far as I was concerned, the more he was willing to slug it out with me, the more likely I'd score an early victory. This was the fight I mentioned earlier in which someone had scrawled "Nail him, Chubby" on a blackboard down in the locker room. The fight was being broadcast on ABC's *Wide World of Sports,* and they had a shot of me shadowboxing in front of that sign. While I was warming up they showed a taped interview with me talking about being called "Chubby" as a kid, but it was the "Nail him" part that was in my head. I not only wanted the world title, I wanted to get it with a knockout.

It took a long time to get all the prefight formalities out of the way in the crowded ring, but eventually everyone was cleared out and we got going. Qawi was the early aggressor and didn't waste much time before coming after me. He was half a foot shorter than me but used it to his advantage, crouching to lower himself even farther so he could punch upward from underneath and go after my middle while giving me less of a target. I spent the first part of the round trying to get his measure, throwing a jab and a hook that missed but told me something about his defensive reflexes. I was moving around the outside of the ring while he held the middle and just turned in place to follow me as I circled him. I was dancing all over the place while he stayed pretty still. Given how the rest of the fight went, I wish I'd not spent quite so much energy that early on.

Qawi was hitting me pretty hard, but I was starting to get a feel for how his punches developed, how his body moved when he threw them, and what he was leaving open in the process. About thirty or forty seconds into the round he dropped both hands slightly, just for a split second, and as he started to bring them back up I faked with my right. He hesitated, so slightly it was barely noticeable, but it was enough to let me shoot out a quick left jab to his face. It startled him and he dropped his hands, so I threw my full weight into another shot. That doubled him over, but I straightened him back up with a left uppercut and he fell away from me.

I have to admit, I was pretty amazed at how quickly he recovered from that flurry. But I'd rocked him good and he became a little more cautious about leaving big openings. We'd started off with me as the young newcomer and him as the veteran who was going to teach me a lesson, but by the time the bell sounded ending the round we were two well-matched fighters angling for openings and trading solid punches. Each of us got off a few good shots, we each made some mistakes, but I was pretty sure I'd won the round. On the other hand, I had a little difficulty telling when the round ended. They were using some kind of toy bell and the noise from the crowd was so loud I couldn't hear it. Neither could Qawi. We both kept fighting until the ref signaled that the round was over. That could be a problem for me: The last time I didn't hear something important in the ring it cost me a shot at an Olympic gold medal.

I started off the second round fighting "inside" a little, standing a bit too close to Qawi. Having a much longer reach than he does, I had the advantage of being able to land punches when he was too far away to hit back effectively. Letting him draw me in close robbed me of that advantage, and I'd have to stay alert not to let that happen again. He was also trying to get me on the ropes, and I had to twist away to get back to the middle where I wanted to be. Neither of us did a great amount of damage in that round, but a lot of punches got thrown and I could feel the effect, not just of getting hit, but of expending all that effort. Both of us were working hard, not giving an inch, and neither of us was willing to clinch and get a second or two of wind back. And, again, neither of us heard the bell ending the round.

I came out for Round Three like a tornado, punching as hard and as fast as I possibly could. I didn't give Qawi a chance to do anything but cover up and try to stay alive. There was no way I wanted this fight to go the full fifteen, because the pace we'd established was so grueling, there was a chance the victory would be based on whichever one of us just managed to stay on his feet while the other keeled over from exhaustion.

But it was a tremendous risk. If I didn't put him down and end it early, I could run out of fuel and have nothing left for the later rounds. Muhammad Ali based an entire fight on a strategy like that, which he called the Rope-a-Dope. Nobody thought he had a chance against an indestructible George Foreman in Zaire in 1974, but Ali essentially spent the first seven rounds up against the ropes with his arms over his face, letting the physically superior Foreman whale away at him. By the eighth round, Foreman could barely lift his arms, and Ali, bruised but fresh as a daisy, sprang like a panther, hit him with a one-two combination and knocked him out.

Qawi wasn't trying to do that to me. I was just overwhelming him, letting it all hang out in the hopes of scoring a knockout or at least doing some serious damage. I staggered him, but he recovered as quickly as he had before, and when I went back to work on him he hit me below the belt. He'd been going for my middle a lot, so it was hard to know if it was deliberate, but it was the only thing that could stop the onslaught and it did. The ref saw it, pulled us apart, and gave Qawi a warning. A few seconds later, with the ref behind him, he did it again, this time three quick low ones, and got another warning. After that, he managed to pull me inside again, and he got off some good punches to my head and ribs. When he hit me low yet again, I gave him a good one right back. We both got warned that time, but those situations are a lot like getting an elbow in basketball: Sometimes you have to serve notice by giving one back, even if it gets you a foul. It lets the other guy know you can't get pushed around. Just before the bell I got in a good round-house to the side of his head and thought I'd probably won the round.

But man, was I tired.

I went back to my corner with newfound respect for Qawi. The guy was an absolute tank. I knew he was tough—he had a fearsome reputation and had whipped a whole bunch of great fighters—but I didn't know he was *this* tough. As I sat down, I started to get a little worried. I was really bushed, and it was only the end of the third round. I'd hit Qawi with everything I had and he was still standing. How could I possibly keep this up for another twelve?

Duva was screaming instructions in my ear but I wasn't hearing him. I was praying. It wasn't anything specific, just trying to put God in my mind.

In the fourth, Qawi got me against the ropes and kept me there for an uncomfortably long time. I couldn't seem to mount an offense of my own, and he was able to get in a lot of hits without me giving any back. But he was doing what I'd done in the third, holding nothing back in an attempt to put me down and risking fatigue if he didn't. I eventually got away from him and managed to land some punches of my own, but on-air commentator Al Trautwig correctly called them "scoring" punches. All else being equal, the judges would award the round to whoever landed the most blows, whether they did any real damage or not. Of course, it wasn't like Qawi was fresh himself, but I think my fatigue showed more than his at that point in the fight. A lot of my blows were missing their targets, and those that were landing weren't landing hard. Qawi was still throwing low shots, but for some reason the ref wasn't seeing any of them. Trautwig told the live television audience, "There's no way I can imagine this going fifteen." I couldn't imagine eleven more rounds of this either, and tried not to think about it, but I couldn't help it. Just before the bell, Qawi hit my left arm repeatedly and I could feel that there had been some damage.

The next round was awful. I couldn't lift my left arm and Qawi seized the opportunity like a snapping turtle, raining punches on me and growing more confident with every unanswered blow. I think he smelled a knockout, because he seemed to get a second wind and his punches became stronger, a sure sign of the adrenaline that comes when you think victory is at hand if only you can mount one last effort. I'd never been in a position like this before, getting pummeled and not being able to do much about it. I was pretty sure I could get out of the round intact, but I was standing at the threshold of something I'd only experienced once before: fighting past the sixth. And I'd felt a lot better going into the seventh of that fight than I was going to in this one.

One of the things that happens when you get tired is that you tend to lose sight of things that might normally catch your attention. It's tough enough mounting the total concentration required to see punches coming before they're barely even thrown, and that much harder to also stay aware of how your opponent's defenses are shifting, whether his offensive style is taking on new notes, what your corner men are yelling and what kinds of things the ref is being particularly watchful for. When fatigue starts to set in, you find yourself changing your priorities, using what's left of your focus on the most important stuff, which is trying to land punches or, when things get really bad, at least trying to not get hit too much by the other guy's. What you don't need is distractions that throw you off. At one point, I hurled a series of about a dozen huge blows at Qawi while he was hunched over twisting left and right trying to avoid them and unable to strike back. At least I thought they were huge. As soon as he got away from me, he held his hands out to his sides, grinned and shrugged his shoulders, as if to say, "I barely felt those." And he looked like he hadn't. I knew what he was doing, which is what he'd been doing all week during press conferences: trying to get my goat and throw me off my game. It surprised me for a second, because up until then he'd stuck to the business of boxing. But I got over it quickly, knowing it was just a tactic.

Another thing that happened soon after was that I didn't hear the bell ending Round Six. Qawi didn't hear it either, and this time neither did the ref. We just kept on swinging until someone started frantically banging on the bell. Qawi and I finally heard it, but the ref still hadn't, and he seemed surprised when we suddenly stopped fighting and turned away from each other. You only get a minute of rest between rounds, and those seconds can be more precious than gold. To lose a handful because of a silly thing like a cheap bell was kind of galling.

And speaking of galling, it was easy to see that Qawi was getting pretty annoyed at how the crowd was on my side and kept yelling my name. But I think the anger is part of what kept him going. (Eighteen years later, when he was inducted into the Boxing Hall of Fame, an interviewer asked him what the worst memory of his entire career was. He answered, "The politics surrounding the . . . Holyfield fight. He was the up and comer and it was in his hometown.") I needed something to keep me going, too, but it wasn't anger—I never got angry in the ring—it was my faith. Before, I'd tried to just put God in my mind, but now my prayers got specific, and I remember exactly what I was thinking: *Lord, please don't let me quit! Help me keep going!* It helped me a lot calling on God that way, knowing he was behind me. I actually felt a little more energized.

Truth is, though, by the middle of the fight both of us were running out of gas in a hurry. Our punches were nowhere near as effective as they should have been, and we were doing whatever we could to try to win. Qawi was throwing low blows all over the place, and the ref just wasn't seeing them. So I gave him back one for every one he threw, but if he felt them he didn't show it, and just kept on laying them on me. He was so tired there wasn't much else he could do, and I think that some of those low shots happened only because he was having trouble lifting his hands to hit me higher. A couple of times each round one of us would rally and throw a flurry, then the other one would do the same. To my amazement, I was in better condition than him. My punches were more effective, and my recovery following a flurry was faster. At some point in the bout it turned from fighting to survival for Qawi, and I started to think about the best way to win. In my career I'd never thought about anything other than trying to score a knockout, but I had enough of my wits about me to know that, before too long, I might need to start thinking seriously about just scoring as many points as possible. Qawi may have been tired but his resilience was almost beyond belief.

The fight was being scored on a "must" system. The winner of a round gets ten points and the loser nine or fewer. No tie rounds are possible. If there's a knockout or TKO, the scores don't matter. But if it goes the distance and you didn't pay enough attention to scoring points because you were so intent on a knockout, you could end up losing a fight you might have won if you'd handled things differently.

While Qawi was resorting to low blows, I had a different strategy, which was to keep working on his left shoulder. It looked to me like he might be having a problem with it. When I got back to my corner Lou told me he'd noticed it, too, and he started shouting, "Hit the target! Hit the target!" at me from the corner to keep reminding me. Spectators probably thought he meant Qawi, but he was talking about the shoulder. It might not seem to you that the shoulder is as vulnerable a spot as the face or belly, but get it sore enough and you essentially take your opponent's entire arm out of play. He won't be able to hit well from that side and he won't be able to defend it, either.

The more tired I got, the harder it became to fight outside and use my reach. Qawi and I were both hunched over a lot, our ears practically touching, trading blows that lacked the power of a fully extended arm behind them. The first half of the eighth was good for me, but when I tried to take a momentary breather on the ropes after a series of combinations that had Qawi on the defensive, he exploded and was all over me. I hadn't expected it, and he got in a lot of good shots before I gathered myself and fended him off. So much for breathers in this bout. As much as both of us needed one, neither was willing to let the other have it.

At one point I grabbed Qawi around the head and held him close for a few seconds, not allowing him any room to haul back. When he broke free he started miming a warning to me not to do that again, and while he was in the middle of it I flicked out my left hand and popped him on the cheek. He didn't like that at all, and came after me with a vengeance. I grabbed his head a few more times and I could tell it was getting to him, which was fine. Believe it or not, getting your opponent angry is not a bad thing. Maybe you've wondered why fighters often goad their opponents in the days and weeks leading up to a fight, baiting them and trying to humiliate them in public. What could be the point of angering a guy who's about to try to knock your head off?

The point is that you can't do your best if you're mad. Sure, a little adrenaline is good now and then. It helps give you strength for a good shot or two when your energy level is down. But, for the most part, anger has a way of taking over and making you forget your plan and your techniques. It's easy to spot when a fighter loses his temper and gets reckless. He wants to smash his opponent's face in so bad he just wades in and starts throwing wild punches. But he usually ends up leaving himself wide open, and if the other guy is patient and keeps his head, he can find that opening and exploit it. One thing you'll notice about most great fighters is that they're almost methodical in the ring. They stay within their game and they don't get drawn into the other guy's style. They may look fierce and determined and serious but they don't look angry. Boxing has been called the "sweet science" and it's usually the "scientific" fighters who become champs.

Qawi had been trying to get my dander up for the whole week before the fight. He told the press I was a baby, that I wasn't ready to fight him, and that I was "mediocre." He told them in detail everything he was going to do to take me apart in this fight. I have to admit I was embarrassed. After all, we were in my hometown, and everyone was reading all of this stuff in the papers and watching it on television. But I try not to react to things like that or talk trash myself—it's the way I was raised and there's no percentage in it anyway—and I think it bothered him that he wasn't getting to me.

And I was pretty sure now that his low blows weren't so much trying to hurt me as to provoke me. I could've complained and started shouting at the ref to pay attention, but as soon as I did, I might as well lay down and give up the fight. Instead, I just concentrated on the job at hand, and when I saw the opportunity to tweak Qawi a little by slapping him in the middle of his lecture, I took it. In the next round, I had him against the ropes for a few seconds and worked him over pretty good, and when he came out of it, he smiled and shrugged again, as though I hadn't hurt him. More mind games.

There was another distraction as well. Both of us were perspiring like crazy. It was a little on the warm side in the arena, and we were working so hard the sweat was flying off with every blow. The canvas was soaking wet, and as the bout wore on it was becoming difficult to maintain sure footing. In the tenth my foot slipped completely and I went down, hard. I got up right away and because it was a slip there was no count. The ref motioned for the canvas to be wiped, and a few towels came out at the edges when we were on the opposite side of the ring, but the whole floor looked like a damp T-shirt and there wasn't much that could be done about it. As the fight wore on and we kept perspiring, it got even worse.

I'd never felt that bad physically during a fight. Just to raise my arms took everything I had, and it felt like I had no muscle left at all, that it had just gotten eaten away and I was moving on pure willpower. I couldn't afford to coast—in a close match, the decision will almost always go to the reigning champ, not the challenger—but it was all I could do to keep moving. My lungs were burning like they'd never burned during all that conditioning Tim had put me through, way beyond the point where I would have fallen off the stationary bike and curled up on the gym floor.

It wasn't lost on me that I was in Atlanta, that the audience was full of my friends and family and supporters. There were people here who'd been with me from the very beginning, people who'd opened their hearts and their wallets because they had faith that I could be the champion. All of those Olympic greats had shown up to be with me, the fight was being broadcast on the most popular sports show in the world, and I felt like I was ten seconds away from replacing that guy who falls off the ski jump during the opening credits of every episode. And it was only the eleventh round.

The good news was that Qawi was worse off than I was. He wasn't covering himself as well as he usually did, and for a great defensive fighter like him to keep letting down his guard was a sure sign he was fading. He could take a punch, that was for sure, but nobody could take as many as I was throwing and not feel the effect.

A pattern had developed and it continued in the later rounds. We'd jab away at each other for a while, then I'd get my strength back and put everything I had into a series of combinations, instinctively trying to end the fight even though I kind of knew that wasn't going to happen. Then Qawi would rally and come back at me while I'd cover up and try to absorb the blows with my arms. Through it all, I don't think he took a single step backward, ever. No matter how many times I hit him or how hard, he just kept coming, like one of those little windup toys that bangs into walls over and over. While I could stop him for a few seconds by throwing a hail of punches, as soon as my strength gave out there he was again, moving forward, looking like I'd never touched him.

In the eleventh, he got to the crowd, too. They'd been on my side all along but started to sense that there was something real special about this guy, about how he just wouldn't quit, and they began chanting his name. That's all fine and well, but did it mean they were seeing more heart and fight in him than in me? Was he showing them more determination? Were the judges seeing it that way as well? I couldn't let that happen. I went into Round Twelve swinging with everything I had, determined to put Qawi down.

It was a good plan, but what actually happened was that I hit him until I couldn't hit him anymore, then he shook it off and came right back after me, same as before. I just couldn't believe this guy. No matter what I did, I couldn't put him down and couldn't make him back off. And I'd spent so much energy trying that all I could do was cover up and try to catch my breath when he took his turn as the aggressor.

But I was even surer now that, even though we were kind of taking turns, we were far from equal. I was throwing a greater number of punches than he was, and landing a lot more as well. The idea of knocking him flat and scoring a knockout was starting to look like wishful thinking, so I tried to concentrate on making sure I was the one getting off the most shots and controlling the action. It was critical that the judges see me as the winner of each round, because the way this fight was going, a decision on points was the only hope I had. The crowd shifting loyalties this late in the fight . . . that wasn't good.

In the fourteenth round I noticed something. The crowd hadn't been chanting "Qa-wi! Qa-wi!" They were chanting "Ho-ly! Ho-ly!" They were still on my side, urging me to give it all I had, pouring whatever energy they could generate right down into me. Then, when the bell rang to start the fifteenth round, I felt my heart soar. I could practically see God smiling and hear him whispering in my ear, "You did it!" Even a bulldozer running over me couldn't stop me from going the distance now. Despite my weariness, I was happy. Win or lose, I'd passed the most significant milestone of my professional career. I now knew for a dead certainty that I could go the distance against a relentless opponent, and my critics knew it, too. Just a few more minutes of reaching farther into myself than I ever had, leaving absolutely nothing left at the end, and it would be over. Whatever it took, I was determined to go down to the wire swinging as hard as I possibly could.

The sweat was still flying off both of us and soaking the canvas. I slipped again, and even though I didn't go down this time, the ref was concerned enough to stop the fight for a few seconds to try to get some of it wiped away, but it was pretty useless. Qawi had to be thinking just what I was thinking, which was that there were only a couple of minutes remaining and there was no reason to save anything. Drawing on his own reserves, he found some hard punches left in his bag and pounded me a few times. The ref gave him a warning, but I couldn't tell for what, and neither could Qawi. He held out his hands, asking what the warning was for, but there was no answer and we kept on going. Then he motioned for the ref to warn me about holding his head. It was a last-ditch, desperate effort to shift the points in his favor, but the ref didn't buy it. Qawi flew at me, hitting me with surprising power this late in the game. I got away from him and, with my back nearly in the corner, saw a perfect opening. I stepped into what was going to be a terrific head shot . . . and slipped again, hitting the canvas hard. Qawi was right there, both hands poised to wallop me, but when he realized I'd slipped he dropped his hands and screwed up his face in frustration while I got to my feet. The ref, knowing it was a slip, grabbed my gloves, putting himself between Qawi and me while he made sure I was steady before allowing us to continue.

I figured there couldn't be more than twenty seconds left in this fight. I bit down hard on my mouthpiece and got ready to give it everything I had. Qawi, as I expected, was heading right for me, but he looked different now, not just physically tired but mentally spent as well. As soon as he got to me I put my hand on his head and he barely resisted, so I let fly with the fastest flurry of punches I could possibly muster. I didn't bother with fancy combinations or try to fake him out. I just machine-gunned blows to the sides of his head with both hands, so fast he couldn't do anything but duck down, put his gloves up and wait for it to stop. As soon as it did, he picked up his head and I hit him again, a hard right to his face, and then I bounced back and forth three or four times, trying to mix him up, like a basketball player yoyoing up and down so the defender has no idea when he's actually going to shoot, watching his eyes to see when he was totally lost . . .

And then Qawi did something he hadn't done once since the opening bell. He backed off. He dropped his shoulder and actually took a step backward. I was so stunned I couldn't quite figure out what was going on. Had the ref stopped the action? Had the bell gone off? But the crowd was screaming and yelling hysterically. They knew what was happening before I did, that Qawi was done, finished, not another ounce of fight left in him.

I finally came to my senses. There were only seconds left in the round, but the rules for this bout said you couldn't be "saved by the bell." If I could get in there while he was stunned and exhausted and hit him with one last piledriver of a punch, I could put him down and get the knockout after all. The crowd sensed the same thing and cranked up the volume even louder as I moved in for the kill.

I should have known better. Qawi hadn't taken a single step backward in almost fifteen rounds. Why did I think he was going to lie down now?

He'd pulled a last-minute fake and drawn me into a trap. As soon as I reached him and jabbed for his head, he detonated like a hand grenade, shooting out a left I just managed to deflect and following up immediately with a tremendous right that I was able to get away from only because I'd already started moving backward from the previous punch. From that point on he was a man possessed, throwing huge shots and flying into me with such determination that I backed up along one edge of the ring, got to the corner and then backed up along another edge. There was no sense hitting him back because he was so wired I don't think he would have felt a howitzer hitting him.

By the time we'd moved another whole length of the ring and reached a corner again, I could feel him losing energy, so I stood still and he just kind of leaned against me, trying to catch his breath, and then he tried to hit me a few mores times. But there was no strength in it, and no heart, and I didn't do much about it and then the final bell rang and it was over.

There's a concept familiar to endurance athletes like marathon runners and triathletes, that no matter what the distance is or how hilly the course or what the weather conditions are, you've got just enough to get to the finish line and not a drop more. It's why you see a runner in a dead sprint for the finish, going at full speed, and as soon as he crosses the line he falls in a heap and can't even lift his head. Exactly the same thing would happen if the race was a mile longer or a mile shorter. It's a purely mental thing, your mind figuring out how to get you just far enough and no farther.

It's a little like that in boxing, too, with one big difference: You don't know the distance in advance. If you score an early knockout,

Carter and Katherine Morgan, when I was thirteen.

Graduation from Fulton High School, 1980.

Working at Epps Aviation helped to finance my amateur career. That's Josephine Abercrombie and Bob Spagnola about to board.

Evander Holyfield

LEFT: In 1988 I became the first undisputed cruiserweight champion of the world.

BELOW: With the legendary trainer Lou Duva, my first fight as a heavyweight, against James Tillis outdoors in Lake Tahoe, July 16, 1988. I knocked James out in the fifth.

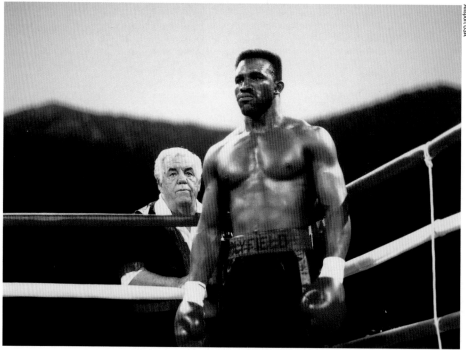

Allsport USA

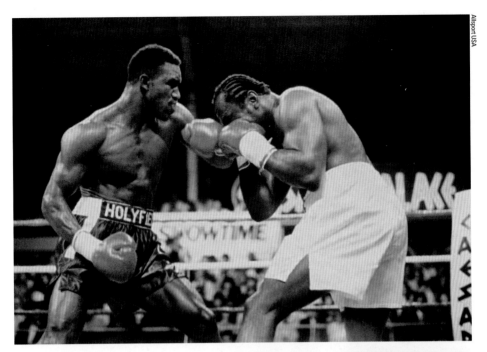

A lot of people thought my fight against Michael "Dynamite" Dokes was my first real test as a heavyweight, March 11, 1989.

ABOVE: Lou Duva talking to me during my world title fight against Buster Douglas, October 25, 1990.

LEFT: My first manager, Ken Sanders, and trainer Lou Duva after I knocked Michael Dokes out in the tenth. It was after this fight that Ken told Don King to let me fight Mike Tyson, "Winner take all!"

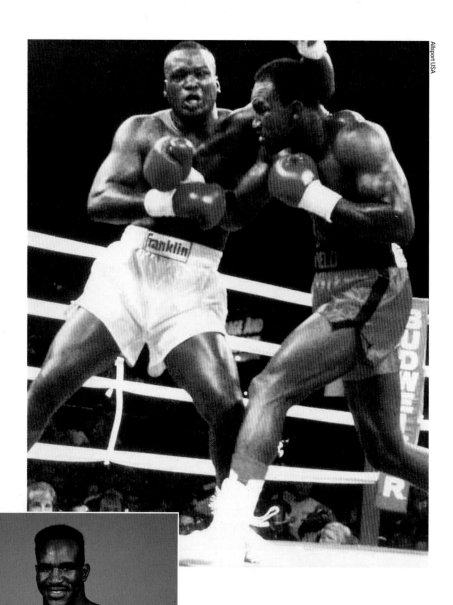

Allsport USA

I knocked Buster out in the third
round to become the undisputed
heavyweight champion of the world.

Tom Casino

Mama getting a service award from her church, 1991.

Evander Holyfield

Evander Holyfield

In church with my son Ewin, 1991.

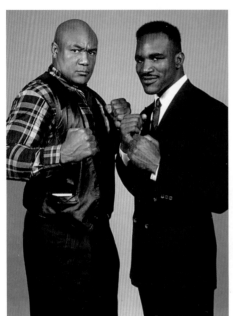

My first defense of the undisputed world heavyweight title was against George Foreman, one of the hardest punchers in the game.

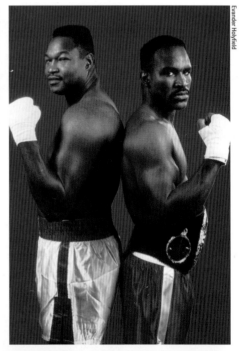

I was almost always the smaller guy in the ring. Larry Holmes, one of ten current or former world heavyweight champions I defeated, outweighed me by twenty-three pounds. Some others outweighed me by more than forty.

LEFT: My mother, Annie Laura Holyfield, 1992.
BELOW:Ashley (Evette), Emani, Ewin, Evander Jr., and Ebonne, 1992.

When you have seven thousand kids over for a Fourth of July barbecue, it means that all the adults work!

In 1992 I suffered my first pro defeat to Riddick Bowe, who won all three of my championship belts. A year later, in a fight interrupted by a motorized hang glider landing in the ring, I fought Riddick again and got two of the belts back.

you might have plenty of juice left, which is why you'll sometimes see guys jump around like rabbits after they've won, hopping up onto the ropes, dancing all over the place and even lifting their corner men into the air.

But when you've fought all the scheduled rounds, you're just like that marathon runner. You gave it everything you had and there aren't five seconds of energy left. The bell goes off and it's like someone opened the drain valve in your gas tank, and it's all you can do to walk back to your corner.

When the fight ended, I managed a weak smile at Qawi and mumbled something nice to him as best I could around my mouthpiece. I was trying to tell him that he'd fought a magnificent fight, that I had tremendous respect for him, that he was truly a warrior of the highest rank. He nodded back his own acknowledgment of me, but I could see in his eyes that he was worried. He was the champ trying to retain his belt, and even though, all else being equal, the win will go to the champ rather than the challenger, he knew that it had been far from equal. The only question in my mind was whether the judges would see it differently and let him keep his title.

As we walked back to our corners, our people did what they're supposed to do, which is to show tremendous support for their fighter. Whenever there's a decision pending, your guys act as though it's the biggest no-brainer in the world, and why even bother to add up the scores? Just give us the belt and let the partying begin.

As soon as the bell rang, both Qawi's people and mine threw their hands in the air, smiling and laughing and high-fiving in a joyous celebration of victory. One of his guys picked him up, and trainer Tom Brooks picked me up at the same time. Qawi's arms hung limp at his sides, but I managed to pump a fist into the air and raise my arms over my head. Contrary to what the critics had predicted, I turned out to be the better conditioned of the two of us. You could see it in Qawi's stricken expression, how all the people who'd told him he could outlast me had been dead wrong. As tired as I was, he was more so. As sore as my body was, his was worse. Where I'd surprised everyone and myself by being able to fight hard through all fifteen rounds, he was stunned that a twenty-three-year-old with only eleven pro fights could go toe-to-toe for seven rounds more than he'd ever fought before. To this day I haven't finished thanking Tim Hallmark for putting me through those six weeks of torture that got me through sixty minutes of hell. (Tim would sell his gym two years later to join my team full-time, and he's been with me ever since.)

I was glad when I was finally set back down on the canvas. It was just too much effort to be held high like that, and it was hard to breathe, too. Lou went over and gave Qawi a hug, and there was a lot of backslapping and handshaking between our sides. How could there not be? We'd just fought what *The Ring* magazine would call the best cruiserweight bout of the decade, and it would also top the "Fight of the Year" lists of a whole string of publications. No matter which of us won, everybody in that arena, including the crowd that couldn't stop screaming, knew that something very special had just happened.

There were over fifty people jammed into the ring when a voice came onto the PA and said, "We have a majority decision." A lot of faces turned anxious at that. The decision wasn't unanimous, so at least one of the three judges had called the fight for me, and at least one had called it for Qawi. It would all boil down to the third judge.

The announcer gave the first judge's tally: "144–140 . . . Holyfield!" A tremendous cheer went up, and the guys around me huddled closer. The more wily veterans put a hand on me, as if to hold me up in case things went south, because they knew that the score just announced was meaningless. Of course there was a judge who'd gone for me. It was a majority decision so there had to be at least one.

The second score was announced; "143–141 . . . Qawi!" Again, no surprise there, but the score spread was smaller. A good sign? No way to tell.

The announcer said the third judge "scores the fight 147–138, for the winner . . ."

Time itself seemed to freeze. Every one of the dozen hands on me tightened in anticipation.

". . . and the new . . ."

My corner exploded with joy. I got hoisted into the air again and people were yelling in my ear so loud I couldn't hear anything the announcer was saying. I didn't need to hear it because there could only be one "new" champion—Qawi would have been "still" the champion—and that was me. It was hard to believe that that arena full of people could have gotten any more crazy than they'd already been, but they did. I was high in the air on a couple of shoulders, and wanted to show my appreciation to everybody for their loud and lusty support, and of course I was elated beyond measure, but I was so wasted I literally couldn't sit up straight. Hands kept shooting out to push me back up every time I threatened to fall over,

Eventually I was set back down, and Alex Wallau of ABC fought his way through the throng to interview me. Before he got his first question out I thanked the Lord for everything, and never meant it more sincerely. Alex pointed out that I'd seemed to give out in the fifth and sixth rounds before getting my wind back. I told him that I'd felt myself starting to give in to the "old Holyfield," the one with the reputation of only having enough stamina for a handful of rounds, but then I'd reminded myself of what I had on the line, and that God was behind me. We talked for about another minute and then I think he realized that I was fading. He mercifully cut it short and let me go.

The rest is a blur. I remember the Olympic champions, and Lou Duva and my other corner guys and a bunch of friends and supporters. I remember noise and chaos and being unable to tell if the light-headedness I was feeling was euphoria, fatigue, or bright camera lights shining in my eyes or forty guys trying to talk to me at once. What I remember very clearly is wanting to get out of there and back to the locker room where I could lie down. I'd been on my feet since the start of the fifteenth round and even after the final bell it still hadn't exactly been restful, and what I needed more than anything else was to just breathe quietly for a minute or two.

I didn't know it yet but this fight still wasn't over for me.

I have no idea how I got back to my hotel. My next memory was being in the shower and getting socked with a series of intensely painful cramps. Not just in my legs and back but my arms and even my neck. My head hurt, too, so bad I thought it was going to explode. I started to double over and grabbed a fistful of shower curtain to hold myself up. I managed to stay upright for a few seconds, but then another wave of spasms hit me and I went down, tearing the shower rod out of the wall. I hollered for Paulette, and a second later the bathroom door burst open and she ran in. It must have looked like the shower scene from *Psycho,* with me squirming around in the bathtub, but she didn't waste any time being scared. Ken Sanders and Shelly Finkel were staying in the same hotel, and she called them to come over. They helped her get me out of the shower and then put some clothes on me.

I knew right away that I was badly dehydrated. Something like this had happened to me four years before, when I was trying to get down to 156 pounds to make an amateur weight class. I'd been taken to the hospital then, and since this was much, much worse, I knew I had to go there now.

I have no recollection of how I got to Crawford Long Hospital, but my personal physician, Dr. Ron Stephens, was waiting for us when we got there. As luck would have it, he worked at Crawford Long, which was only six blocks from my hotel. One of the first things he did was weigh me. After he tweaked the little slider on the scale and got it balanced, he screwed up his face in confusion and said to me, "How much did you weigh going into the fight?"

"Are you serious?" Sanders said. Half of Atlanta knew what I weighed going into this fight.

"One eighty-six, wasn't it?" Stephens said to me, and I nodded.

"What's the problem?" Finkel asked him.

The doc looked back at the scale, like he was trying to make sure of something, then said, "Problem is, he weighs 171 now."

Sanders did a quick mental calculation, then his eyes got wide. "You telling me he lost *fifteen pounds* during the fight?"

"What hurts, specifically?" the doc asked me.

I didn't know where to start. Everything hurt. Not only was I exhausted and dehydrated but I'd also just taken a thousand punches from a world champion fighter, which Stephens knew because he'd been at the fight. It was hard to sort out the "normal" pain from the kind that told you something else was wrong. But I'd just gone to the bathroom and there was something he probably needed to know about that. "I think I peed some blood," I told him.

That's not so unusual after a fight when you get hit in the kidneys a lot. Except . . .

"I didn't see you take any kidney shots tonight, Evander."

The doc was right. I hadn't.

A few minutes later I was in a bed with an IV in my arm. When the first bag was empty, they slapped another one on the pole. Then another, and another. After a while I lost count. The doc came in several times to check on me. One of the things he told me was that it wasn't blood I'd seen in my urine.

"You ran out of all your reserves," he said, "so you were burning up muscle toward the end. What you saw was the residue of that." He also said my kidneys weren't working right, just from being so dried out, but that there wouldn't be any long-term effects.

Once I'd gotten stabilized and could think clearly, Ken and I talked quietly. I remember telling him, "Man, I don't know if I want to be the champion anymore. It's too hard!"

He nodded, but made me promise not to make any big decisions while I was still laid up. It was good advice. We talked for a few more minutes, and soon after I fell asleep.

Ken was there when I woke up the next morning. "You hungry?" he asked.

I hadn't taken in any solid food since a few hours before the fight. I was starving. "Forget this hospital food," he said, standing up. "What do you want to eat?"

I knew exactly what I wanted: A Burger King Whopper with cheese, a ton of fries and a strawberry shake. I must have fallen back asleep because it seemed like only a few seconds before Sanders had it all laid out on one of those little rolling tables that slides over the bed. I stared at it for a while.

"What're you gonna do?" Ken said after a minute or two. "Just look at it?"

That's all I could do. I was hungry but couldn't bring myself to take a bite. "You eat it," I said to him, and he did.

Later that day they pulled the IV out and weighed me again: 195 pounds. One of the nurses said they put over two gallons of saline solution into me to replace what I'd lost. When I was discharged later that day, I still hadn't made up my mind if I wanted to keep fighting. But when I got home, the first person I saw was Evander Jr. and that was all it took for me to decide that I would. After all the lessons I'd tried to impart to my son, what was I going to tell him when he got older . . . that his old man had been a quitter? "When I stop fighting," I was to tell him later, "it'll be because the time is right and because I want to. Not before."

In 2004, Dwight Muhammad Qawi was inducted into the Boxing Hall of Fame. An interviewer mentioned that I'd said he was the toughest opponent I'd ever fought. Qawi said, "Yes. I put him in the hospital for two days." It was only one day, but I don't mind. Qawi became a dedicated substance-abuse counselor, and I admire him for that, especially considering what a rough start his adulthood had. By the way, I fought him again the following year and knocked him out in the fourth round, on the same night that Ebonne (pronounced "Ebony") was born to Sheryl and me.

I knocked out a lot more guys out after that, too, but that title fight against Muhammad Qawi was still my best.

A quick word about boxing titles. Unlike most pro sports—tennis, golf, skiing and the like—boxing has no single international sanctioning body. There are three separate organizations, the WBC (World Boxing Council), WBA (World Boxing Association) and the IBF (International Boxing Federation). They each have their own world titles, so there are three world championship belts up for grabs at any time, and they could be held by one, two, or three fighters. If one fighter holds all three, he has "unified" the title and is "undisputed" champion of the world. But just because you beat that guy in a title fight doesn't mean that you automatically inherit all three. Sanctioning fees have to be paid to each organization and prefight approval obtained before they consider it to be a title bout for their particular title. A unified title is a rarity, and highly coveted. Hold all three belts and you truly are the undisputed champ. (There are actually other organizations in addition to the big three. The World Boxing Organization in particular has come into its own and the WBO titleholder is now recognized as a legitimate world champ.)

Qawi was the WBA world champ when I fought him the first time, and that's the title that was on the line in that fight. Over the next two years I fought and beat the best fighters in the division, and when I defeated Carlos De Leon in April 1988, I became the first undisputed and undefeated cruiserweight champion of the world. There wouldn't be another for seventeen more years, and to this day all cruiserweight championship belts carry my likeness.

The bout against Carlos was my last in that division. I moved up to heavyweight for my fight against James Tillis three months later and have been one ever since.

The decision to move into the heavyweight division wasn't a hard one. There wasn't much else to accomplish as a cruiserweight and too few opponents who could face me and still give the fans a good fight. It was time to move on and give myself some really huge challenges.

Not everyone was in favor of it. A lot of sportswriters said that I would always be too small to take on the kinds of monsters who dominated the glamorous "big man's" class. They said I'd be nothing but a "blown-up cruiserweight" and wouldn't have a prayer of ever getting a title shot against the "real" heavyweights. That was just the kind of talk that got my blood pumping.

Young fighters often ask me what I did to become a heavyweight. Truth is, what I really did was stop trying so hard to stay a cruiserweight. The more I trained, the bigger I naturally got. It became a serious struggle not to grow out of cruiser. It got to the point where I was eating only one small meal a day and dehydrating myself to make weight. Average body fat for a healthy American male under thirty is around 15 to 18 percent, optimum is 10 to 15 percent, and an elite athlete's might be down in the 5 to 10 percent area, depending on the sport. Mine was 3 percent, and that was just downright unhealthy. There were times during training when I felt weak and dizzy from hunger.

So becoming a heavyweight wasn't much of an effort for me. Tim Hallmark designed a program to make sure I did it gradually and in a way that would contribute to my overall health. It consisted primarily of changing and intensifying my weight workouts and also modifying my nutrition. As Tim put it to me, "What you need is *more* nutrition." He got me up to three squares a day and made sure I was getting some fat in my diet. Fat is generally a dirty word, and for most people it should be, but some fat is necessary and I didn't have nearly enough. To this day I eat very little for someone my size, but it sure was a relief not to go around hungry all the time.

Following Tim's regimen I eventually tipped the scales at a few ounces over 200 pounds, but the sportswriters were right about one thing: I was destined to always be the smallest guy in the ring. My first fight was at 201, my second at 202 and even twenty years later I was barely hitting 216. It wasn't unusual for my opponents to outweigh me by as much as forty pounds.

But I sure shed the "blown-up cruiserweight" label pretty quick when I beat my first ten heavyweight opponents, eight of them by knockout.

CHAPTER 10

Breaking Ranks

Four months after I won my first cruiserweight world title, twenty-year-old Mike Tyson became the youngest world heavyweight champion in history. He spent the next three and a half years storming his way through the heavyweight division without a single loss. And he wasn't fighting pushovers, either. He defeated Tyrell Biggs, Larry Holmes and Michael Spinks before meeting James "Buster" Douglas in Tokyo in 1990.

I was in the audience for the Douglas fight. Since turning heavyweight I'd knocked out all six of my opponents and was the number-one contender in the world, so I was scheduled to fight Mike in June. It hadn't been easy setting that fight up. As badly as I wanted to fight him, it seemed that Don King just as badly didn't want me to. There were a couple of possibilities as to why, one of which had to do with the fact that King and Lou Duva weren't exactly bosom buddies. But I don't think that was the main reason. The main reason was that King was afraid I'd beat Mike. Or, to put it another way, he felt that I had a better chance of beating Mike than a lot of the other contenders. It wasn't so much that King thought I was a "better" fighter. It's that I was different.

Mike was a brawler. By that I mean that he liked to fight inside, standing toe-to-toe with an opponent and trading punches, relying on his power, his conditioning and his ability to absorb a lot of punishment. Also called a "fighter" (as opposed to a "boxer"), a brawler is looking to land a knockout punch as soon as the opening bell rings. It's the kind of style that Howard Cosell warned me not to pursue at the Olympics, because amateur fights are only three rounds long and victory is generally won on points, not knockouts. One thing about being a brawler is that you risk not racking up a lot of points, so if you don't get the knockout, you might lose the decision.

"Boxing," on the other hand, is an outside style. You circle, dance and jab, staying out of the way of power punches and stepping inside only when you spot an opening or have your opponent worn down and properly set up. Boxing is a lot more technical than brawling, and takes a lot of concentration. It was also hard to do against Mike because he had a real knack for drawing you into his style. King knew that a skilled boxer who wasn't intimidated by Mike was a serious threat. He also knew that boxing was my strength and that I wasn't scared of anything.

So the negotiations with King hadn't gotten very far, until a couple of key dates began creeping up on him. Mike was obligated to fight the number-one contender in each of the three governing organizations within a year. Since I was the contender in two of those, the WBA and WBC, he had to fight me or he'd be stripped of those titles. Any hopes that King had that I might lose my number-one rank as the deadlines approached soon evaporated, and he had no choice. June would see "The Brawl For It All."

The Douglas fight in Tokyo was a nothing bout for Mike, just an easy payday, and was such a mismatch that it had to be held in Japan because none of the big venues in Las Vegas, Atlantic City or New York wanted anything to do with it. The Vegas oddsmakers had Tyson as a 42–1 favorite, about the same as you'd get for Godzilla versus Winnie the Pooh.

The fight went as expected, all the way to the eighth round when

Mike uncorked a massive uppercut. It sent Douglas sprawling and the count began. When the ref called out "Nine!" Douglas scrambled to his feet and Mike swooped in to finish him off, but the bell rang before he could do it. Douglas staggered back to his corner to try to regain his senses and I guess he did, because in the tenth round he launched a huge right uppercut of his own and this time it was Mike who hit the deck. Unlike Douglas, though, Mike didn't get back up in time.

It was one of the biggest upsets in history, but a bigger one came ten months later. My fight with Mike was off because he was no longer the champion, so I fought Douglas instead. Everybody had assumed Mike was going to wallop the daylights out of me, so they naturally thought my fight against the guy who'd beaten him wouldn't last thirty seconds past "Good evening, ladies and gentlemen . . ." It was a reasonable as-sumption, so an awful lot of money changed hands in Vegas when I knocked Douglas out with one punch in the third round and became the undisputed heavyweight champion of the world. "A fluke," some writers said. "A lucky punch." Over the next few months I guess my "luck" held up, because I successfully defended the undisputed crown by beating former world champions George Foreman and Larry Holmes and knocking out a third challenger for good measure.

But I still wanted Mike Tyson.

A lot of sportswriters thought it pretty remarkable that I'd beaten the man who'd beaten Tyson, but if they'd had any idea what had been going on in the weeks leading up to the fight, they would have thought it downright miraculous. While I was getting ready to fight the bout of my life, I was also in the process of losing both my manager and my wife.

There had always been conflict between Ken Sanders and Main Events. Uncomfortable as it became at times, I put up with it because that kind of tension can be a good thing, competing interests keeping everybody honest. But in recent years it had escalated to the point where the Duvas tried to get me to line up with them against Ken, and Ken tried to get me to line up with him against Main Events, each of whom wanted the other gone. I would come to realize later when I was running my own businesses that putting me in the middle of all of that was Bad Management 101 on both their parts. You don't put pressure and burden on the guy you're supposed to be shepherding to a world championship. One of their jobs was supposed to be keeping me away from distractions and handling them for me. I didn't know enough at the time to be able to recognize that, much less try to do something about it, so it was doomed to become a choice of one or the other of them sooner or later. It finally happened as the Douglas fight was approaching.

It wasn't easy for Ken to be my friend. He was a good old southern boy with a lot of good old southern boy buddies. While I was an amateur and he was a prominent local businessman, those friends didn't pay it much mind, but when I went pro and started winning all my fights, Ken became a bit of a big shot around town because he was my manager. Some of his "friends" became envious and started looking for ways to bring him down a notch, like giving him a hard time about me making more money than him. At first it was just kidding around, but at times it got vicious, some of his business associates even making nasty racist cracks. Ken stuck by me through all of it, but it cost him and it wore him down a little. It also made him feel that he needed to be seen as in control, and that's probably why things had to come to a head.

I broke training for a day to honor a speaking engagement, and ended up on the same plane as Ernest Evans. He'd just seen me fight and came over to introduce himself. You probably know Ernest better as "Chubby Checker," a name he gave himself based on "Fats Domino." Chubby had rocketed into the celebrity stratosphere in 1960 on the strength of the Twist, probably the most wildly popular dance craze of all time. But he'd just as quickly plummeted back into obscurity, having been bankrupted by managers not just once but twice.

We got to talking—the conversation started when I told him my childhood nickname had been "Chubby"—and at one point he asked me a few questions about my business affairs. He listened carefully, especially to my story about the auto dealership, and then said, "Evander, you're going down the same road I did." When I asked him why he thought that, he held up his hand and counted off on his fingers. "You and your manager got the same attorney, same accountant, same banker, same everything." He shook his head. "Don't do that, man. I'm tellin' you."

That made me think, and in the next few weeks I sounded out some people about it. To a man they warned me that I shouldn't be using the same financial and legal professionals as my manager, that it was standard procedure not to do that. I didn't do anything about it at first. Then just a few months later I ran into Chubby on another flight. He asked me if I'd taken care of separating those services out, and I admitted I hadn't. I still trusted Ken, and I just didn't think I needed to do that.

"Got nothin' to do with trust," Chubby said. "Guys I was with, I trusted them with my *life*. Didn't make any difference." He ended the conversation a little later by saying, "Listen, do me and do yourself one favor, okay? At least have a different accountant."

I knew he was right, and decided to make the switch. My first step was to call Ken and talk it over with him, but he got insulted and didn't handle it very well. I guess all of the pressure on him had been building for a while and I'd picked the worst possible time to bring up a subject like that. Even though it had no financial or other impact on him, he got really angry. I listened for a while, but when he cursed me, I hung up on him.

A few days later when I called him about something having to do with the upcoming Douglas fight, Ken said, "I thought we were over, you and me." I told him no, we weren't. He was surprised, and explained that his feelings had been hurt, which was why he went off on me. I said I understood, then added, "But don't ever curse me again." I was willing to work with him, but I couldn't forget the things he'd said. And that's when we agreed to part. I felt really bad about it, and when the Duvas told me they were happy that Ken was out of the picture, I felt even worse.

After that, and a short-lived stint with the rapper M.C. Hammer managing me, I didn't feel I needed a manager guiding my career, just business guys and lawyers to do negotiations and handle matters requiring special expertise. One of the problems I kept running into was that so-called "managers" assumed I was just going to do whatever they advised. But that's not how I looked at the role of managers. Their job was to give advice and counsel, but the decisions were mine, as were the consequences. Whatever I decided after listening to everybody, they needed to get behind it and support it, not feel insulted if I didn't do it exactly their way.

The Buster Douglas bout was the first fight of my pro career that Ken wasn't with me, but as soon as I got back to Atlanta I went to see him and handed him a check for $1.2 million, 15 percent of the $8 million I got for the fight.

"What's this for?" he asked. "I wasn't even there."

I told him that it didn't matter that he hadn't been there. He'd been my manager through everything it took to get there, and had rightfully earned his cut. My own thing is never to let a rough moment or two wreck a valuable friendship, and I'm truly thankful that Ken and I are still very close friends. People are trying to get him back into the boxing game because he had such a nice way of handling fighters, and they're right. Once in a while he asks me to take a look at a young fighter and I'm always glad to do that for him. The sport can only benefit by Ken's presence.

The other thing that happened just before the Douglas fight—a week before, to be exact—was that Paulette filed for divorce. Her lawyers had suggested that bit of timing strategy, probably thinking that it would do maximum damage to my head and make me vulnerable in the negotiations. The whole thing felt like some kind of plot. Paulette didn't handle money well, and while I paid all the bills and rarely questioned anything she spent, she didn't have direct access to the accounts. A lawyer told her that if she divorced me she'd have half of everything all to herself. He also advised her to wait and hit me with all of this just before the Douglas fight. I wonder if he was also the one who told her not to let me know that she'd filed. I didn't find out about it until a reporter who was interviewing me said, "So what's with your wife filing for divorce?" I mumbled something vague, because I had no idea she'd done that.

My lawyer thought her lawyers were crazy and would have done better by their client if they'd waited a week. "Don't they know how much you're going to get paid for fighting Douglas?" he asked in amazement.

It didn't matter. I had no intention of negotiating. I told my lawyer to give Paulette anything she asked for, and that's what we did. Even when she demanded custody of the kids, I gave in. As painful as it was, I wasn't about to make my children the subject of a court fight, and I also didn't think it right to tear kids away from their mother. We ended the matter quickly and without the kind of bloodshed you see in a lot of divorces.

Not having the kids with me was every bit as awful as I'd thought it was going to be, but it didn't last long. A couple of things led me to believe that all wasn't going well and before too much time passed I sat Paulette down to talk about the kids. She didn't argue back when I told her I'd noticed signs that there were problems that could easily get out of hand. One of them was that the kids talked disrespectfully to her and weren't obedient. I told her that one of the surest indicators of how a kid was going to turn out was how he behaved toward his parents. Paulette's relationship with her own parents was strained, and she was smart enough to see the connection when our kids started to fall into the same patterns.

There were other things as well but there was no need to beat her over the head with them. My argument was a simple one: If she wanted the kids raised right, we both knew they'd be better off with me.

I had strong feelings about how I wanted my kids to be raised. I didn't want them to think that they were successful because I was successful, without having accomplished anything on their own. I didn't want them to get everything handed to them, because then there'd be no reason for them to strive to do things themselves. That's no kind of preparation for life. I wanted them to be ambitious, to have goals and to work hard to achieve those goals. That's the only way anyone ever feels good about himself. The easiest way to shortchange your kids is to give them everything they want but nothing that they really need, and that's one road I didn't want our children going down. They might be grateful for the moment when you give them stuff, but that shallow gratitude will turn to resentment as soon as bad things start happening to them that they're not equipped to handle. If you don't believe me, pick up a supermarket tabloid and read about the antics of rich, famous children of rich, famous parents who overindulged them and never taught them how to live. Those kids never accomplished anything on their own and became self-destructive because that's what happens when you have nothing to live for. And if you think those kids love their parents because of all that money they give them, I'm willing to bet you're wrong.

"If you want those kids to grow up loving you," I told Paulette, "let me bring them up. Let them come and live with me."

When she resisted, I assured her that she could see them any time she wanted, with no restrictions, and then I said, "I'll continue to pay full child support, no questions asked. Just let me have them." I wasn't trying to bribe Paulette; I was just trying to show her how serious I was, that the money didn't matter compared to making sure our children got their lives started off right. When she saw that, she became convinced. I give her a lot of credit for making that very difficult decision.

It's a sign of how much she loved them that she let them come live with me. And it's not like I took them away from her. She saw them all the time and there were no hard feelings between us. Evander Jr., Ashley and Ewin have been with me ever since, and have been a never-ending source of joy, for Paulette and me both.

There are a lot of theories about what it takes to raise a kid right, like having a father around. The thinking is that if a boy doesn't have a father in the house, he's doomed.

I don't think it much matters whether it's a mother or a father or both or a grandmother or an uncle. What matters is that *someone* is there, all the time, and loves you and cares for you so much that they're willing to take the time to raise you, not just feed you. That old line about "a roof over your head and food on the table" just doesn't cut it with me. A kid needs a lot more than food and shelter to grow up right. He needs structure and discipline and a strong hand at the tiller to make sure he learns what he needs to know. It doesn't mean parents have to do it all themselves, but they need to be careful about who else has influence. I grew up with no father in the house, but I had Carter Morgan, and a mother who understood that you couldn't ask for a better man than Carter to take her son in hand. I had the Boys Club, one of the best things ever to happen to me, a place where good behavior was rewarded and it wasn't at all cool to have been in jail or have a gunshot wound. My childhood wasn't easy but I was blessed because Mama, Carter and the Boys Club gave me what every kid needs to grow up right: structure, discipline and love. Now I feel it's my obligation to provide the same for my own kids, and to support people and organizations who provide it for other kids.

About seven years after the kids came to live with me Ashley turned twelve. She came to me and said she wanted to change her name. I said, "Go ahead," but she shook her head and said, "I mean for real." When I asked her why she said, "'Cuz everybody's got an 'E' except me!"

It had become a tradition in the family. All of Ashley's brothers and sisters had names beginning with E and she wanted to be part of it. I was really touched by that, so I went to court and made official the new name she'd picked out for herself: Evette.

God would eventually bless me with eleven incredible—and incredibly sweet—children and there's not a day goes by that I don't thank Him for the gift of Evander Jr., Ashley/Evette, Ebonne Esheal, Ewin Ezekiel, Emani Winter, Eden Eloise, Eleazar Evan, Elijah Esaias, Elijah Jedidiah, Eli Ethan and Eve Elizabeth.

Mike Tyson was far from finished after losing to Buster Douglas. Four months later he fought Henry Tillman, who'd taken his Olympic spot in 1984, and knocked him out in the first round. He did the same thing to Alex Stewart, then beat Donovan "Razor" Ruddock twice the following year. While I was busy defending my titles, he was doing everything he could to get a shot at taking them away from me.

And even though he was no longer world champion, he was still the man to beat. The thing about Mike isn't just that he was a good fighter, it's that people were absolutely terrified of him. You can see it when you watch tapes of his fights, how tentative his opponents were, almost like they were afraid to make him mad. The prefight interviews didn't help, either. Reporters were always asking scary questions: "Are you worried you're going to get hurt? Have you thought about whether you really want to do this? Do you realize it's only a matter of time until Tyson kills somebody in the ring?" By the time the opening bell rang, a lot of his opponents were already toast. He wasn't just respected as a fighter, he was feared, and that probably contributed to a lot of his wins.

So even after he lost the crown, Mike was still the guy you had to beat to prove you were the best. Even if you'd just won the fight of your life, it was always the same thing in the postfight press conferences: What about Tyson? When are you going to fight Tyson? Like it was more important than being champ. And in some ways, it was.

CHAPTER 11

———

"Iron Mike"

Mike Tyson called himself the "Baddest Man on the Planet" but it's hard to know exactly what he thought that meant. In the 'hood, *bad* usually means *good,* like "Man, that movie was so bad, you just have to see it!" So was Mike saying he was the best man in the world? Or did he mean "bad" in the usual sense, like rotten or nasty? I think he liked the bad boy image, a guy from the projects who made good but never lost his inner-city roots. When we met for the world championship, he didn't enter the arena the way most fighters do, in the middle of a royal procession and wearing flowing silk robes. He kind of sauntered in, like he'd accidentally stumbled on the place but didn't care because he could whup anybody at a moment's notice anyway. Instead of a robe, he was wearing only a torn sweatshirt with the sleeves cut off. Was that a clue to what he meant by "Baddest Man on the Planet"? My guess is that Mike himself hadn't given it as much thought as I just did. It just sounded right to him: tough, ornery and invincible.

Mike had a rough start in life. He lived in Brownsville, one of the meanest sections of Brooklyn, and by the time he was ten or eleven he was already creating chaos. He discovered boxing in reform school. Vet-

eran trainer and fight commentator Teddy Atlas describes in his autobi-
ography how he met the young future champion.

Bobby Stewart, a former Golden Gloves champ and Mike's counselor at the corrections facility, got him only so far in boxing and then
knew he couldn't take him the rest of the way. So Stewart got in touch
with Teddy, who was working in Cus D'Amato's camp in Catskill, New
York, and asked him to have a look.

Mike arrived at D'Amato's in a prison van, and when he stepped out,
Teddy's eyes almost bugged out of his head at the size of him. Mike was
about five-nine and weighed 190 pounds.

"Just how old is this kid?" Teddy asked.

"Twelve," Stewart replied, and pulled out a birth certificate to prove it.

Teddy agreed to take the kid on and see how it went, so every week
for three months the prison van would pull up to D'Amato's and Tyson
would spend the day training. He had a lot of behavioral problems and
was a handful around the camp, but Teddy, who had himself done time
in Riker's for violent crimes as a teenager, had overcome those same issues in his own life. That left him with a gift for seeing deep into the
heart of kids who were like he used to be and knowing just what to do to
get them back on track. Teddy took a stern but caring approach and
Mike seemed to respond. After three months, Mike was released on pa-
role under the condition that he stay at the camp under Teddy's super-
vision.

Teddy had a whole batch of troubled kids at the camp and was doing
a remarkable job of straightening them out. His approach to them was
very much like my mother's was to me, giving them goals to shoot for
and letting them know that at least one person in the world cared about
them, and it was working. On weekends he'd drive them down to New
York City so they could compete against other fighters. The bouts were
usually in seedy little gyms on streets you could hardly find, filled with
thick tobacco smoke and bad smells and a crazy assortment of oddball
characters betting on the fights. The kids were matched up by age, but

nobody would believe for a second that Tyson was twelve, so Teddy had to put him up against kids as old as sixteen to get him fights. It didn't matter. Mike worked so hard in training and was so strong and talented that he knocked everybody out anyway.

By this time Cus D'Amato, who'd guided Floyd Patterson and Jose Torre to world championships, was getting on in years and had given the run of the camp over to Teddy. Cus would show up at the gym once in a while and give some advice, but was pretty much out of things.

Until he saw Mike Tyson. D'Amato's fight radar was as sharp as ever, and he soon realized that this kid had championship potential. He knew that Mike was troubled, but also saw that he was responding to the tough love he was getting from Teddy, who agreed that Mike could go all the way if handled right and given enough time. And that right there was one of those great turning points in life, those critical moments at which everything can change depending on which path you take.

The problem was that Cus didn't have time. He was getting old, and didn't know how many years he had left. If he was going to produce one last champion before he checked out, it had to happen soon.

So he threw himself into the middle of Mike's training, and that's where he started crossing swords with Teddy. Whenever Mike got into trouble, which was pretty often, Teddy would sit him down, give him a stern talking-to and not let him fight for a while. Every time that happened Cus would get upset, because he saw the clock ticking and didn't want Mike wasting a second of time being unproductive. So he started overriding Teddy, and not just in camp, either. If Mike got into trouble at school, Cus would go to the principal and try to smooth it over. Same thing with the local police, who knew and admired Cus. It didn't take long for Mike to figure out that he could get away with pretty much anything as long as he worked hard in the gym and kept knocking guys out. Cus looked the other way and made sure everybody else did, too, and if Teddy tried to interfere, well, Cus still owned the camp.

Mike knew that Teddy was still on his case, and since that was the only obstacle there was to his behaving any way he wanted to, it was the one he pushed on the hardest. It came to a head one day when Mike went way over the line and Teddy had to stick a gun in his ear to make his point. Mike got the message, but Cus didn't, and Teddy was no longer able to stand by and watch as Cus, intent on producing one last champion, insisted on indulging Mike's bad behavior. Teddy had simply had enough, and when he left the camp, he probably took with him Mike's best chance to become as good a man as he was a fighter.

It's amazing how those moments can affect an entire life. When I was little my mama worked twelve hours a day as a cook and when she came home she was so dog-tired she could hardly keep her eyes open, much less spend time with all her kids. But by the time I was six she'd worked herself into a heart attack and could no longer do her job. So for the rest of my youth I had her practically all to myself, and it's because of all that love and attention that I was able to accomplish all that I have. I sure hate to think of her heart problems as having been part of a divine plan for my benefit, but the plain truth is, maybe they were. We didn't have money but I had Mama, and without her there for me, who knows where I might have ended up?

Mike wasn't as fortunate. With Teddy gone he was left without someone who would love him for himself rather than for his accomplishments. He discovered that the world was his oyster as long as he kept winning. No matter how bad his behavior, he was still surrounded by adoring fans holding out autograph books and rich supporters holding out money. When he became the youngest world heavyweight champion in boxing history (ironically, without Cus, who'd died the year before), the adoration became so fevered that, as happens with so many big celebrities, Mike thought he could get away with just about anything. And he was mostly right. But given Mike's history of pushing the envelope, it was inevitable that there was going to come a time when he pushed too far.

But that was still a ways off. Before that, Mike was a big inspiration to me as a boxer. He may have been gigantic as a twelve-year-old, but as an adult heavyweight he was very small. I started watching him in 1986 and was impressed by what he was able to do in the ring. He had an arm length of seventy-four inches and was fighting guys with eighty-four inches. He weighed 215 pounds and was going up against fighters who weighed 235. He was short at five-nine but was taking on monsters who were six-four. And he was kicking the stuffing out of all of them.

I watched every one of his fights. I wanted to figure out how someone who was undersized like that could keep winning. How was he able to reach up high with those short arms and throw head shots at someone half a foot taller? How was he able to rock guys who outweighed him by over twenty pounds? I had to know because I would have the same issues if I ever became a heavyweight, and since Mike had a three-year head start in that division, I watched to see how he did it. Studying him carefully and comparing his skills to my own, I came to believe that I could do it, too.

I also came to believe that I could beat Mike himself. Even though our strength, speed and skills were fairly evenly matched, the attitudes we would bring into the ring with us were not. Those were created by how we were brought up. When it came down to the mental aspects of a fight, I felt sure I'd have the edge.

I wanted to fight Mike, but there was a situation underway that was making it difficult to set up a match. To explain it I have to touch on the business side of the boxing world, and that world is so bizarre there's almost no way to keep this simple, but I'll try. Just bear in mind that the whole story is about eight times more complicated than I'm going to make it sound.

Part of the problem is that the three major governing bodies—the

WBA, WBC and IBF—all have different rules, as do the boxing or athletic commissions of all fifty states, and sometimes those rules are in conflict with one another. In this case, we were mostly concerned with the WBC, the World Boxing Council.

Every champion is obligated to defend his title within a certain amount of time. You generally have a year to face the number-one-rated contender, but for your first defense you can fight anybody in the top ten. After I beat Buster Douglas at the end of 1990 and won all three titles, Lou Duva set up a fight against George Foreman. George wasn't the number-one contender—Tyson was—but he was tremendously popular. The promoters thought there'd be so much money in a bout between the two of us that they offered me $20 million for the fight, the biggest payday in boxing history. If I won, which Lou was sure I would, I'd probably get even more to fight Tyson a few months later. He set the Foreman fight up for April 1991, and everything was looking rosy. I should have known better.

Since losing his world crown, Mike had fought four matches, won them all, and was ready to get his titles back. Looking around at the field, I guess he and Don King thought that Mike now had a better chance against me than against any of the other contenders. If I lost to one of those other guys in the coming months, Mike would have to fight him instead of me, and King wasn't willing to take that chance. So they wanted to fight me before I fought anyone else. Problem was, I was set up to face Foreman.

As badly as I wanted to go up against Mike, it didn't make any sense to do it as the very first defense of my new title. I was going to be paid a fortune for fighting Foreman, would probably beat him, and would then still be able to fight Mike. But if I fought Mike first, that would be a tougher match, and if I lost and never got the shot at Foreman, I'd be out $20 million. To me it was simple arithmetic, and a few extra months before fighting Mike was no big deal.

Don didn't see it that way. And when Don King doesn't see something "that way," he doesn't just sit around. He, Mike and the WBC filed a lawsuit against me and everyone on my team to stop the Foreman fight.

You need a reason to file a lawsuit other than your own self-interest. There has to be some legal basis, and King had come up with a doozy. It had to do with Mike's loss to Buster Douglas in Tokyo back in February. Mike knocked Douglas down in the eighth, but Douglas beat the count in getting back to his feet and went on to win. According to the lawsuit, however, the ref had counted too slowly. By the time he called out "Nine!" he should have been way past ten, the suit said, and Mike should have been the winner by knockout.

Don had protested Buster's victory at the time of the fight, but it had been denied. (What made that especially interesting was that Don was not only promoting Tyson, he was promoting Buster, too!) Whether or not he had a valid point at the time, the supposed "long count" had happened months ago. Were they really trying to reverse the outcome of the fight?

No. They couldn't do that. Instead, they were using an obscure WBC rule that gave the council the power to order an immediate rematch if there was a "controversial or irregular" result. The WBC also had the power to order a rematch after an "intervening" bout. What that meant is that if the winner of the controversial bout gets beaten in the next match, then whoever beat him has to fight the guy he beat before he fights anybody else.

I can hardly follow that myself, so let's try it again. If the winner of the controversial bout (Douglas) gets beaten in the next match (which he did, by me), then whoever beat him (me) has to fight the guy he beat (Mike) before he fights anybody else (Foreman).

Bottom line: The WBC was ordering me to fight Mike before I fought Foreman, and the purpose of the lawsuit was to make me follow that order. Now, in America, you can't legally make anybody do anything. You can only make them *not* do things, or you can have things taken away from them. The WBC wanted the court to issue an injunction to stop the Foreman fight, and if I didn't then fight Mike they were going to take away my WBC belt.

They didn't get the injunction, so the Foreman fight was still on. But that didn't mean they couldn't still strip my title, so *we* got an injunction to stop the WBC from doing that until we had a chance to try to settle it. That wasn't going to happen overnight, though, so the judge suspended the case until after the Foreman fight.

Don King is a hard guy to figure. There are so many layers, so many different personalities he can adopt at a moment's notice depending on the situation at hand, that there's no easy way to tell who the real Don King is.

He's definitely one of the shrewdest businessmen I've ever dealt with, and one of the toughest. He's happy to negotiate all day long but if you try to call what you think is a bluff, the odds are pretty high it wasn't a bluff at all. He's walked away from some pretty big deals when they didn't go his way. Part of the reason he's willing to let a deal go is that he's intensely competitive, to the point where winning is as important as landing the best deal. That makes it difficult for him to back down from a position once he's dug his heels in, even if it's the right thing to do from a business standpoint. While it's generally a good negotiating tactic never to back your adversary into a corner he can't gracefully get out of, with Don it's absolutely critical.

Main Events was very good at doing deals, but they were by the book, using fairly standard contracts and terms. Don King never did anything by the book and was enormously creative. He had a great vocabulary but if the right word wasn't at hand, he'd make one up, and if you couldn't understand it, he was ready with a definition so convincing you'd swear it came right out of a dictionary.

I understand Don King because we grew up in similar circumstances and learned a lot of the same lessons about getting things done. Don's motto is "Fake it till you make it." To be successful, act like you already are. Don always shot very high, so even when he had to scale back his expectations, he still ended up with more than anybody else would have. He inspired others to do the same, too, making people more willing to shoot for the moon. To do it he'd put on a great show: "This will be the greatest fight in history!" or "You've made me madder than anybody ever has!" People knew he was showboating but there was still the feeling that at least some of it had to be true. And he did the same with his fighters, playing up how much one hated the other, to throw some anger and malice and excitement into the battle.

But I never played that game, for two reasons. The first is that I never hated any of my opponents, any more than two chess players had to hate each other in order to have a good match. The second is that there's no going back from a public stance like that. If I glare at an upcoming opponent and bad-mouth him, how do I then turn around and say he's really a nice guy and we're actually friends? How do I pretend to be stupid and then expect people to react to me any other way? So I tried not to get into that game, and King thought I was hurting myself because of it. "You can't draw flies to a picnic!" he told me over and over. It's not enough to be a good fighter, he warned. You have to be an attraction, a personality, somebody who somebody else wants to kill and you want to do the same to him. He loved fighters who hollered and pounded their chests and carried on for the cameras. Mike Tyson was especially good at that, and King always pointed to Mike when he was trying to get me to do the same kinds of things, like intimidating opponents weeks before the fight even started.

That kind of thing could ruin a fighter's reputation, making him a clown or a fool in the eyes of the public, but for Don, it was money in the pocket. Nobody wanted to see two nameless men fight each other. One of the things that makes sporting events so much fun is rooting for one side. There aren't that many fans, of any sport, who are so into the science and technique that they don't care who wins. Millions of people who watched Muhammad Ali fight didn't know a left hook from a right jab but they sure knew who Ali was, and it wasn't just that he was a great fighter. He was a personality, a rare combination of talent, attitude and show business, the kind of champion who created new fight fans and put fortunes into the pockets of his promoters.

I wasn't like Tyson or Ali, so Don didn't think much of me early on. But the public did, and I won fights, so he had to deal with me but wanted to do so on his own terms. I wasn't buying it. He even went so far as to call me an "Uncle Tom" on national television, in an effort to light me up and get some cheap publicity. I knew what he was doing and I didn't rise to the bait. It wasn't me, wasn't my way, and I was having none of it. When the media reacted as he knew they would, and confronted me about it, I told them I didn't believe King meant what he said. He was probably insulted that I didn't take it more personally but, as far as I was concerned, it was strictly business.

Besides, getting into it with King on a personal level is a bad strategy because there's no backing away from it. He'll look you in the eye and tell you how badly he wants it to work, that he wants everyone to get a fair deal, and on and on. If you give in he'll keep taking and taking, but if you resist he'll make you out to be the bad guy, the stumbling block who blocked the deal while he was the one who'd do almost anything to make it happen.

None of that made him a crook. No matter what he pulled, it was always my choice how to respond, or whether to respond at all. He never out-and-out tricked me or lied about factual matters, so as far as I'm concerned, the best way to negotiate with Don King is to keep your ego out of it and stick to the numbers.

You can imagine how it galled Don when the guy who couldn't draw flies to a picnic became undisputed heavyweight champion of the world and started earning the biggest paydays in history for himself and his promoter, Main Events. He switched gears and now started saying I couldn't fight anyone who wasn't "over forty-two or had drug problems."

On April 19, 1991, I did fight someone over forty-two. It was George Foreman, in Atlantic City. That "over the hill" former world champion had knocked out twenty-three of his last twenty-four opponents and was the hardest puncher I'd ever faced. It was the first time since fighting Muhammad Qawi five years before that I didn't win by knockout, but I did win. It was a great fight, a great night, and my twenty-fifth straight victory since turning pro, but when all the celebrations were over, I stepped back through the looking glass to deal with Don King and Mike Tyson.

One thing you can rely on about Don: He's a businessman to the core. Here he was knee deep in this lawsuit against us but did that stop him from trying to set up a fight between Mike and me? Of course not. Business is business. And if that was good enough for Don, it was good enough for me. I had no problem negotiating the deal. Besides, my lawyers told me that it was likely the suit would be dropped if we came to terms on the fight.

As it turned out, there would be more money if I fought Foreman again instead of Mike, because Don would demand too much for his side. But after banking the proceeds from the Foreman fight, the difference didn't seem very important. I wanted to meet Mike in the ring, so I told my guys to strike the best deal they could and get it set up.

Over the next few weeks there was a tidal wave of posturing, grandstanding, bluffing and threatening. Don tried to stall things so we would begin to panic as the best pay-per-view dates started to disappear. He also knew that the drop-dead date for a Foreman rematch was approaching, and tried to use that as leverage. People were flying around on airplanes, pulling each other into private meetings in hotel rooms, playing one side against the other, making promises left and right and using some amazingly creative accounting to try to justify various splits in revenue.

Don had pulled out all the stops trying to intimidate me in the court of public opinion, too. Nobody did that kind of thing better, and this was when he called me an "Uncle Tom." After my second-round knockout of Adilson Rodrigues in Las Vegas, back when King was doing everything he could to prevent me from fighting Mike, ABC had Ken and me linked up by satellite to Don and Tyson. (This was the year before the Douglas fight so Ken was still with me.) There was all kinds of the usual nonsensical baloney that nobody really buys, and then all of a sudden Don pulled something new out of his bag. He said that everybody thought I was such a nice guy but that I was really just an Uncle Tom. He said I'd always had white people helping me and working for me, and what kind of a proud black man does that? With Tyson snickering "Yeah, yeah" into the camera, Don asked how come I wasn't like other black fighters who had black managers and promoters?

I knew exactly what he was doing, and it had nothing to do with racial politics. He just wanted me in his own stable and thought that he could humiliate me into leaving Ken by making it look like I was a traitor to the race, and the only way to redeem myself would be to join up with a black man, namely Don King. It wasn't the only time he pulled something like that on me. He once referred to a decision I'd made as "bearing the wounds and scars of slavery." I didn't fall for any of it. I didn't even get angry, or let him draw me into trying to defend myself. He was right about one thing: White people had helped me all my life, starting with Carter Morgan and the businessmen who supported the Boys Club. I decide what people to deal with based on their skills and integrity, with never a thought to color or ethnicity or what God they believe in or if they believe at all. I've had a white coach, black trainers, Muslim promoters, a Jewish manager and a Mormon real estate consultant, and I wasn't going to let Don King use racial politics as an excuse to not let me fight Tyson.

Ken wasn't quite as cool about it, though. You could practically see steam shooting out of his ears as Don lit into me, and while I patiently waited for the tirade to pass, Ken jumped in and said, "Fine! Winner take all!" It was the only time I'd ever seen Don King speechless, before or since. He finally managed to go "Huh?" and Ken said it again. "You heard me! Tyson versus Holyfield, winner take all!"

I was speechless, too. After the show I grabbed Ken and said, "Why'd you do that!" He shrugged and replied, "Well, you can beat him, can't you?" I said something like, "Uh . . . um . . . yeah, sure, I can beat him," but I wasn't prepared to bet $15 million or $20 million on a winner-take-all arrangement.

Ken let me fidget for a few seconds, then he laughed and threw his arm across my shoulders. "Don't worry about it," he assured me. "There's no way Don King takes a chance like that. He'd work things so the loser still makes a ton of money, believe me."

Eventually, cooler business heads won out, and an agreement was crafted for Holyfield versus Tyson to take place November 23, 1991. The payouts would be the biggest ever: $30 million for me, $15 million for Mike, with the two of us splitting the gate profits sixty-forty. Sportswriters all over the country had declared that whoever won this fight would be crowned heavyweight of the decade. Everybody was happy, there was a lot of handshaking and backslapping all around, and things were looking rosy again.

Three days later George Foreman's people filed suit against all of us to stop the fight. They claimed that Lou Duva had made an oral agreement for me to fight George and then we breached it by signing the deal to fight Mike.

The suit was filed in Houston, where I lived while training, so everybody scrambled to fly down there and figure out what to do about it. We had to hire local lawyers to represent us, and the judge in the case put us on a "fast track" to get it resolved. We all agreed to half a day of mediation as well, to see if we could resolve things on our own and avoid a drawn-out legal battle that was in nobody's best interest. The half day wasn't enough, so with the judge's permission everybody agreed to keep trying. After a few days—and nights—of hard work and good faith all around, we worked it out and got it settled.

That was the last barrier. There was nobody left to come after us and get in the way. We had the contracts in place, the releases signed, approvals from all three governing organizations, and the venue all set up. In the immortal words of the builder of the *Titanic* . . . what could possibly go wrong?

As it turns out, plenty. On September 9, 1991, Mike was indicted on a charge of rape, and that changed everything.

Only two people know exactly what happened in Mike's hotel room in Indianapolis on July 18, but the rest of the facts were not in dispute. Mike had met a Miss Black America contestant at a pageant rehearsal and they'd gone out afterward, stopping at Mike's hotel late at night and going up to his room. Three days later she filed a complaint with the police alleging that Mike had raped her, and two weeks later a special grand jury handed down an indictment. A trial was scheduled for the following February.

Our fight was set for November. There was a lot of talk about whether it should go on, but all the lawyers were united on one point: An accusation is not a conviction, and Mike was innocent until proven guilty. He insisted that he'd done nothing wrong, and whether he had or not was up to a jury and nobody else. Bottom line, no matter what anybody's personal feelings might be about what had happened, we had a signed contract, and not to follow through would leave a lot of people open to lawsuits for breach of contract. So the fight was on.

Or so we thought. A few weeks later—I remember the date because it was my birthday, October 19—we got a message that Mike had injured his ribs while training and the bout would have to be postponed.

For how long? Nobody knew. He wouldn't be able to train while he was healing. How much time would he need to get himself back into shape? That would depend on how long a layoff he'd had, which nobody could predict. So there was no way to begin doing any rescheduling yet. Because of lead times for things like promotion and arranging for facilities and television coverage, even under the best of circumstances the fight couldn't take place before March or April.

But Mike's trial was scheduled to start in February. There was no way to know if he'd be found innocent or guilty, and if guilty, whether he'd go to jail. Everybody, including Don King, knew we were paralyzed and that the contracts were now meaningless.

The richest fight in history, and the most eagerly anticipated since Ali versus Frazier, was off.

CHAPTER 12

You Can't Win 'Em All

It was a terrible blow for my fight against Mike Tyson to get canceled. It wasn't just the money, but the fact that I wasn't going to be able to defend my title against the number-one contender. Not only that, it was also too late for a rematch against George Foreman. We decided to see if we could quickly make a deal with a legitimate contender who was in line for a title shot and could be in shape by November 23.

An Italian named Francesco Damiani fit the bill. He was a big strong guy with a good record who wasn't terribly fast but had great punching power. While that deal was being made I found some sparring partners whose styles resembled Damiani's and went to work getting ready for him. Damiani showed up in Atlanta well in advance of the fight to get acclimated and participate in some promotion. During one press conference he asked if he could come watch me work out in the gym.

"Sure," I said. "I'll be sparring tomorrow morning."

Damiani came to the gym and watched me for about an hour, then got up and left without saying a word to anybody. That night he was on a plane back to Italy.

"They said he got injured," Lou Duva told me. "Fell out of the ring."

"Injured? What ring? I was the one who worked out today!"

Lou just shrugged: *What can I tell you?* "Thing is, we got the arena, paid for all the ads in advance, TV time is booked . . ."

"Everything except an opponent."

"Yeah. Short notice, but I got a couple of ideas."

It had to be a quality fighter, I insisted. I'd rather call the whole thing off, even though it would cost us a fortune, than fight someone who wasn't a legitimate contender. And he had to be in fight shape, too.

Lou nodded his agreement. "I got a guy in mind."

That was good news. So why did Lou look troubled? "Who?"

He took a breath before answering. "Bert Cooper."

Oh, boy. Now I knew why Lou was less than thrilled. Cooper's style was wildly different from Damiani's, whom I'd been training for ever since the Tyson bout got canceled. Where Damiani was big, slow, hard-punching and relatively young, Cooper was small, fast as lightning and a very crafty veteran of the ring. Damiani may or may not have been scared of me—we never did find out for sure why he'd left town—but Cooper definitely wouldn't be. If we were to give him this shot to fight for all three world titles, he would go at me the same way I'd gone at Buster Douglas.

"What do you want to do?" Lou asked.

I wanted to fight Bert. That wasn't the problem. I just wanted enough time to prepare properly. Boxing loves an underdog, and there had already been two major upsets in the last year. I didn't want to be on the wrong end of a third one.

I got an idea. "Let's do it," I told Lou. "But let's move it to Atlanta."

It was a mad scramble but we booked the Omni in Atlanta, site of my first world championship, and sold it out almost immediately. I wound up TKOing Bert in the seventh, but it was far from a cakewalk. He was so hungry and so aggressive that I was having trouble staying outside and boxing, and kept finding myself brawling instead. A minute into Round Three he caught me with a big right hand and wobbled me a little, then followed it up right away with a series of fast, hard shots. I still hadn't gotten my balance back after that right and was up against the ropes just trying to cover up and survive while he kept up the barrage. I wasn't doing it very well, and pretty soon he had me off balance and launched a tremendous, arcing right hook toward the left side of my head. I put up an elbow to try to stop it, and kind of half did, but he'd thrown it so hard and had so much body into it that the momentum knocked me right into the ropes. I felt myself going down, fast.

Something lit up in my brain, like a big neon sign saying, "You haven't gone down once in your entire pro career!" It was true. I'd never been put on the canvas. I saw that sign and in a split second resolved that I wasn't going to go down now if I had to tear a muscle staying on my feet. I almost did, too. I hit the ropes face-first, and just before my left glove touched the canvas, I caught the top rope with my right and managed to hold myself up. It twisted me around into an awkward position, left elbow on the bottom rope, but no part of me ever touched the mat.

I bounced back up as quickly as I could and got into fighting stance, but referee Mills Lane was pumping a hand at me and counting out loud: "Three! Four! Five . . . !"

He'd ruled it a knockdown and it was the right call. It was also the first time I'd ever been counted. I dropped my arms and used the mandatory eight count to get my breath back. As soon as we resumed, Bert went after me again, big time. The HBO commentators started shouting that I was in trouble, that Bert had almost knocked me down again, and it was just about that time that I got reoriented and wobbled *him* a few times. It was an exciting round and the crowd had really come alive. They hadn't expected to see me so close to getting knocked out.

In the fifth I went after Bert and landed a series of very effective uppercuts. But it wore me out, and by the middle of the round I was too tired to throw big punches. Bert had taken a lot of blows, but when he realized I was fatigued, he called up his reserves and started hitting me hard. I covered up, trying to buy time to get my strength back, when all of a sudden Lane called for time. He then came over to me and lifted up my right glove to have a look. There was a boomerang-shaped cut about three inches long right through the leather, exposing the padding inside.

I got a good rest sitting in my corner while Lou Duva changed the glove. "Haven't seen this since Ali and Cooper," he said. That was a different Cooper, though: Henry. And it happened between rounds, probably because Ali's trainer, Angelo Dundee, was trying to get Ali some extra time to rest. Mine was a result of those uppercuts I'd hit Bert with. I'd really clocked him and don't know how he managed to stay standing. I'd opened a cut above his right eye, too, but his guys weren't allowed to tend to him while he waited for my glove to be changed. That had to wait until after we resumed and finished the round.

It wasn't until the end of the seventh round that I saw some openings and got a fresh burst of energy at the same time. I hit Bert with everything I had, as hard as I could, and it was working. The more I hit, the less he was able to defend himself, and that energized me even more. I had to knock him out, because if I didn't get him down soon, it was back to the corners and a rest I didn't want him to have. I knew I was taking a chance of completely draining myself with this all-out effort and leaving nothing for another round, but I was too committed to stop now, and I couldn't slow down, either, because I didn't know how much time was left in the round.

I was raining a series of unanswered rat-a-tat shots, and at the exact moment that I thought Lane should step in and stop the fight, he did just that. It was no surprise. He was one of the best refs who ever lived, and his judgment was absolutely uncanny. Fighters loved to have him in the ring because they knew that he would be completely fair and wouldn't miss anything.

I got my win, the hometown crowd got more than its money's

worth, and I was glad we'd decided to go ahead with it. The best part for me was that, even though I'd gotten drawn into fighting Cooper's fight and not my own, I was able to make adjustments and win.

But, like I said, it was no cakewalk.

Sure enough, in the postfight interview right there in the ring, Larry Merchant turned from me to Lou and asked him if we were going to "go on ice" until Mike Tyson's difficulties were resolved. Lou set him straight on that score and told him we weren't sitting around waiting for anybody. "We'd like to fight Tyson tomorrow if we could," Lou said, "but if he's not available, then we'll go on to somebody else."

Mike wasn't available. The following February he was found guilty of rape and two related charges, and the month after that he was sentenced to six years in prison. So, as Lou had put it, we went on to someone else, and that someone else was Larry Holmes, one of the greatest heavyweights ever. He'd held on to the world title for an incredible seven years and had lost only three fights since turning pro nineteen years before, two to Michael Spinks and one to—wouldn't you know it—Mike Tyson. After that last loss he hung it up for four years but then decided to come back, and he did it in style, beating all six of his opponents. Three days before Mike was found guilty, Larry won a decision against Ray Mercer, who'd been unbeaten to that point.

Four months after that, I beat Larry in Las Vegas in the third successful defense of my titles.

Still, 1992 was to prove a hard year for me.

My older brother Willie was one of those quietly special people a few of us are blessed to have in our lives. He was the artist in the family, and although he never really fulfilled his creative promise, he had something of the artist in his heart. As a child I didn't know my father, but between

Willie and my coach, Carter Morgan, that important role managed to get filled.

Willie, whom we all called "Bo," was fiercely protective of all of us, especially my brother Bernard and me, the two youngest. I have a hazy memory of one incident, but Bernard remembers it more clearly and has told the story often. He and I were walking home from the local golf course where we caddied on weekends. Two neighborhood rough-necks, who were notorious for hanging around the golf course and beating up and robbing caddies, came up to us on the street and demanded the money we'd just made. Neither Bernard nor I was ready to hand it over just like that, and we put up some resistance, but there wasn't any doubt that we were going to lose the money. The only question was how painful we were going to make it for ourselves.

That's when Bo showed up. "What's going on?" he asked.

Bernard pointed at one of the thugs. "They're gonna take our money!" he said.

Bo looked at the other two kids, each of whom was the same size as him. "That so?" he said.

One of the kids stepped up and said, "And what're you gonna do about it?"

Willie stared at him for a second, then turned to Bernard and me. "You two go on home," he said.

I didn't like the sound of that. Willie was pretty tough, but he was so good-natured he never got into fights, and taking on two big guys wasn't something I wanted to see him try. A few bucks wasn't important next to seeing my brother take a beating. "Come on, Bo," I said. "Isn't worth it."

"I said, you go on home."

Reluctantly, Bernard and I turned and walked away.

I don't know what happened—Willie never said, and he wasn't the type to brag about things like that—but those two guys never so much as looked at Bernard or me again.

After I became a professional fighter, Bo became an important member of my team. He laid out training plans for me and was always pushing me to get in the best condition possible. When it started to look like I'd be going up against Tyson pretty soon, he stepped up the workload even more. A lot of guys tried to get me to do one more rep or another minute on the treadmill, and I usually just did what I thought was best. But when it was Bo standing over me on the weight machine yelling, "Gimme two more!" I gave him two more. I loved my older brother with all my heart and I loved having him around.

Willie lived with his fiancée, Renee, and her kids. One night about 2 A.M. someone started banging on the door of their house. Renee's older son Dante got up and went to the door, and when he saw that it was his uncle Michael, Renee's brother, he let him in.

Michael pushed Dante aside and stormed across the living room to a bedroom where Renee's younger son Larry was sleeping. He started banging on the door and yelling something about the kid having stolen part of his income tax refund. Larry got up and opened the door just as Willie came out of his bedroom in time to see Michael point a shotgun at Renee's son.

"If I don't get my money back," Michael was shouting, "somebody's gonna be dodging bullets!"

"Michael!" Willie said. "Are you nuts? Get that gun offa him!" Willie stepped forward. "Come on, man," he said. "You ain't gonna shoot anybody." Willie and Michael were good friends, and Willie thought that some calm talk might defuse the situation.

But Michael whirled around and pointed the shotgun at Willie. "You lookin' for somea this, too?"

His words were slurred and he was unsteady on his feet. Willie, probably realizing Michael was very drunk, took another step forward, his hands up and his palms facing out. "You don't need to do this, Mike," he said softly, soothingly. "Come on now. You been drinkin', you ain't thinkin' straight . . . come on now."

Michael, weaving unsteadily, pushed the barrel up against Willie's chest.

"Now you know you ain't gonna shoot me," Willie said, "so why don't you just—"

The gun went off with a deafening blast, and just like that, in front of Renee and her kids, my brother Bo's chest exploded and he was dead.

Renee was in a bad state of shock when she called me. I dressed quickly and got into the car to drive to Willie's house. It was raining, and the flashing lights from the police cars were reflecting from every surface, disorienting me. When I got out of the car the cops recognized me. One of them started to wave me through the line they'd set up, but a higher-ranking officer overrode him. "You need to stay out here, Mr. Holyfield," he said.

"Why?" I asked him. "That's my brother."

"That's why," he answered. He was afraid I'd get all crazy and go after Michael, even though they had him in custody and had already removed him from the scene. I wouldn't have done anything like that, but the police officer didn't know me well enough to know that.

A few minutes later two men came out carrying a body bag on a stretcher. "At least let me see him," I said to the officer as they put the stretcher in an ambulance. He nodded, and one of the guys zipped open the bag so I could see my brother's face. Bo's eyes were open, and there was no damage above his neck, so it looked like he was alive. It was hard to convince myself that he was gone. After the ambulance left they let me inside the house. It was an awful scene. Somebody had come for the kids, but Renee was still there, still in shock, my brother's blood soaking into the carpet, flashing red lights bouncing off the walls and mirrors.

Willie died just eight weeks before I ran headlong into a brick wall called Riddick Bowe. He was far and away the biggest, toughest, strongest fighter I'd ever met in the ring, outweighing me by thirty pounds.

When the camera was at certain angles, you couldn't even see me standing behind him. I had to start training while my brother's funeral arrangements were still being made. It was hard; I was so used to having Bo around, it was like this big emptiness was following me around where he used to be. It didn't help that Riddick's last name was "Bowe," and every time I heard it, I was reminded of my brother.

It was the first time I ever lost my cool during a fight. I'd taken a lot of criticism for not knocking out Holmes or Foreman, even though I'd beaten them both. Some writers had dismissed the two former world champs as washed up and not worthy of title shots, and I thought that was unfair to me and, more important, to them. They'd gotten back into contention by beating the best fighters of the day, and I'd fought them the way I thought I needed to in order to win. Knock out George Foreman? The guy was 254 pounds of power and guts and if he didn't want to go down, he wasn't going down. I had to box him for the points, not fight him for the knockout, and that's how I won.

I have to admit that the criticism had gotten to me. Still, as much as I wanted to knock Bowe out, for the first two rounds I stuck to my plan and boxed him from the outside. Then, toward the end of the second round, we clinched, and after the ref told us to break, Bowe hit me. It didn't do any damage, but it was a cheap shot and I guess I was ripe to be aggravated. I made up my mind to knock him out and did about the dumbest thing you can do against a guy who is bigger, stronger and younger than you and outweighs you by thirty pounds: I moved inside and tried to outpunch him.

From that point on, the bout evolved into an epic battle that is still shown on television as a classic. We each dished out enough punishment to fuel a dozen fights. Just about everyone who was there or saw the video says the same thing: It wasn't a boxing match. It was all-out war.

The climax came in the tenth round. Bowe hit me harder than I'd ever been hit in my life, an uppercut right smack on the chin. I saw stars, and I mean that literally. They were dancing all around my head, like in one of those old cartoons when somebody gets hit on the noggin with a frying pan. When I finally pulled myself back together, I turned the tables on Bowe and served up some mayhem of my own. When the bell sounded to end the round, we got a standing ovation like I'd never experienced before except at the end of a fight. It would come to be regarded as one of the greatest rounds ever fought.

I managed to go all twelve rounds but took a bigger beating than I ever had before. The Qawi fight in 1986 had been a death march that almost killed me, but that had mostly to do with exhaustion and extreme dehydration. He hadn't hurt me very much. Bowe, on the other hand, hurt me a lot. I wasn't surprised when the decision was announced and Bowe was declared the winner.

It was my first loss as a professional, and much has been written about this fight coming on the heels of my brother's death, and how that must have affected me. Many writers said it was why I lost. But it's not true. I trained hard, I fought hard, and the simple truth is that Riddick was better than me that night. To lay it off to some excuse on my part is to unfairly shortchange a truly great heavyweight.

Either way, though, I was no longer champion of the world.

Losing isn't the dirty word most fans—and a lot of athletes—think it is. Losing is an important part of a competitive life. And while nobody enjoys losing, the trick isn't to be 100 percent perfect all the time. It's to deal with the occasional loss in ways that make it less painful and less counterproductive.

Losing can often be turned into something positive, if you come at it the right way. For one thing, it takes some pressure off. Think back to when you may have seen a baseball player or a golfer on a hot streak. When newspaper and television reporters are swarming all over them, do they look happy and satisfied? Are they absolutely delighted at what's going on?

Not often. They might be enjoying some of the attention but they're usually half-crazy with anxiety, terrified of what's going to happen when the streak, as it eventually has to, ends. When it does, everybody's disappointed, the spotlights go dark, it's like some kind of great tragedy has occurred. Somehow it seems like the guy is worse off than he was before. What is it about human nature that causes that?

Sometimes streaks can even distract you from more important things. Whacking more home runs in a season than Babe Ruth may get a lot of attention, but if you become more interested in belting them out of the park than getting safely on base, you can hurt your team.

I've spoken with a lot of guys in a lot of sports who've had big streaks end, and you know what? Almost every one of them says the same thing, at least in private: "Man, I'm so relieved that's over! I couldn't stand it anymore!" And you can take this one to the bank: A lot of them, consciously or otherwise, ended it on purpose, or at least stopped trying so hard, because it just wasn't worth the stress. They wanted to get back to business and stop trying to fulfill everybody's unrealistic expectations for them.

The great tennis player Chris Evert won 125 consecutive matches on clay, including 24 tournaments, over a six-year period starting in 1973. When she finally lost one, the press was all over her, asking if she was going to retire now that she was washed up. I don't remember her exact words but I remember basically what she said, that losing a match now and again didn't mean she wasn't a champion, and she still had a lot of big wins left in her.

Losing doesn't make you a loser. Only a losing attitude does. Being a great golfer doesn't mean you never hit a bad shot. It means that, when you do, you stay calm and figure out what you're going to do to get out of it.

How you deal with a loss brings out your true colors. You can only show great sportsmanship when you lose, because anybody can be a good sport when he wins.

Losses are especially tough when you think you've been dealt an unfair hand. This happens a lot in judgment sports. If you're bowling or playing darts or pool, you pretty much have only yourself to blame if you lose. The results speak for themselves. But if you're a competitive figure skater and a judge has it in for you or was bribed, or if you're a basketball player and some guy keeps stomping on your toes when the ref's not looking, then when you lose there's a great temptation to go nuts and make sure the world knows it wasn't your fault.

Something that happens that sports fans are less aware of is an athlete setting himself up to lose, usually without realizing it. You'll read about a guy who went out drinking the night before a ski race or pulled a muscle playing touch football before a big game and then lost. You wonder how somebody can be that crazy stupid, especially when everybody knew that he had it in the bag, that all he had to do to win was stay upright. Why would a guy throw it all away like that?

Hard to say, but when I see something like that happen, the first thing that pops into my mind is that the guy was so terrified of losing he went out and manufactured an excuse in advance. "Yeah, it was stupid, but my head hurt and I was dizzy and that's why I lost." Not because he just didn't have the right stuff or the other guy was better. It was because he was hung over or his arm hurt too much. That way he thinks everybody will assume he's still the best and only lost because of this one dumb thing he did.

That is a losing attitude. When you act out of fear rather than strength, when you make up reasons to fail, you might as well get out of the game.

One thing about champions, they always want the ball. In the last minute of the last game of an NBA Final, a guy like Magic Johnson or Larry Byrd will put himself right in the coach's face and beg for the ball. They're not afraid of missing the last shot or looking like idiots or getting blamed for blowing the championship. None of that matters.

And neither does losing, at least not when you keep the bigger picture in mind. Besides, my own thing is that setbacks pave the way for comebacks.

At the same time that reporters were writing about my heart and courage, they were also calling for my retirement. This was the first time I ran into the phrase "For his own good" and I was to get mighty tired of it over the coming years. I was too small to be fighting heavyweights, a big guy like Bowe was going to kill me someday, I'd already been undisputed champion of the world so what did I have left to prove, my title win and three successful defenses had been lucky or the challengers weren't adequate, yada yada yada.

When asked what I was going to do after losing to Riddick, I said, "I'm going to get back in line." And that's what I did. A year later I fought Bowe again. The sporting press went nuts when that fight was set up. Since beating me in our first match, they said, Bowe had gotten bigger, faster and stronger, while all I'd done was win a twelve-round decision over Alex Stewart to get myself in contention for another title bout. I wasn't just going to get whupped, I was going to get killed.

I was bothered by the mistakes I'd made in the first bout. I watched the fight film many times and was convinced that, had I stuck firmly to my plan and not blown my cool, I could have beaten Bowe. So I wanted to fight him again and this time do it my own way. I did, and beat him, and I was the world champion again, only the third time in history anyone had ever gotten the heavyweight title back after losing it. (The other two were Floyd Patterson and Muhammad Ali. George Foreman would later become the fourth.) Unfortunately, not too many people were talking about what an historic fight it had been, because they were too busy talking about something else that had happened.

It was during the seventh round. I'd been dominating the fight since the opening bell, and now had Riddick against the ropes. I heard this weird sound from somewhere up above, like a vacuum cleaner or something. I tried to stay focused, but then noticed that the crowd had gone a little quiet, and I glanced over to see that a lot of people were looking up in the air. I had no idea what the heck was going on, so I shoved Riddick away and stepped back to separate us, then looked up just in time to see something floating down into the ring. It was a parachute, except that instead of hanging from it with his feet dangling, this guy was sitting in some kind of contraption that looked like a seat in front of a big house fan. The chute snagged on the massive rigging holding the overhead lights, and the first thing I thought of was lights just like them collapsing onto the stage during a Curtis Mayfield concert, hitting the popular singer and leaving him paralyzed from the neck down. I jumped to the other side of the ring just as the parachutist hit one of the ring posts. A bunch of people in the crowd dragged him down and started beating him, and kept it up until a squad of security guys swarmed in and got him out of there. I thought he'd gotten roughed up pretty good, but he was released from the hospital that same night. Turned out his name was James Miller but he'd forever after be known as "Fan Man."

The fight was stopped, and it took more than twenty minutes to get it going again. I was annoyed because all the momentum had been on my side, and Riddick now had a chance to get rested up. It was getting chilly, too—the arena had been set up outside to accommodate the enormous crowd—and I was worried that my muscles would start to tighten. Another thing was that I gradually began to notice some aches and pains. I knew that the adrenaline of a bout protects you until it's all over and things start to sink in, but I didn't realize how important that was until I had to stand down for a while before a fight was over. With every minute that passed I felt less and less ready to get going again. My shoulders were especially achy. Riddick was huge and heavy, and sometimes when we clinched and he leaned his full weight on me, it bent my arm back. It was kind of like when you high-five somebody who's much bigger than you and you feel like your shoulder wants to come out of its socket. You can get little muscle tears when you do that and that's what I was feeling. Then again, Riddick had to be hurting, too.

When we finally got the go-ahead to resume, I fell back into the groove pretty quickly. Riddick made me go all twelve rounds, but I got the decision and had my world title back. Then Michael Moorer took it away in a twelve-round decision during which I tore a bunch of ligaments in my shoulder. While I was in the hospital for that, they also diagnosed a heart defect, and I was forced to retire. But then I unretired (I'll tell you about that later), got back in line, and won a decision over Ray Mercer. Then I fought Riddick Bowe for a third time while also fighting hepatitis. The illness knocked me out in the third round and Bowe finished me off in the eighth, and all the noise started up again: Holyfield has to retire, for his own good. That one was my own fault. I stayed quiet about being sick because I didn't want to take anything away from Bowe's victory and I didn't want to make excuses. Maybe if I'd disclosed that I'd had hepatitis, the sportswriters would have cut me a little slack. Unlike being over the hill, you can recover from being sick.

I got back in line. In May of 1996 I beat Bobby Czyz, which put me in contention for another title shot, and that's when the real fun began, because Mike Tyson had been released from prison the year before. He began his comeback by knocking out Peter McNeeley eighty-nine seconds into the first round. In March of 1996 he knocked out Frank Bruno and won the WBC crown, and in September he KO'd Bruce Seldon in the first round to win the WBA title.

So in the fall of 1996, five years after my original bout with Mike had been canceled, he was the world champ and I was the number-one contender. It was like the planets had purposely lined themselves up to bring about this situation. What nobody could know at the time was that it would lead to one of the most bizarre sporting incidents of the last half of the twentieth century.

CHAPTER 13

———

"Finally!"

A lot of people thought it a crime that Mike Tyson had even been allowed back into the sport. Boxing already had enough of an unsavory reputation in a lot of circles, and a convicted felon sitting at the top of the pinnacle wasn't doing much to improve it.

I didn't feel that way. Whatever Mike had done, he'd paid the price that a judge had determined was appropriate for his crime. That's why we have the law instead of mob rule. After all the emotions are played out, it's the courts that make the final decision about how to deal with the situation. So it seemed to me that, once the price was paid, the debt was cleared. You didn't have to like the guy. You didn't even have to agree that the sentence was appropriate. What you think and feel is a personal choice. But once the "official" decision was made, once the law of the land had spoken about how Mike was to be treated from a legal point of view, there was no reason not to let him get on with his life and career.

As Lou Duva had said after I won the world title the first time, we weren't going to sit around waiting for Mike Tyson. Instead, I moved on, lost the world championship, won it back, lost it again and was now ready to try to win it for a third time.

The clamor for me to quit the game had grown deafening. Since being released from prison, Mike had scored four KOs in less than eight rounds of fighting. If anything, he was even more devastating than before, and for sure he was a lot hungrier. Add to that some questions about whether I had a heart problem, and the sportswriters were near unanimous: If I was dumb and deluded enough to get into a ring with the Baddest Man on the Planet, I wasn't going to make it out of the first round any other way than feetfirst.

And was it worth the risk? Because it wasn't like beating him would make me undisputed champ. Mike held only one belt at the time. The reason for that goes back to this crazy business of three separate governing bodies.

When I fought Riddick Bowe in Las Vegas for the first time, I held all three belts and was the undisputed champion. That title passed to Bowe when he beat me. The next guy in line for a title shot, according to the WBC, was Lennox Lewis. The press reported that there was a lot of bad blood between Bowe and Lewis, and in fact there was plenty of swaggering talk about a match, but when it came down to setting up the fight, Bowe wouldn't do it. He claimed that Lennox wasn't a worthy opponent, and he also said that the WBC sanctioning fees were too high, but nobody believed him. For one thing, Lennox had beaten Bowe at the 1988 Olympics in Seoul, and for another, the WBC fees weren't even a rounding error compared to what he'd make on the fight. The feeling in the boxing community was that Bowe was simply afraid of losing to Lewis.

I don't think any of that was true. Riddick is a friend of mine, and let me tell you right off, Riddick Bowe isn't afraid of anything. The problem wasn't him. It was his manager.

After Riddick beat me, he and I had a long talk and I gave him some advice based on my experience. I remember exactly what I said to him at the beginning of the conversation: "Don't take any fights for less than $15 million. You're the champion of the world now and you don't have to." I explained that if you didn't set the bar high right at the beginning, it would be very hard to climb back up there later. I used the $15 million figure because I knew he could get that for fighting Lewis. And even if he lost, the payday for a rematch would be huge. "Just like it's gonna be when I fight a rematch against you!" I told him. We had a good laugh over that and he appreciated my advice.

His manager, however, had other ideas. He thought that losing would be the worst thing in the world and he wasn't willing to risk it, so he talked Riddick into taking easier fights at a fraction of what he could have earned fighting Lennox Lewis.

But Lewis had the right to contend for the title, so the WBC threatened to strip Bowe of the crown if he didn't take the fight. Bowe beat them to the punch. In a display of pure showmanship, his manager called a press conference and had Riddick literally throw the WBC belt into a trash can. That meant that the title was now vacant. Lewis would later pull the belt out of the trash when he beat Tony Tucker.

All of that not only robbed Bowe of the serious money he could have made fighting Lewis, it robbed me of my chance to become undisputed champ again with one fight. Even though I fought Bowe again and beat him this time, he only had the WBA and IBF titles, so that's what I won.

I lost them to Michael Moorer, who lost them to George Foreman, who lost the IBF belt when he refused to fight Axel Schultz in a rematch of a controversial fight. In a really convoluted series of oddball events, the belt eventually ended up right back where I'd left it, in Michael Moorer's hands.

Meanwhile, the WBC belt eventually worked its way around to Mike Tyson. He was obligated to defend it against Lennox Lewis, but even though he was offered an astounding $45 million, Mike wouldn't do it. In response to a court order to fight Lewis or lose the WBC title, he surrendered the belt on the same night he won the WBA title.

Did you follow all of that? Doesn't matter. The point is that the titles were no longer unified, but were in three separate hands. Were I to
fight Mike Tyson, the only belt up for grabs in that bout would be the
WBA. If I wanted to be undisputed champ again, I'd have to fight and
beat three different guys.

Well, you have to start somewhere, and I wanted to start by fighting Mike. Turns out I'd have to fight some other people first, including
the Nevada Athletic Commission. We wanted to put the fight on at
the MGM Grand in Las Vegas, one of the greatest boxing venues in the
world and one of the few that could hold an event of this size. But the
NAC had doubts about my health and demanded that I go through a
series of tests at the Mayo Clinic before they'd renew my license. When
one of my guys looked at the list, which filled several pages, he threw
it down and said, "An astronaut couldn't pass these!"

But I took them anyway. One of the doctors at Mayo confirmed
that I had an "abnormal" heart: "It's so strong we weren't even able to
test its limits," he said, and gladly signed a letter stating that I was fit to
fight.

There was only one obstacle left, and that was negotiating with
Don King. Since the original fight with Mike had been canceled, he'd
had a lot of opportunities to see me fight. He watched me beat George
Foreman and Larry Holmes, then lose the world championship to
Riddick Bowe, then win the rematch and regain the title, then lose it
again and just keep on going. So while the rest of the world thought
Tyson was going to pulverize me, and Don did, too, he was savvy
enough to know that it was far from certain. That left him with a
problem: Mike was the prime thoroughbred in his stable, and if he
lost, Don would be left without a heavyweight champion.

So Don let the complex and heated negotiations go right to the
wire before he sprang his final condition. "If your guy beats my guy,"
he said to my attorney, "he has to come fight for me, at least as long as

he stays the champ." That kind of thing is done all the time in boxing. It's a way for a promoter to ensure good bouts for his fighters and protect himself at the same time.

I agreed to the condition and the fight was set.

★ ★ ★

We got to Las Vegas two weeks before the fight, which the promoters had named "Finally!" A week later the town began filling up, and I'd never seen that kind of media frenzy in my life. The big running joke among reporters greeting each other was "Are you here for the funeral, too?" meaning that they'd come to see me get killed. *Newsweek* ran a headline, NICE MAN, NASTY BUSINESS: WILL EVANDER HOLYFIELD'S BEST QUALITIES—COURAGE AND FAITH—GET HIM BEATEN TO A PULP BY MIKE TYSON? The conclusion the writer reached was that, Yes, I would be beaten to a pulp

I asked a reporter whom I'd known for a while, "If you're all so sure I'm going to lose, how come there's so many of you here?"

"Because," he answered, "we figure you're going to go down in style."

It was a good thing I don't pay much attention to what people write or say about me, because the press really was treating this like a suicide mission. I didn't want to get distracted doing interviews, but every time one of my guys predicted a win for me, reporters would look at each other funny or just laugh right out loud. The question wasn't *if* I would lose, but in which round, and nobody was taking bets beyond the third. Officially, the line against me was 17–1, just like for the Douglas fight. Which had to make you wonder why Vegas was crammed to the rafters with people who were willing to pay thousands to scalpers for a single ticket to the fight. What was the point of paying that kind of money just to watch two or three rounds of some has-been getting his head handed to him? Yet high rollers continued to pour into town all week. The ramps at the airport were so jammed with private jets they had to be towed to overflow areas.

My team stayed at Caesars Palace instead of the Grand because we'd heard that Mike's guys liked to do things like bang on his opponent's door at all hours so he couldn't get a decent night's sleep. They did everything they could to intimidate me, even to the point of having someone I'd never seen before scream threats at me during a press conference, telling me all the barbaric things Mike was going to do to me during the fight. That one backfired on them, though, because every time he opened his mouth I started laughing. I didn't do it on purpose; I just thought the guy was half nuts. The reason it backfired was that he turned out to be a professional motivator they'd hired for Mike. Why he would need a professional motivator to get himself pumped for the fight was beyond me, but it couldn't have helped to have the opponent crack up every time the guy started talking.

I wasn't affected by any of that trash talk. I kept telling myself that eventually it was just going to be the two of us in the ring and all the talking would end. At one point I even grabbed a mike from one of their guys and said that to Tyson, too.

But that didn't stop the mind games. Right after the weigh-in, somebody in Mike's camp told the Nevada Athletic Commission that Mike wouldn't fight unless I took a steroid test. The implication was that I'd juiced myself up to become a heavyweight and then stayed juiced in order to outmuscle bigger and stronger fighters.

It seems that this same professional motivator had been at our press conference months before when the fight was announced in New York. I hadn't trained that day and when I haven't been working my muscles, I look a whole lot smaller than when I have. Before the weigh-in in Las Vegas, I had a long, tough training session, including a lot of weight work. I was pumped up like a bodybuilder, and when Mike and I took off our shirts before stepping onto the scales, it showed. Mike especially couldn't seem to take his eyes off me. He'd seen me shirtless back at the Olympic Trials in 1984 but since then I'd gained a lot of muscle, and it didn't come out of some bottle, either. It came from endless hours of hard work under the direction of my conditioning trainer, Tim Hallmark. But Tyson's on-staff motivator convinced him that I couldn't be stronger than him unless I'd cheated.

My guys went nuts at the demand that I take a drug test, especially Tim, who is one of those health buffs who believes the body is a holy temple and knows I feel the same. I would no more put a steroid or any other illegal substance into my veins than put poison in my mouth. Regardless, Mike's camp had no right to demand such a test, and my team was ready to march right into his camp and explain that to him in very straightforward terms. I'd never seen them so hopping mad.

Me, I hardly ever get mad. There's rarely much percentage in it. Instead, I try to stay calm and consider the larger picture. How can I turn the situation to my advantage? While my guys fussed and sputtered and stormed around the room, I got an idea. "What are you smiling about?" my attorney at the time, Jim Thomas, fumed at me.

I pointed to the phone. "Call back and tell Tyson's people I'll take the steroid test."

Jim didn't reach for the phone. He knew there was more coming.

"But Mike doesn't get the results until after the fight," I added.

The big night, when it finally arrived, was very big indeed. Paid attendance was over sixteen thousand people, making it the highest-grossing gate in Nevada's history at more than $14 million. And that was just the people who bought their own tickets.

There were so many celebrities in the audience—actors, athletes, writers, politicians, you name it—that it looked more like the Academy Awards than a prizefight. The jewelry in view could have financed a small country for a year. It was a great event for everybody, and still holds the record for the biggest pay-per-view audience of all time.

As of eight o'clock that night only one fighter in heavyweight history had ever won the world championship for a third time, and that was Muhammad Ali. At eight-forty-five I became the second when I TKO'd Mike in the eleventh round.

If I thought the postfight hysteria in Las Vegas was through the roof, it was nothing compared to what went on in my hometown of Atlanta. Mayor Maynard Jackson proclaimed November "Evander Holyfield Month" and threw a huge parade for me. It ended in a park where a stage had been constructed. My friend Magic Johnson got up to introduce me and said some very flattering things that somebody other than me will have to tell you about. When it was my turn to speak, I first gave thanks to God, as I always do after a fight, win or lose, and then found myself talking about my mother, reminiscing about the many lessons she'd taught me.

My upset of Mike stunned the world, but to me there was no "upset" involved. I call it that only because that's what it's called when everyone thinks you're going to lose and instead you win. To me it wasn't an upset at all, because I knew I was going to win. I've never gotten into a ring without thinking I was going to win. Once in a while I'm wrong, but that doesn't matter.

The usual carping began right on schedule. Tyson hadn't trained enough, I head-butted him and opened a cut over his eye, I was still just a blown-up cruiserweight . . .

What did I have to do to get some respect? I was supposed to have *died* in that ring, and instead I won. I was heavyweight champ of the world and had beaten three former champions on the way to getting there. Everybody I'd fought was bigger than me and I beat them thirty-four out of thirty-six times anyway.

As for this "blown-up cruiserweight" business, didn't anybody realize what a compliment they were paying me when they said that?

How does a guy who belongs down in the 190-pound weight class wind up knocking out all those heavyweights? Fighters don't try to fight above their class. They practically kill themselves trying to make weight to stay down in the lower ones so they don't get creamed. Here I am, the smallest heavyweight in the business, barely a ham sandwich above the 200-pound line, and I keep winning. So how is "blown-up cruiserweight" a criticism?

The media coverage started getting interesting at this point. Not too many people were saying, "Wow, he's the world champ! What a great fighter!" And it wasn't just because that kind of thing is so boring. It's also because if they did that, all of those sportswriters would be admitting that they'd been wrong. And not just some of them but all of them, with the single exception of Ron Borges of the *Boston Globe,* the only one who predicted I'd win. How do you write a bunch of columns predicting a massacre and calling for someone's retirement ("for his own good," of course) and then turn around and tell your readers he's really a great fighter after all? There had to be some other reason why I won other than that I was the better fighter and the writer simply blew it. Which brings me back to that steroid test Mike's camp had demanded.

Jim Thomas had been asking why I didn't want Mike's guys to see the results of the steroid test until after the fight, and now that it was all over I explained my thinking.

"Cheaters can't stand for other people to cheat," I told him. If they wanted to believe that I was on the juice, that was fine with me. That way, when I started pushing Mike all over the ring, maybe he'd assume I cheated and that he couldn't beat me, and that would give him a good excuse for losing. Once it was shown I'd been on steroids, I'd be disqualified and he'd be declared the winner.

After the fight that was one noisy camp, all excited to see the results because they were sure I just had to be on the stuff. When the results were revealed and were, of course, completely negative, you never saw a bunch of guys quiet down so fast.

The negative results also removed another possibility for why all of those writers might have been wrong. Even so, what I was still hearing was, "Fight Tyson again and prove it was for real." At least when they weren't calling for me to retire.

That was fine by me. I beat Mike once, and I knew I could do it again.

By the way, I haven't even gotten to the weird part yet.

CHAPTER 14

The Weird Part

My cut for a rematch had been preset at $20 million. Now, $20 million is plenty of money, and I wasn't one to turn my nose up at a sum like that, but I wasn't interested in the number so much as in being treated fairly. By this time everyone knew that the rematch was going to be far and away the richest prizefight ever, and a lot of people were going to make an awful lot of money on it, in part because the deals had all been set up before the first fight.

But the reason it was going to be so lucrative was that I'd won, contrary to all expectations, and everyone wanted to know if it was just a fluke. It didn't seem right to me that fans were prepared to pay sky-high ticket prices to see me get my head beaten in and yet other people were going to make more money on the fight than I was. I wanted to fight Mike, sure, but I wasn't half as bothered by the skeptics who were calling for a rematch as you might think. It was annoying, but no more than that, and I didn't run my life according to what other people told me I should do. If we couldn't negotiate a fair deal, I wouldn't fight Mike and that would be that, as far as I was concerned. I didn't have to prove anything.

Jim Thomas understood that but said there was a legal problem. "You already agreed to the $20 million number," he pointed out. "It was right there in the first contract." Jim knew that there was no way I'd violate an agreement, written or otherwise.

I told him I understood that. "But you tell Don King that if he doesn't renegotiate the deal, I'm going to retire."

Jim smiled. He'd written that piece of the contract himself. It said that I had the right to retire any time I wanted to without any negative financial consequences. When Don heard that, he blew his stack and started screaming at the top of his lungs. But by that time I'd come to understand him a lot better and knew that it was just his way of saying, "Okay, let's roll up our sleeves and figure this thing out."

Which is just what we did. Jim and I got together with Don and a couple of Showtime people and we all made the best cases we could. Jim ran down a full set of detailed financial projections for a rematch and proved conclusively that Don would make enough money to buy the planet Mars. Don pulled out his own projections and proved beyond a shadow of a doubt that he would be penniless and homeless and that his kids would starve if he paid us what we were asking. And who said accounting wasn't an art?

As the evening wore on we gradually worked our way to the middle and agreed on a package of about $34 million in cash plus $1 million worth of other stuff. Jim did a little research and said that it was the largest amount ever paid for a single performance of anything in any field anywhere on earth. That sounded pretty fair to me.

The fight was scheduled for the following April, but Mike suffered another training injury and we had to push it back to June. It would be back at the MGM Grand once again. I didn't need any special motivation to get up for this fight, but I got some anyway. The oddsmakers had made Mike the heavy favorite, and the sportswriters were lining up the same way. They said Mike had underestimated me and hadn't trained properly, and that he wouldn't make that mistake again. They'd seen him in camp and reported that he was training as hard as he ever had in his life, and when it comes to Mike Tyson, that's saying a lot. Think what you want about him, but when Mike put his mind to it, nobody trained harder. He could work himself into exhaustion day after day and it showed in the ring.

As hard as it was to imagine, Las Vegas was even more crowded and crazy than it had been for the first fight. There were reporters there from countries I never even heard of, and hundreds of them had shown up without credentials for the fight. I don't know how they thought they were going to get in. A lot of extra security people were put on to keep the peace.

Mike looked pensive during the prefight ring ceremonies, pacing rapidly, like he couldn't wait for the formalities to be over. He looked a lot fitter than he had the last time. There was a lightness to his step and his occasional shadowboxing flurries were so fast his gloves blurred under the bright overhead lights. The MGM Grand arena is huge, and was packed to the rafters—the gate broke the previous record set by our first fight—but if Mike noticed any of it, it didn't show. The swagger he'd had back then was also completely gone now and in its place was seriousness and resolve. There was fear, too, or at least worry, and I think that anxiety might have been contributing to his impatience. But whatever it was, this man had come to fight, not posture, and he was all business.

Mills Lane was the referee. He wasn't scheduled to be originally, but in what looked to be another mind game just like the demand for a drug test in the first fight, Mike's camp had insisted on a change of refs at the last minute. They got no argument from me. Mills Lane in the ring meant one less thing for me to worry about.

When the bell rang to start the first round, Mike wasted no time. He came to the middle and threw a hard right. I deflected it and threw one of my own. His hands moved faster than I've ever seen them move and his body movements were quick, too. He seemed to snap back and forth like a plucked string and his reflexes were tuned to the max. On the other hand, I sensed that there was something timid and tentative in him that I hadn't seen before.

As I danced around and threw some jabs and straight rights, he was moving to anticipate my punches and at the same time feinting with his shoulders to throw me off. At one point in the first round we faced each other twitching and faking and not throwing a single punch for almost ten seconds, looking for the right opening or waiting for the other guy to go first. When it was clear neither of us was going to fall for anything, we started throwing again.

I felt I had Mike's measure now and began to get aggressive. My jab was working and I used it to set up some rights and a few uppercuts. Mike was throwing some solid punches as well, but I barely felt them and I could tell that was worrying him. I was also backing him up a lot, something he swore he wasn't going to let happen, but there wasn't much he could do about it. He wasn't hurting me so I kept stepping into him and pushing him around the ring.

His defense was to clinch more often than he was used to, and our arms kept getting tangled up. Lane was having a tough time prying us apart, and it only got more difficult as we started retaliating against each other by hanging on much more than we should have, clamping our arms down on each other like some kind of interlocking puzzle. To me this was just tactics, and I tried to figure out how to deal with it. Mike, on the other hand, was quickly growing frustrated, and he started abandoning his fundamentals in an effort to just sock me, not as part of an overall strategy but because he was irked. It didn't help when my head banged into his eye during a particularly aggressive clinch. It wasn't a head-butt, just an inadvertent collision, but when it opened a cut over his eye, he started pointing to it and complaining to the ref. A cut not caused by a punch is pretty good evidence of a head-butt, and Mike's eye was bleeding, but I knew something Mills Lane probably didn't, and that is that Mike had cut his eye in practice, while sparring. That was the injury that had delayed this fight for six weeks, and what he had now wasn't a new cut from colliding with my skull. It was the old cut reopened when my head rubbed against it as he held me in the clinch. Blame his sparring partner, not me.

Back in the corner, my guys were confident that I'd taken the first round, and I was, too. I was forcing Mike to fight my style, not his, and I was landing more and better punches than he was and controlling the action. The second round was much the same. Mike complained about head-butting again, and also about something else, but I couldn't tell what it was. When Lane didn't react, Mike threw a low blow at me but it did no harm and I just let it go. I wanted a victory, not revenge, and wasn't about to get distracted just because Mike was getting exasperated. I won the second round, too, and started thinking about how I was going to knock Mike out. I wasn't interested in winning a decision.

The third round was a different story. Mike was so rattled that he came out of his corner without his mouthpiece and had to go back for it, but his corner men must have had some words with him because he hunkered down and came at me hard, throwing a lot of solid shots and getting out of the way of a lot of mine. Using all of his speed, power and wiles and staying in control of himself, he was getting the upper hand. I had to step up my own game to meet the onslaught, but Mike was ferocious, especially with his left. Two minutes in, I thought he was winning the round, and when we clinched I wrapped my right arm around his left to keep him from launching another bomb at me. After we broke I got some solid punches in, and while he was slightly off balance I threw a hard right and followed it up with a left. It was supposed to be an uppercut starting way down low but Mike saw it coming and dropped his forearm to deflect it. My fist slid off his arm and landed on his trunks below his right hip. It was a clearly inadvertent low blow but a few seconds later Mike retaliated with one of his own anyway.

Conditioning trainer Tim Hallmark's son Mitchell brought me to my knees. It was a low blow.

My friend 1984 Olympic gold medalist Mary Lou Retton at a charity function in St. Louis, 1995.

Ashley (Evette) and Ebonne, around 1995. Fighting Mike Tyson was easy compared to raising teenage girls.

In our first fight, I put Mike Tyson down in the eleventh round
and became world heavyweight champ for the third time.

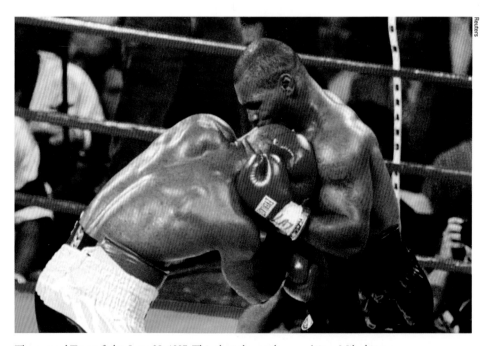

The second Tyson fight, June 28, 1997. This shot shows the *second* time Mike bit me.

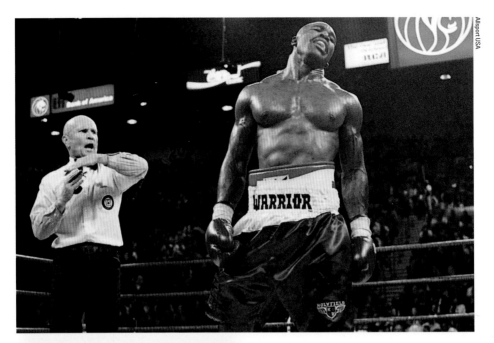

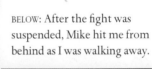

ABOVE: Mills Lane suspends the fight after he sees my ear.

BELOW: After the fight was suspended, Mike hit me from behind as I was walking away.

Allsport USA

Reuters

Visiting with South African president Nelson Mandela the week after the second Tyson fight.

Don King, one of a kind.

On March 13, 1999, Lennox Lewis and I fought to a controversial draw. It was the only time I've ever gone into the ring angry at an opponent.

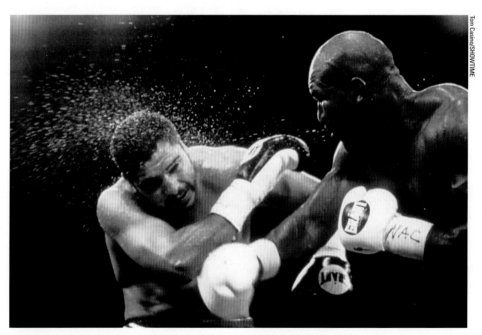

John Ruiz and I fought three times. The first time I won and became heavyweight champion for the fourth time. The next time John won, and the third time it was a draw.

Lee Gruenfeld

LEFT: Relaxing after a workout in Willie Savannah's Houston gym before I faced Jeremy Bates as the first bout of my comeback, "Holyfield V."

BELOW: Conditioning trainer Tim Hallmark and boxing trainer Ronnie Shields watching me shadowbox. With good people in your corner, the battle is already half won.

Lee Gruenfeld

Lee Gruenfeld

Tim is a great believer in balance and flexibility.

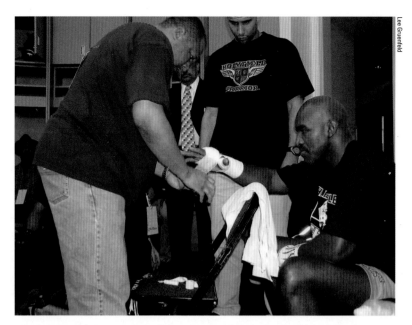

Every trainer has his own way of wrapping his fighter's hands. Ronnie Shields is one of the best in the business.

Almost the entire clan, in 2006. (Emani was visiting relatives and wasn't around for the picture.)

Shadowboxing in the locker room just before a fight.

We were both fighting well, and even though neither of us seemed to be gaining much of a points advantage, I thought Mike's aggression could win him this round unless I scored some decisive shots or knocked him down. That he had finally found his rhythm made what happened next even more mysterious.

With about forty seconds left in the round, we clinched again. Mike's face was at the side of my head and he started doing something odd, kind of working himself around until his mouth was close to my ear. He didn't seem interested in getting in a few rib shots while we were waltzing around, just in maneuvering his face to the side of my head.

At just about the time I was starting to wonder if this wasn't something I should pay a little attention to, I felt a pain like someone had just stuck a red-hot poker into the side of my head.

Now let me tell you, I've felt my fair share of pain in the ring. I've had my nose smashed, my shoulder muscles ripped, my kidneys nearly destroyed and my chin crunched by some of the hardest-hitting guys alive. I was well familiar with every type of pain you could possibly experience during a fight, but this . . . this was different. For one thing, I didn't know it was coming, so there was surprise and shock thrown in. For another, I didn't know right away what had happened. All I knew was that one of the sharpest pains I'd ever felt was lancing into me from the vicinity of my right ear. I spun away from Mike and jumped high into the air, looking like a cat that had just stepped onto the third rail. I was in agony, and as I danced around trying to deal with the pain, I noticed that there was blood streaming down my face and shoulders. What the heck had happened? Did I get shot by a sniper? I hadn't heard any guns being fired.

"He bit him!" someone was shouting, a note of hysteria in his voice. "He bit him!" I touched a glove to my ear but it was like putting a blowtorch to it. I pulled my hand away quickly and blood flew from my glove.

Meanwhile, Lane had made a T of his hands, suspending the fight.

While he was trying to figure out what to do, I walked to one side of the ring and tried to touch my ear again. But Mike wasn't finished. With my back to him and before Lane had a chance to stop him, he ran at me and with both hands gave me a hard shove, throwing me into the ropes and almost knocking me off my feet. Had the fight been restarted? I immediately turned and saw him on the other side of the ring. If the fight was back on, why had he run away? I didn't care. I sprinted across the ring to get at him, but Lane jumped in front of me and confirmed that the fight was still suspended.

I didn't need to complain to him about Mike hitting me from behind while we were on hold. He'd obviously seen it. Once he determined that Mike was going to stay put this time, he came over to see me. It's the only time I've ever seen Mills Lane look like he wasn't sure what to do. Then he said, "I'm going to disqualify him."

"Don't do that!" I pleaded. That would be a lousy way to end this fight.

Lane thought about it for a second, then put his hand up on my neck and turned me so he could have a look for himself. He didn't like what he saw and walked over to the other side of the ring where he motioned for the doctor and the boxing commissioner to come in.

The doctor, Flip Homansky, turned my head to look at my ear, then pulled back in surprise when he got a good look. "You okay to fight, Evander?" he asked.

"Huh? What do you mean?"

"Your ear," he said, pointing to it.

It hurt. So what? "Let me fight," I said. "I'm gonna knock him out." I had no idea yet that Mike had actually bitten part of my ear off, but it wouldn't have mattered anyway.

While Homansky looked me over, Lane spoke with the commissioner, Marc Ratner, and the microphones picked it up.

"He's disqualified!" Lane told Ratner. "He bit his ear! He's out!"

Ratner, the same boxing executive who'd passed on the news that

Mike's camp had demanded a steroid test from me, asked him if he was sure.

"He bit his ear!" Lane grabbed his own ear to demonstrate. "I can see the bite marks!"

"So you *are* disqualifying him?" Ratner wasn't arguing with Lane. He just knew that there was a lot involved here and wanted him to be sure.

"Well, let me ask the doc," Lane said, and turned to Homansky, who'd finished examining me. "He bit his ear . . . can he go on?"

The doc said I could. Lane came over to my corner and told us that he was going to deduct two points from Mike and let us keep fighting. Then he went over to Mike's corner and told him the same thing. Mike started to protest, and Lane . . . well, you have to understand Lane's knack for quickly getting to the heart of the matter. He spat out a profanity, cutting Mike off instantly. "Two points deducted, and if you do it again, you're disqualified!"

Lane called us to the middle, and he looked angry. After he got us going again, we tried to get back into our rhythms. It seemed to be working, but thirteen seconds into the restart we fell headlong into the Twilight Zone. Mike grabbed hold of me, pulled me in close and clamped his teeth down on my other ear.

The pain was blinding, but I was so shocked that he would do that again that it took about two seconds for it to sink in. I jumped away but this time I wasn't going to hop around and take a chance on having the fight stopped. I was going to knock Tyson out right now. As I launched myself directly at him, he was standing there beckoning to me with both hands and yelling "Come on!" I realized at that moment that he was out of control, and I grabbed hold of myself, hard. This was no time to get angry and emotional. That's exactly what he wanted me to do, forget my technique and my training and just stand there swapping punches with him. That would take me completely out of my game. There was only one course of action open to me, and that was to resist the temptation to land the big haymaker and do what I do best: box, not brawl.

It took me less than two seconds to get completely refocused. I was fighting to keep my world title and none of Mike's antics were going to stop me from doing it. Let everybody else sort it out later . . . I had a fight to worry about. I got back into position and started throwing jabs. Mike tried to draw me inside but I wasn't buying it. My ear hurt like blazes but I avoided the temptation to swipe at it. There were only a few seconds left in the round anyway and soon we were back in our corners.

Lane thought he'd seen Mike bite me again but wasn't sure. "He bit him again!" the same guy from before started screeching, even as my corner men worked on both my bleeding ears. Lane came over to see for himself, and that was it. He went over to Mike's corner and informed them that he was stopping the fight and disqualifying Tyson.

The ring began filling with people: my guys, Mike's guys, fight officials, wives, uncles, who knew what all, plus a truckload of security people. I didn't think anything of it but couldn't see much from my sitting position. Then I realized that half the people in the ring were fighting each other, and when I stood up, I saw the reason why.

Mike had come completely unglued. He was clawing and fighting his way across the ring to get at me, throwing wild punches at anything in front of him. His own people were trying to hold him back, but he still managed to deck a security guard. Then fights began breaking out in the seats just outside the ring, and more security guards started swarming in that direction. When the irate audience started throwing junk into the ring to protest what had happened, the security people decided to clear it out as fast as possible, starting with me, because Mike was still flailing around and nobody knew when he was going to stop. Eventually, a whole platoon of security guards backed him into his corner and kept him surrounded.

Down in my locker room there were several dozen people in various states of panic, fear and outrage. The first thing I did was wave them all to silence and lead a quiet prayer, in which I forgave Mike. I figured that if I could find it in my heart to do that it might have a calming effect on the others, and it did. Then someone came in and held up a plastic bag. "Got a piece of his ear in it," he said as he handed it to Tim Hallmark. Seems that Mike had spat it out onto the canvas. Tim buried the bag in some ice and then I was hustled upstairs to a waiting ambulance.

The security people were clearing the stadium, and a surging mob now surrounded the hotel. There were numerous reports of shots being fired but I didn't hear any while waiting for the ambulance to pull up and take me to the hospital to get my ears looked after.

"How're you doing, Holy?" Tim asked me before they closed the doors.

I smiled at him. "Still the champ, ain't I?"

And that, my friends, was the weird part.

PART III

Mountains, Valleys, and Everything in Between

CHAPTER 15

Atlas Shrugged

There was a whole lot more going on during the time of the Tyson fights than just the Tyson fights. The highest highs of my life were taking place at the same time as the lowest lows.

It actually started when I fought Michael Moorer on April 22, 1994. Michael was a good fighter who'd exasperated several trainers into leaving his camp. It takes a tremendous amount of motivation to do the work necessary to be a champion boxer, and if you have doubts about how much you want it, you can't possibly push yourself hard enough to do what's necessary. That's why champions seem so driven, in any sport. It's rare to see an athlete with so much talent that he doesn't have to work. You might think that Magic Johnson strolled onto a basketball court one day and took over the whole sport using his natural gifts, but that's almost an insult. He worked his tail off for years to get into the NBA, and when he got there, he worked even harder to become a champion, because he wanted it so bad. Nobody had to push him.

Based on what other people have told me, Michael didn't have that kind of motivation. Which was really too bad, because he had a lot of potential, at least on the physical side. He was very big, very strong, very

189

fast and he could take a punch. Those are the things that got a lot of trainers interested in him early in his career. When he was able to get himself to a place where he could prepare properly, he was a terror in the ring. It was only later, when they had to spend a lot of time cajoling and pushing him and sweet-talking him into working out, that they got fed up with the process and left. There were plenty of fighters out there who were aching to realize their potential, and Michael just didn't seem worth the trouble to them.

Then Teddy Atlas entered the picture. Teddy was the guy I told you about who'd been Mike Tyson's trainer until he'd gotten crosswise of Cus D'Amato. He'd been on the verge of training a world champion with Tyson, and it nagged at him to have missed that opportunity, so he was ripe for another one.

Teddy had a reputation as what fight trainers call a "psychology guy." He was great at all the standard training stuff, but he was also terrific at sniffing out an individual fighter's mental side. What motivated him, what inspired him, what was missing in his psychic arsenal and what was needed to round him out. If a fighter needed some warm consolation now and then, Teddy knew just what to say to him. If he needed motivational pep talks or just required some private space, Teddy sensed that, too, and made sure it was provided.

I'll give you an example of how Teddy was able to climb inside a fighter's head. Remember when I told you that Mike Tyson had insisted on a change of referee for our rematch? The day before the fight several sportswriters called Teddy in New York to tell him about it and ask him what he thought. It only took Teddy a few seconds to absorb the news and interpret it. "Tyson's setting up an alibi," he told the reporters. "An excuse for losing. And he's making sure everybody knows about it in advance." To Teddy, it meant that Mike was taking a loser mentality into the bout, and it led him to make an amazing prediction, one he repeated the next night at a fight party at sportswriter Jack Newfield's. "If Tyson thinks he's losing," Teddy told the partygoers, "he's gonna foul himself out on purpose." When asked how, he said either by head-butting, hitting low or biting, which are the most common fouls. So "The Bite" might have stunned the world, but it didn't surprise Teddy one bit.

What Michael Moorer needed was someone who could smack him upside the head fourteen times a day yet still be there to soothe his fragile ego and constantly reinforce his self-worth. That's a pretty tall order, and it's what drove his previous trainers away, but Teddy thought he was up to the task. In addition to his uncanny insight into a fighter's mind, he wasn't afraid of Michael, and that helped a lot when he had to get tough, or even threatening.

I meant that last part literally. People who watched the HBO broadcast of our fight were shocked at how Teddy was treating Michael, and fight fans don't shock easily. He screamed at him and cursed at him. After the third round when he thought Michael wasn't being aggressive enough, he got right in his face and yelled, "Now you start doing what we trained to do! Otherwise, don't come back to this corner!" Later when the bell ended the eighth round, Michael came back to his corner only to find Teddy blocking his way. "You want me to fight?" Teddy said, and sat down on the stool while Michael just stood there. "You want me to trade places with you? Do you?" It went on like that the whole fight, Teddy hurling profanities and generally treating Michael like an overgrown fourth-grader. And you know what? That's exactly what Michael needed to hear. Whatever you might think of Teddy's tactics, he was reading his fighter like a book, and it worked. Teddy had an ocean of desire to win this fight, and he poured every last drop of it into Michael. Whether that made Michael want it, too, or just made him too scared to face Teddy at the end of every round, I can't say. I only saw all of this on the tapes later, because I was having problems of my own during the fight. All I know is that Michael fought the bout of his life that night, and was better than he'd ever been before. By the time it was over, he had taken away the two world championship belts I'd won in my rematch against Riddick Bowe. But I'm getting ahead of myself.

I knew going into this fight that it was going to be a lot tougher than most people thought it would. I never made the mistake of taking any of my opponents for granted, but there were some I trained harder for than others. This wasn't going to be some easy-payday title defense. I was very aware of Michael Moorer's potential. I'd seen him fight and knew that he had all the physical gifts. Put that together with a savvy trainer like Teddy Atlas and a world championship on the line and it made for a potent combination.

About two weeks before the fight I hurt my shoulder in training. It wasn't a complete surprise. I knew I'd done something to it during my rematch with Riddick Bowe, but I didn't know what. In the weeks after the fight the shoulder nagged at me a bit, but I tried not to pay attention to it. Then in training it started getting worse.

I didn't want to go get it diagnosed because it might've resulted in the fight getting canceled. I tried to work around it but that only made it worse, so I laid off a little to see if time would help. It did, kind of, at least to the point where I thought I could deal with it. My camp was concerned, but over time they'd learned that I didn't like to be second-guessed once my mind was made up. I appreciated criticism and wanted people to sound off on their opinions, but once I made the decision, it was like a pro golfer picking a different club than the one his caddie suggested. Once he's made his decision, all the caddie can do by continuing to suggest something else is mess him up.

The first round was pretty tame, Michael and I kind of feeling each other out and not trying to do too much. I got the impression that he wasn't fighting instinctively and was a little uncomfortable, and then it occurred to me that he was probably following instructions from Teddy. That was good, because if I could switch gears before Michael had a chance to get back to his corner for new marching orders, it was possible he wouldn't be able to adjust in time on his own. Then, after he was in his corner, I'd switch gears again and confuse him even more.

Teddy knew I liked to stay on the outside, dancing and throwing jabs, so at the end of the second round I marched right into Michael and hurled a giant right hand at the side of his head. He wasn't able to get out of the way or block the punch, and I followed it up with a hard left and got ready for that sweet slap of leather and some Leaning Tower of Michael. Before the blow even landed I was already visualizing how I'd follow up. My right foot was forward now so I'd take a step with my left, hit him with a right hook, two quick jabs and another left. If I put my whole weight into it, I might even knock him out.

Boxers coat the sides of their head and their faces with Vaseline before a fight. That makes the glove slip a little when you get hit so that you have less chance of an impact cut opening up. But when a shot comes at a perfect right angle, like mine was coming at Michael, there's no slippage. That's a satisfy feeling, at least for the guy who threw the punch, and what would have made this one even more satisfying was that it put Michael down on the canvas.

I say "would have" because even though I knocked him down, I didn't get to savor the moment. Just as my left hand connected, I felt like someone had hit me in the shoulder with a machete. Pain shot up and down my arm, and it was like nothing else I'd ever felt in the ring, not even getting my ear bitten by Mike Tyson later. That would be just as acute, but it calmed down to a manageable level after a while. This didn't. Normally, adrenaline protects you from the full pain of getting hurt, and I don't usually show by my expression that I've been hurt, but I couldn't help it, it was so excruciating. I grimaced and hitched up my shoulder as I backed up to the neutral corner.

Tim Hallmark knew instantly that something bad had happened. He jumped forward, his mouth open and his eyes wide, and he stayed like that at the side of the ring for the rest of the round. I had a few seconds to myself while Michael took the eight count from ref Mills Lane, and then it was a matter of trying to survive. I didn't know what exactly was wrong, so I decided to test the shoulder out, despite how much it hurt. But when I tried to throw a punch, it looked like I was swatting a fly. It just plain didn't work. I could hold my hand up and move my arm a little, but pulling the trigger was out of the question. I did my best to stay out of Michael's way without my injury becoming obvious and managed to get through the last few seconds of the round.

Before the bell even finished sounding Tim was through the ropes and shouting at me. I couldn't hear what he was saying, so I leaned into him and whispered, "My arm's hurt!"

"I know!" he whispered back. "I think you separated your shoulder!"

As far as my trainer Don Turner was concerned, I might as well have broken my arm. "We got to stop the fight!" he said after I'd sat down.

I shook my head hard. "Don't do that!"

"You only got but one arm!" he insisted.

"Then I'll fight him with one arm!"

While that was going on Tim was massaging my shoulder. It hurt like all get out but it was hurting before anyway, and maybe rubbing it might do some good. It was better than doing nothing.

I had about forty seconds left to figure out how to deal with a double dilemma. On the one hand, I had to create a way to keep fighting with half my weapons gone. I couldn't hit Michael with my bad wing, and blocking punches wasn't going to be easy, either. I had no idea what would happen if he caught me a good one in the shoulder or the upper arm.

The second problem was trickier. I had to make sure no one found out how badly I'd been hurt. If the ref saw it, or if one of the judges or doctors or commissioners did and pointed it out to the ref between rounds, he'd stop the fight, and I didn't want that to happen. I still thought I could beat Michael, even with one hand, and my own thing is, I didn't want anyone else but me deciding that the fight should end. And it wasn't only the officials I had to worry about, there was my own corner, too. Those guys weren't flunkies, they were seasoned professionals, and not only that, they were my buddies. If they felt in their hearts that my health was at risk, they'd throw in the towel in a New York second. Yeah, they'd figure I might get bent out of shape about it, but no way would that stop them. How did I know that? Because I knew they loved me, and that they cared about me more than they cared about me getting angry with them. I never in my life thought I'd wish that someone would love me a little less, even for a few minutes!

So there I was, fighting Michael Moorer, fighting the ref and fighting this awful, terrible pain. Then when I went back to my corner, I had to fight my own guys so I could continue. Meanwhile, I wasn't sure if Michael had noticed anything on his own, but I knew it had probably taken Teddy Atlas all of ten seconds to figure out that something wasn't right. I kept trying to make adjustments, to anticipate what Michael was going to do and defend against it from my right side. For the most part it was working, but it was taking its toll. Boxing is tiring enough as it is, but nothing wears you out quicker than fighting pain or protecting an injury. Every once in a while I had to force myself to throw a left, even though it was agonizing, because if Lane saw me using only one hand, he'd know something was wrong and would stop the fight for sure.

As if all of that wasn't bad enough, a cut opened on my left eyelid in the fifth round. I hadn't brought a cut man to this fight, which was something unheard of. Don called them the biggest scam in boxing, and said "Save the twenty-five grand. I can take care of anything myself." But before this fight was over I was to develop a whole new appreciation for the art of stopping bleeding. Don did his best but Michael kept going after the cut and reopening it, and I had blood dripping into my eye the whole night.

I don't know how many rounds were being scored my way, but it was pretty clear a decision was going to be risky. If I wanted to win this fight, I had to knock Michael out. Normally you set up a knockout punch with a lot of lefts and rights, hoping to stun or at least disorient the opponent long enough for you to find a good opening, but I couldn't do that. And no matter what else I did, I couldn't seem to generate an opportunity to land the big one. Just trying not to get knocked out myself was a full-time job. It went on and on and on, and my shoulder kept getting worse and worse. I could hear Pernell Whitaker, the WBC welterweight champion and my longtime friend from the 1984 Olympic team, yelling over and over from ringside, "Move to the right! Throw the right hand!" Moorer was left-handed and so was Pernell, so he knew what he was talking about. The next day Dave Anderson of the *New York Times* wrote, "Maybe if Evander Holyfield had listened to Whitaker yelling at ringside, he wouldn't have been hit with Michael Moorer's right jab so often." I *had* been listening. But after fighting ten rounds with only my right hand, I just couldn't throw it anymore.

I don't know how I made it to the end of that fight, but it went all twelve rounds. When that final bell sounded my shoulder was on fire. The last of whatever adrenaline had allowed me to go the distance drained away completely and all I was left with, all I could think about, was how bad the pain was. I hardly cared if I won or lost. I just wanted to get out of that ring and away from those lights and the noise and do something to lessen the agony.

The split decision went to Michael, by the narrowest margin possible, a single point on one judge's scorecard because he hadn't credited me for the knockdown in the second round. As Michael's corner was celebrating the new world champion—and the first lefty ever to hold the title— and after I congratulated him with as much sportsmanship as I could summon up, I begged Tim and Mike Weaver to get me away from there as soon as possible. Down in the locker room I was met by Ronald Stephens, the same doc who'd taken care of me after the Qawi fight. He hustled me into an ambulance and over to the hospital, where they gave me morphine for the pain and saline IVs to get me rehydrated.

As the morphine kicked in and dulled the pain at least enough for me to think straight, I talked to Tim and Doc Stephens about what was likely wrong with my shoulder. None of us knew as we chatted quietly in the emergency room that the shoulder was about to be the least of my problems.

CHAPTER 16

—

Affairs of the Heart

"Evander had a heart attack in the ring."

Dr. Stephens had his back to me and was talking to Tim and Mike, like I was already dead or something. They still had the morphine going, so maybe I just hadn't heard him right.

Tim looked over at me with a scared expression, but Mike was still looking at the doc and said, "He had a *what?*"

"I don't know exactly when," Stephens said, "and I don't know precisely what the nature of the episode was, but he was fighting in a state of heart failure."

Mike had a little trouble absorbing the news. "How did he fight twelve rounds with a heart attack!"

Stephens shook his head. "I don't know. But one thing I do know." He folded his arms across his chest. "That he went twelve rounds in his condition is nothing short of an absolute miracle." By then a reporter from the *Atlanta Journal-Constitution* had arrived. He overheard that comment and it appeared in the paper the next morning.

Tim was still looking down at me so I pointed toward the doctor and wiggled my finger. Tim got his attention, and when he finally turned to me, I asked him the only question I cared about. "What do I do? To fix it?"

He started in trying to explain it to me, and said something about a "stiff heart" and an "atrial septal defect." I asked him what that meant, and he did a pretty good job of describing the condition in simple terms. The part I remember best is him telling me I had a little hole in my heart. When he was done, I said I understood and asked him again, "What do we do?"

"First thing we do, we're going to airlift you out of here," he said. "Get you to Emory as quickly as possible."

"And then . . . ?"

He frowned and looked around.

"He wants to know how soon he can fight again," Tim said.

"Fight?"

"Yeah, fight," I said. "When can I go back in the ring?"

This very confident doctor all of a sudden didn't look so confident. "Evander," he said, "we have to wait for all the tests, naturally, but . . . you're not going back into the ring. Not ever."

Flying to Emory in Atlanta with tubes still in my arm was like traveling to my own funeral. I spent half the flight trying to deal with my career being over and the other half trying to come up with reasons why this doctor was off his rocker, like I could talk my way out of his diagnosis or something. And behind all of that was the idea that there was this broken thing in my chest and if I sneezed or turned my head the wrong way, it would just up and kill me. The thought I finally settled on was that if Dr. Stephens had been real sure, he wouldn't have been flying me to one of the most prestigious hospitals in the country.

He said one interesting thing to me before we left. "Do you realize how lucky you are?"

Lucky? My career was over and I'm lucky?

"If you hadn't hurt your shoulder," he said, "you never would've come here. We wouldn't have done a routine EKG and you wouldn't have known about this problem. But now that you do, you can take steps to get it treated and stay alive." He smiled at that point. "Somebody must be watching over you."

It was a good point, and it made me think. It also gave me comfort. If my fight career really was over, maybe this was God's way of making sure I didn't foolishly try to continue it or waste a lot of time in denial. Just *wham*, that's it, get over it and move on.

The staff at Emory was waiting for me when I arrived. They reviewed all the tests that had been done in Las Vegas and the diagnosis was confirmed. The good news was that I could live a fairly normal life with only a few precautions, but the bad news didn't change. I was finished in boxing, and there was no choice about it. Even if I wanted to take a chance, no state would license me.

I didn't need to hear that last part. I may be obstinate, but I'm not an idiot and I'm not selfish. I had kids who loved me and depended on me, a girlfriend I cared about deeply and wanted to marry, a mother and brothers and sisters who would be saddened if I left this world before my time . . . and a God who I thought was trying to send me a clear message. If the experts said I could die in the ring, then that was that.

Like I said, setbacks pave the way for comebacks. After I had surgery for the rotator cuff I'd torn in the Moorer fight, I was determined to get on with whatever God had in store for me, with the same determination that had guided my fighting career. I didn't have to think hard about what that direction would be, either.

The first thing that guided me was my faith in God. It was the anchor of my life and influenced everything I did, and had never let me down, not even once. Sometimes it took a bit of time for the overall plan to make itself apparent to me, but it always did, and my faith kept growing stronger. That didn't mean I was perfect, but I was sure trying. Later on I would take a lot of heat for having kids out of wedlock, and I didn't mind that because I was wrong and I deserved it, but it did bother me a little when people called me a hypocrite. I never once told people how they should live their own lives and I never once made the claim that I was living mine well or tried to make it out that I was better than I was. All I ever did was publicly give thanks for all the gifts God bestowed on me and proclaim the Word to anybody who chose to listen. I may have sinned and been weak, but that doesn't make me a hypocrite.

The second thing driving me was that, from the very first day that I had more than two pennies to rub together, I looked for ways to use it to help people. It started with my mother and the rest of my family, and soon after I was giving money to organizations and people I believed in. There's a principle in Christianity I believe in and practice called *tithing*, which means giving 10 percent of whatever you make to the church.

The third factor was that I felt very strongly about children. I love kids and think that it's impossible to do too much for them. Everybody only has one childhood, and it sets you up for life. If a child isn't nurtured and supported in the right way, then as an adult he isn't going to have the tools needed to deal with a tough, demanding world. Sometimes parents aren't in a position to bring their kids up right, maybe because they don't have the means, or more likely because they themselves came into adulthood without the right tools. Lord knows my mama didn't have the means—we lived in the projects and everybody had to work just so we could stay together and have any kind of life—yet she brought me up as good as any kid could ever hope for. Even so, if it hadn't been for the Boys Club and the generosity of a lot of other people, I might have grown up much different than I did. So I knew firsthand the value of reaching out to less fortunate kids and lending a hand. That was hard for me to do one on one, though. My first priority was my own kids, and between them and my career, there was simply no time. Besides, I was just one man and could only do so much, but I had enough money to support people and organizations who could put it to good use.

When I considered all of these things, it was natural that the best way to combine my faith, my love of children and my wish to use my wealth to do some good in the world was to get involved in a ministry. I didn't know exactly how to do that, or what form it might take, but I wasn't ready to make those decisions. The first thing I had to do was get myself straight with the Lord. Until I had a better understanding of what my place was in the greater scheme of things, how could I help kids to find theirs? I was also concerned about my home life. I wanted badly to be married, to have the kind of stable family I'd always envisioned. That my first marriage hadn't worked out weighed on me heavily, and I blamed no one but myself for it. I never blamed anybody for anything that happened to me. If it looked to the outside world like someone had done me wrong, that's not how I saw it. To me, the problem was that I had let them do it. Most people can't help the way they are, or don't care to change things in themselves that need improving, but it's up to me to not allow a situation to develop that would hurt me.

As much as I wanted to be married, I knew that it was important to think a lot more carefully about it than I had the first time. I had a girlfriend at the time, Sandy, whom I was very much in love with. Marriage was in the wind, but all these things that had happened to me were like a warning that I needed to hold off on major decisions until I got myself squared away. I also didn't think it was fair to Sandy to marry her before the matter of my heart condition got resolved. I still didn't know exactly what the long-term outlook was or what I needed to do to stay healthy.

It was a confusing time, and I needed some help to sort it all out. Most of all, I wanted to hear from the Lord before I took the next step. A friend who was working with me suggested that I might want to talk to evangelist Benny Hinn. I asked my pastor about it and he said that Hinn was an anointed man and that I should seriously consider going to meet him. The idea of a man of God helping me was very appealing, so I went to Hinn's Philadelphia Miracle Crusade.

After the service began Hinn called me up on the stage and said, "I heard you had a problem fighting."

But I hadn't come about that, and I'd never mentioned anything about my heart condition to him. I'd already put my boxing career behind me and was ready to move on. "No," I answered. "I just need to hear from the Lord."

I stayed up on the stage during the service, and toward the end Hinn said to me, "You said you want to get close to God." He put his hand out and reached for my head, and the next thing I knew, I was on the ground.

I had no idea how I got there. I looked around and didn't see anybody who might have hit me. I came to my feet and got into a boxing stance, to make sure I didn't get blindsided again. This time when Hinn raised his hand I was balanced and alert and ready.

"You are healed," he said.

Wham! Down I went again.

Lying on the floor, I couldn't figure out what had happened. I'd been heavyweight champion of the world twice and somebody at a prayer meeting had decked me?

I got to my feet again. "How long was I down?" I asked. I figured maybe five or ten seconds.

"Thirty-five minutes," someone answered.

I couldn't believe it. It was only when I saw film of the incident that it really sank in that I'd been slain in the spirit, something that happens when you personally encounter the power and glory of God. It was only the first of several surprises that night.

"You're worried because you want to be married," Hinn said when I'd gotten back to my feet and pulled myself together. He turned me toward the audience and waved his hand toward them. "Evander," he said over the PA system, "your wife-to-be is sitting in this very meeting, getting the Word of the Lord just like you are."

I looked out over the vast crowd, as though a ray of light was going to shine down on the Chosen One or something. Nothing like that happened, of course, but I did notice one thing. Hinn had a large entourage consisting of musicians, singers and assorted staff members. There were about fifty or sixty of them seated in the section closest to the stage. It was a sea of white faces except for two black men and one smallish black woman about three rows back. Me being black, I felt a kind of connection and somehow felt it appropriate that I should at least say hello to them at some point.

Before the service ended I told Hinn about my heart condition. I explained to him that my boxing career was over because of it, but that I'd made my peace.

"There's nothing wrong with your heart, Evander," he said confidently, with the whole audience listening. "You go back to those doctors," he insisted, "the very ones who told you that your heart was bad. You tell them your heart has been healed, and let them run as many tests as they want."

I kind of wish Hinn had told me about my future wife privately instead of announcing it. Once I left the stage, about three dozen women came up to me at various times during the rest of the meeting. They were smiling brightly and making all kinds of meaningless small talk, all of it by way of saying, "He meant me. I'm the one." A lot of them said that God had told them this was so.

There was a private reception after the main meeting. I spotted the black female staffer I'd seen earlier. She was sitting by herself and I went over to introduce myself. Her name was Janice Itson and she was very intelligent and accomplished and a bit shy. She was a physician and had gotten her medical degree from the prestigious University of Chicago.

She wasn't a singer and didn't seem to be bustling about like a lot of the other people on Hinn's staff, so I asked her what she did.

"I examine people who claim to be healed," she said. "To make sure there's no trickery."

Now that was interesting. You see these charismatic evangelists "healing" people and it's often pretty obvious that there are some shenanigans going on. What Janice would do was make sure people had the infirmities they claimed to have before they went onstage, and then check to make sure they were really gone after they were healed. As shy as she was, once we started talking about the Bible she seemed to turn into a different person. I couldn't believe how knowledgeable she was, and how well she understood the meanings of passages that had puzzled me. She may have been a doctor by profession, but her first love was teaching the Bible, and she was very good at it. Some girls I'd dated would go to church with me, but it was usually just to make sure I didn't meet up with any other girls. Janice went on her own.

She lived in Chicago. When I got home a few days later I gave her a call and we got to talking. I didn't hang up until about eight hours later. It was mostly me listening and Janice talking about the Bible.

Somewhere along the line I told her about all those women who'd come up to me at Benny Hinn's reception, a lot of them saying, "God told me I'm going to marry you." In order for that to be true I'd have to marry an awful lot of women and have them die so I could eventually marry them all. So all but one or maybe two had to be lying, and that disturbed me. By that time I was a good deal less naïve than I used to be, but it still rattled me when people looked me in the eye and lied. So it really blew my mind when all of these women who were participants in a Christian crusade could say things like that with straight faces. And it wasn't like they were just making up harmless stuff. They were claiming that God had spoken to them. I thought you had to be cursed or something to do a terrible thing like that. I said to Janice, "Do you think they were lying?" She said she didn't know. I asked her if she heard from

God herself and she said yes, she did. So I asked her, "What did God tell you about me?" And she said, "That you're going to be my husband."

That was the last thing I expected to hear. I find it almost impossible to lie, even though it's gotten me into some trouble, and so I was honest with Janice now. "Why would God allow you to keep yourself for Him all these years just so you could run into a guy who's got five kids with three different women and was only married to one of them?"

And I hadn't changed, either. I had a girlfriend I loved, but it wasn't a monogamous relationship. I was taking care of all my kids and I was close with their mothers, too, and still saw two of them occasionally. Sandy knew about it and said she had no problem with it, but I knew that if we got married it would create trouble. It wasn't like I was still adding to the problem, though. I'd known these women for years and cared for them deeply, and I just didn't know how to break things off. It's part of this thing I have when it comes to people I've been close to. No matter what they might do to me, if they came and asked me for forgiveness and wanted me back in their lives, I forgave them, even if maybe I shouldn't have. It took me a long time to figure out that forgiving people didn't mean that I had to continue associating with them and doing things for them just because they asked. I think that was because I came from a large and close family, and if somebody did something nasty to you, you didn't get rid of them. You found a way to accept them back, because that's what families do.

"So I have this problem," I told Janice. "It's why I went to Benny Hinn, to get past that before becoming involved in a ministry." Janice said it was okay, because she knew I was going to get better. But I wasn't yet, and that's why I wouldn't get married again. I knew how much it had hurt Paulette when I had a child out of wedlock, even though our marriage was on the rocks. I didn't ever want to put anyone through that again. It didn't matter that someone knew that about me up front, either. I knew that God was going to help me change, but I didn't know how or when, and I wasn't going to get married until I did.

Janice had no such doubts. She told me over and over that God loved me, that I'd had this great anointing in my life, that I was *chosen* and was going to do great things. She said, "All of this that you're going through, it's preparation for the person you're going to become. You're going to be delivering people *from* things like that because you've been through it." That was pretty heady stuff for a believer like me, especially coming from someone as authoritative in these matters as Janice.

The question was, when? Whenever I started dating a woman, this need to take care of her popped up and I found myself doing things for her, and kept doing them even when we weren't dating anymore. Every time one of them got bent out of shape it ended up costing me a lot of money to take care of it, which is one of the problems you have when you have a lot of money. People think you can buy your way out of problems, and pretty often it's true. I was trying to please everybody and not hurt anybody and it was all getting to be too much.

Janice called it a "generational curse," the same expression Mama used to use, and said I could break it. How? "Because you love your kids so much. And if you continue to be that way, your kids are going to be that way, too."

I thought about my boys, and knew she was right. But before I even got a chance to say anything, she said, "I'm not talking about your boys. I'm talking about your girls." She said that girls look at how their fathers behave, too. "Every time a boy messes around, he does it with a girl, right? Well, where do you think your daughters are going to learn how to behave?"

It's hard to believe, but that had never occurred to me before. I was always worried about being a bad role model for my boys, but as Janice spoke, a picture of my daughter Evette rose up in my head and I got sick at heart thinking that my behavior might affect her life in a negative way, because my whole thing with my kids was to do exactly the opposite. It was an awful feeling, and I think a whole chain of events got kicked off right then and there.

* * *

Once Janice and I would get to talking, we just kept on going, and we talked two or three times a week. I learned as much about the Bible from her in one conversation than I did in my regular Bible studies class in a month. Being a doctor, she was also able to explain to me in ordinary language what my heart condition was all about.

I decided to take Benny Hinn up on his suggestion that I go get my heart checked again. I went back to Emory, to the same doctors who'd seen me when I got off the plane after the Moorer fight. The first few tests they did came up completely negative. So they did some more, and those were negative, too. After about a week of this they finally said that there was absolutely nothing wrong with my heart. They couldn't explain it, but there was no doubt in their minds.

The state of Georgia reinstated my boxing license after they got the test results. Normally that would have been good enough for the Nevada Athletic Commission, too, but it wasn't. I don't know why, but it probably had something to do with the fact that it had only been a few weeks since I almost died in the ring. I gave them all the test results and they still didn't believe it. They said that if I wanted my license back I'd have to go to the Mayo Clinic in Minnesota because it was the best medical facility on the planet. Whatever they said there, NAC would consider it final. I felt the same way.

To make a long story short—and it was a long story; I don't think a sitting president was ever put through more tests than I was that week—at my final meeting with the Mayo doctor who was coordinating everything I settled in for a long session because he had a stack of results about six inches thick on his desk. "So what's it all mean?" I asked. "What's really going on with my heart?"

The doctor stood up and stuck out his hand. "Nothing. Go home."

I made no move to take his hand. "What do you mean, nothing?"

"I mean, nothing. Good-bye. Go home."

I still didn't take his hand. "What do I do when I get home?"

"What you've been doing your whole life."

"I've been boxing."

"Well, there you go. Do that."

Here was this guy telling me there was nothing wrong with my heart, so why was it pounding at about two hundred beats a minute? "Are you telling me to go back into the ring?"

"No. I'm a doctor, and people get hurt in the ring, so why would I tell you to do that?"

"Doc . . ."

He laughed and sat down, and that's when I knew he was toying with me, having a little fun while he told me some of the best news I'd ever heard.

"You're telling me I'm healed?"

He shook his head and leaned back. "I can't say that one way or the other. All I know is, there's not a thing wrong with you now. I can also tell you that, whatever was wrong with your heart, it wasn't anything you were born with."

I orbited the earth a couple of times, and when I got back a few seconds later a million questions were bouncing around in my head, but I wanted to get one big one out of the way first. "Are you clearing me to fight again?"

"Yep."

He gave me a second to let that sink in, then explained his conclusions. "It was tricky trying to piece the puzzle together," he said, "but what we think is that it was the treatment you got after the fight that caused the problem." Among the things I remember him saying was that I had received far too much saline and morphine. He also said that he would not have let me get on a plane. "I would have kept someone in your condition in the hospital. You could have gone into cardiac arrest." He thought it was a miracle that I lived through it all.

* * *

So did Benny Hinn heal me? Was it a miracle?

No, Hinn didn't heal me. God healed me, working through Hinn.

All healing comes from God, just as everything does. But God heals in many different ways. Sometimes healing is done through surgery, sometimes through medicine, sometimes with only the passage of time. If we can see a direct connection, like a heart valve replaced by a surgeon, we don't think much of it. If the method isn't that obvious, we might consider it a miracle. It doesn't really matter to me what you call it, and it doesn't really matter to me who or what gets the credit, because the real credit goes to God, who works through people.

In my case, God chose to bring me together with Benny Hinn to complete a healing process that actually began way back in the emergency room in Las Vegas. I believe there was a reason for us being brought together, and the reason is that God wanted it that way, so that's the way it was. And as for a miracle, as far as I'm concerned, there was more than one involved. It was a miracle that I didn't die in the ER, a miracle that I didn't die on the plane and a miracle that my heart was healed and didn't show a single sign of the damage that had been done to it only six weeks before. One of the reasons I went back to fighting is that I knew that no one would believe my heart had been healed if I didn't. Once my license was restored and I was back in the ring, it put all doubts to rest.

But being slain in the spirit was about much more than finding out my heart was okay. When Hinn said "You are healed" he was referring to all of me, not just my heart. From that point on, my relationship with God deepened and my life got better. I began to learn how to benefit from past mistakes, how to correct my old ways and how to become a better person.

By the way, I also became world heavyweight champion two more times, and I give the credit to God for that, too.

* * *

People sometimes ask me how someone who calls himself a spiritual man, a Christian man, can be a professional prizefighter. Being a Christian doesn't mean that I belong to a specific church, but that I try to take Christ's life as an example of how to live my own. Put that way, it really does sound at odds with what I do for a living.

But there's no contradiction at all, for a couple of reasons. First of all, God gave me these gifts, and I believe he meant for me to use them, the same way he meant it for anybody else who chooses to be a fighter and has the skills and talent.

And speaking of "choosing" to fight, that's exactly what everyone who goes into the ring does: They *choose* to do it. It's not like boxers go around beating up people at random. Everyone I fight has made the conscious decision, of his own free will, to get into the ring with me.

I know that sounds self-serving, an obvious excuse. After all, when you get right down to it, I'm still standing there trying to smack someone silly, trying to hit him so hard he can't stand up. And even though he's trying to do the same thing to me, that might make it fair, but it doesn't necessarily make it *right*.

So what would Jesus think? If He walked through the door right now, would He approve? Could I hold my head up and answer with pride if He asked how I earn my living? It's a great question, and in order to answer it, I'll tell you something about boxing that may be hard to understand if you're not close to the game.

When most people think about "fighting," they picture two people who hate each other and want to cause each other pain. They think about anger and rage, big emotions that drive people to do irrational, inhuman things. One of the definitions of "fighting" is people trying to settle something using violence.

But that's not what boxing is about, at least not to boxers who have their heads screwed on right, which is most of them. When I box I don't hate my opponent, not by a long shot. I don't hate him any more than a pro tennis player hates her opponent or a chess player hates his. It's just competition, like any other sport, except a lot more physical because you throw punches instead of a baseball. If I see that George Foreman isn't keeping his left up, I might go to work hitting his arm as much as I can to weaken it even further, just like Michael Moorer did to me. I'm not trying to permanently maim him so he can never lift a fork again. I'm just trying to take away one of his offensive weapons, like a pitcher purposely walking the other team's best batter so he doesn't get the chance to hit a home run. And George understands that perfectly. If he sees that he's opened a cut over my eye, he'll go to work trying to make it worse so the ref stops the fight and he wins by TKO. I don't get mad at George for that. I expect it. It's fair and it's just, because each of us chose to play this game of our own free will, using a strict set of rules we both agreed to.

The point of a boxing match isn't to maim the other guy or humiliate him or end his career. The point, as in any other athletic contest, is to *win.* In order to do that, you do anything and everything that the rules say you can. It isn't personal . . . it's business, just two guys doing their jobs. Just because they're hitting each other doesn't mean they hate each other. One very visible proof of that is what happens at the end of almost every fight. The two boxers give each other a hug, a few complimentary words, even shake hands with each other's corner men. They might even get together afterward and swap critiques of how they performed.

Now here are two guys who seconds before were trying to knock each other's blocks off, and all of a sudden they're embracing and telling each other "Great fight" or "Good job." That's not the behavior of men who blew up and got into a fistfight over a parking space or a drunken insult in some bar. It's two athletes expressing mutual respect after a well-fought contest, just like two tennis players meeting at the net after a match and shaking hands. It's why I could knock Henry Tillman out in Reno and go to his wedding in Chicago a few weeks later.

If you fight a sanctioned bout under clear and time-honored rules against an opponent who chooses to enter the contest voluntarily, I believe that God approves. In fact, I think He more than approves. I believe He smiles on people who are willing to test themselves under very difficult circumstances, when they know there's danger and risk and have worked very hard to meet the challenge.

That's why I'm completely comfortable praying right in the middle of a fight. I don't worry that God is going to be mad because I'm throwing punches at another guy. I try to fight with a pure heart and good intentions, not anger, and I think that pleases Him. When I get into trouble in the ring and look to God, I don't ask him to let me win. I don't ask Him to weaken the other guy or throw a crimp into his game. All I ask for is the strength to do my best and the will to keep going no matter how much I hurt. If I can do that, then even if I lose, I can walk away satisfied knowing I gave as much as I possibly could.

That's what I was asking for when I fought my first world title match against Dwight Muhammad Qawi. I was so exhausted I could barely stand up. I ached all over and was so wasted I couldn't see straight. But my fear wasn't about pain or losing or getting hurt, it was about weariness. It was that I might have to quit before it was over. That to me was far worse than losing, and I remember exactly the prayer that was running through my mind: "Dear God, please help me keep going!"

Did God actually hear me and do something to allow me to keep going? To tell you the truth, I don't know. What I do know is that praying itself reminded me of God's presence, of what I'd come to understand was His plan for me, and that gave me strength. I prayed because in the later rounds I honestly didn't know if I could continue. I'd never gone that distance, so I had no history to assure myself that I had it in me. But I feel that God doesn't throw anything at us that we're not equipped to handle. Praying made me remember that, and gave me the answer right then and there: Yes, I could go the distance. If I couldn't, God wouldn't have put me in that position. That didn't necessarily mean that I would win, but that was beside the point. I wasn't asking for that.

Now, I don't want to sound naïve. I know that boxing isn't like other sports, and I'm not trying to get you to think it is. While you can win a bout on points, meaning that ringside judges have determined that you fought better than the other guy, the ultimate victory is a knockout, which means that your competitor is unable to pick himself up off the canvas. Not exactly the same as putting a ball through a hoop. But there are surprisingly few serious injuries in boxing, whereas athletes in some other sports get badly banged up all the time. At any given time during the football season there are hundreds of players on the injured list and you'd be hard-pressed to find an ex-player who isn't living with chronic pain of some kind. But everything you do in life carries risk, and we each make our own choices about the risks we're willing to take.

Boxing is not for everybody, and that's fine. Neither is hockey or rugby. But even if you're not a fan, boxing deserves your respect. If you visit a gym, you won't find a roomful of bloodthirsty thugs looking to break heads. You'll see a bunch of people—including a lot of kids—working themselves harder than you'd ever believe young people would be willing to. They're punching bags, skipping rope, shadowboxing, sparring . . . they're covered in sweat, panting and fiercely determined. Boxing isn't something you do for thirty or forty minutes in a ring a few times a year when you're competing in a bout. It's something you do every day, and not just in the gym, either. In addition to workouts and sparring, you have to be careful about what you eat and drink, even how much you sleep. You have to take direction from your trainer, and that translates into a special kind of respect that is sorely lacking among today's youth. Boxing is first, last and foremost about discipline, and if a kid doesn't have that, or isn't willing to learn it, he won't last twenty minutes in this game.

You might have noticed that a lot of boxers seem to come from very poor circumstances. Some of them have been in trouble with the law, or were obviously headed in that direction, what we call "at risk" kids. It's natural to think that these kinds of people bring an unsavory reputation to the sport.

I think just the opposite. Life is about capitalizing on opportunities, and some people have a lot more than others. It's hard for most of us to imagine the hopelessness and despair that exist in a lot of our inner cities and poor rural areas. Kids in those kinds of places don't do tennis or golf or anything else that requires money and well-maintained facilities.

Boxing is a way out for them. It provides discipline, direction, mentoring and an outlet for youthful energy. You don't have to be a title contender to achieve these benefits, either. There are literally thousands of gyms scattered all over the country. Look under "boxing clubs" in your local phone book and you'll be amazed. They're often sponsored by schools and youth associations and, yes, even churches. A lot of Boys Clubs were originally created for the purpose of starting boxing programs.

If you visit one of these clubs, the kids you'll see there—both boys and girls—aren't looking to break heads. They're looking to test themselves against other kids who are as ambitious and determined as they are. They want to be champions, they hope to make a living doing something they love, and they're willing to pour their hearts and souls into it, driving themselves to exhaustion day after day to be the very best they can. They help each other out, too, giving advice and support and encouragement. The amount of respect floating around a boxing gym is enormous. At sparring sessions where onlookers are present, there is usually a round of applause when it's over. It's not for winning—sparring is practice, not competition. It's acknowledgment and appreciation for hard work and the courage to step into the ring. For some of those inner-city kids I mentioned before, it's the first applause they've ever gotten in their lives.

Respect, dedication and devotion. Now I ask you: What kind of God wouldn't smile down on that?

CHAPTER 17

A Year of Living Dangerously

Things were looking pretty good that summer, but there was one big situation that was threatening to unravel my life. Sandy and I were getting close to a decision to get married, but the more time that passed, the more I started to wonder whether Janice hadn't been dropped into my life for a reason. Janice had also met Tamie, my daughter Eden's mother, who was working for me, and they liked each other a good deal. Tamie was very well aware of my beliefs and had started to explore her own spirituality. Janice turned out to be the ideal vehicle for her to continue that. As a Bible scholar and natural-born teacher, she became a kind of personal guide for Tamie. Everything she did seemed to be some kind of sign that she would be the ideal woman for me. She was smart and well-spoken and strong in her convictions, and I loved talking to her on the phone every few days and learning about the Bible from her.

There was just one problem. Whenever I saw her in person, for some reason I couldn't quite figure out, there was a total lack of what you might call "chemistry." Much as I wanted to, I couldn't muster up that kind of feeling. I'd get all excited whenever we talked on the phone, but when she visited me or I visited her, unless we were talking about God or the Bible or some other spiritual subject, there was this big blank space, because we didn't seem to have anything else in common. What made it all the more difficult was that she'd let me know at the very beginning that she thought she was the woman Benny Hinn was talking about at the revival meeting that night, and that it was fine with her. She wanted to marry me.

I prayed about it a lot. I was in love with Sandy but I didn't want to make a really big mistake, and what I prayed for was that God would make me fall in love with Janice. I had this strong feeling that my meeting her was preordained, and that's why Benny Hinn had seen it, or at least a hint of it. On paper, as the expression goes, she was perfect for me, but I just couldn't get myself to the point where it felt right as well. I couldn't marry her and then just talk to her on the phone for the rest of our lives.

I broke up briefly with Sandy later that summer after a minor spat. During that time, I brought Janice to Atlanta to meet my kids. They got along great, but I still felt no romantic love for her. Then Benny Hinn asked me to go to Jerusalem with him. He was putting on a crusade there and was taking about four hundred people. Janice was one of them, so I said yes, because I figured that if God was going to make something happen between us, He'd probably do it in the Holy Land. But He didn't. If we weren't talking about God or the Bible, there just didn't seem to be anything else to say.

Just before I left Israel I talked to Benny Hinn's brother about it. He was also a pastor, and he said, "Evander, don't ever marry somebody you're not in love with. You'll wake up one day just wishing one of you would disappear." When I got home I spoke to my own pastor and he said the same thing.

There wasn't enough depth of the right kind of feeling to make a marriage, and I was still in love with Sandy, but every time Janice spoke, she brought me peace. It was killing me, and I had to be honest with her.

When she got back to Chicago I called her and told her I wouldn't marry her because I didn't love her. Right in the middle of telling her that, something suddenly occurred to me: Maybe Janice didn't love me, either. Maybe she just thought God wanted her to marry me, and if He did, it wouldn't matter to her if she loved me or not. So was it possible that God had spoken to her, but not to me, because her faith was stronger than mine?

I needed time to sort all of that out so I didn't say anything more. I was thankful that despite my telling Janice that I wouldn't marry her, our friendship continued.

It was a giddy time for me. I was very happy to be fighting again after that awful scare with my heart.

I got my license back and in May of 1995 won a ten-rounder against 1988 Olympic gold medalist Ray Mercer after knocking him down in the eighth, the only time in his career he ever hit the deck. Six months later I fought Riddick Bowe for the third time and this time it was his turn. He TKO'd me in the eighth round.

No problem. I just got back in line and got a fight set up against Bobby Czyz for early the next year. If I won, it would be an important step toward regaining the world title. I had some time before serious training needed to begin, so about three or four weeks before the fight I attended a black college basketball tournament in North Carolina on behalf of Coca-Cola, which was a sponsor of mine. It was there that I received one of those phone calls that everyone dreads.

It was from Lennie Weaver, my nephew Mike's wife. Mike was my sister Eloise's son, and Lennie was calling because Mike had gone to the hospital. When I asked her why, she said, "To see your mama and Eloise. There was a car accident on the way home from church."

The world seemed to freeze, but just as all kinds of horrible thoughts started to work their way up into my head, Lennie said hurriedly, "But don't worry! I don't think it was serious. They just went to the hospital to get checked out."

"How do you know that?" I asked her.

Her answer was hesitant and unsure. "I don't know. That's just what Mike seemed to think."

Later in the day someone else called to tell me that Mama was still in the hospital, banged up but not too bad. I was having trouble getting specific information and got the feeling that they weren't telling me everything, so the next morning I flew home and went straight to the hospital. One look at Mama and I knew I'd been right. All I could see of her was her face. It was badly bruised and she wasn't moving. There was a tube taped to the side of her mouth and connected to a machine that made a wheezing sound.

"Is that thing breathing for her?" I asked the doctor when he came into the room.

He nodded. "She was conscious on the way over here, but slipped into a coma as we were checking her in."

I was supposed to be in Houston to start training but I stayed in Atlanta instead. Over the next few days they did two brain operations to try to relieve pressure inside Mama's head. After the second one she seemed to respond; Bernard read to her from the Bible and said she smiled and squeezed his hand. After about a week I decided to go to Houston, but first I made sure the hospital understood that they were to do everything possible for her. There was a little uncomfortable foot shuffling, and then one of the hospital people told me that Mama's care was costing a fortune and she had no insurance. I assured them that I would cover all the costs.

I went at my training extra hard to make up for the lost week, but it wasn't easy to stay focused, not knowing what was going to happen with my mother. After about two weeks Bernard called to tell me Mama had taken a turn for the worse and was never going to come out of the coma. The doctors wanted to know if they should take her off life support. I told him to tell them absolutely not, then called Benny Hinn. He said to head on up to Ohio where he was holding a revival meeting. I went, and after the meeting he and I and a few friends got together to pray for Mama. Benny asked me, "What exactly is it you want to pray for, Evander?"

Up until that point, I hadn't given it much thought. I did now, and said, "For the right thing to happen." It was one-thirty in the morning.

The next morning Bernard called. "Mama passed," he said, his voice raw with fatigue and emotion.

"When?" I asked him. He said the official time was one-thirty that morning.

I took great comfort in that, and made up my mind not to grieve for Mama but to celebrate her life. I also thanked God for not taking her right at the accident scene but giving her enough time so that everyone in the family could say good-bye.

I fought two-time champion Bobby Czyz on May 10. He weighed the same as me and it was almost an unfair fight, because I was so used to fighting guys who outweighed me that Bobby looked like a middleweight to me. I dominated him from the opening bell, throwing punches at will while he hardly hurt me at all. Only problem was, even though I had the decision in the bag, I couldn't knock the guy out. I wanted a knockout because that kind of performance would give me a better chance at a title shot against Tyson. I tried everything, throwing enough at Bobby to whup three guys, but man, could that guy take a punch.

I was so anxious to score a KO I didn't really fight my best, and got overexcited and sloppy. I started going to toe-to-toe, trading big punches instead of using my jab, and for a moment in the third round I thought I was finally setting it up properly. I had Bobby against the ropes and was raining blows on him that he couldn't answer. But just as I was getting ready to land the big one, the ref suddenly jumped in between us. I thought he was going to stop the fight, but instead he gave Bobby a standing eight count. I looked at him in amazement, thinking, "I'm finally about to put him away and you're giving him a rest?" There was no justification for a standing eight.

As usual, I kept my mouth shut, and then it was time to go back to work. I kept "loading up" on every punch, trying to score the knockout, but fighting inside like that, flat-footed and graceless, wasn't my style. Not only didn't it work, I was wearing myself out in the process, just as bigger guys had worn themselves out trying to do the same thing to me. I'll tell you truthfully, I'd made such a mess of this fight that after the fifth round I was about ready to quit. It wasn't because I was tired— I had so much energy I didn't even sit down after the round and my corner men had to work on me standing up—I was just frustrated. Here I was trying to prove to the world I was still championship material, but I'd gotten sucked into fighting somebody else's fight and couldn't put my opponent away. I thought to myself, "Boy, I must look terrible. One more round of this and I'm heading back to the locker room."

It was a really low moment feeling like that, wanting to quit in the middle of a fight. Then the bell rang to start the sixth round . . . and Bobby didn't come out of his corner. He said his eyes were burning, so his trainer told the ref to stop the fight and, after a few seconds, Bobby agreed. They also demanded that the ref check my gloves, accusing me of having some substance on them that was getting into Bobby's eyes. So the ref came over and rubbed his fingers on my gloves and on my chest, then rubbed them into his own eyes, and when nothing happened, that was the end of that ridiculous accusation.

Talk about your basic blessing in disguise. Not only did I win the fight because Bobby quit before I did, but I looked so awful that Don King decided that *now* Mike Tyson could beat me.

And that's how my first fight against Tyson came about.

* * *

The Tyson fight was scheduled for November of that year, 1996, and it gave me a little logistical problem. Sandy, who by then had moved to Atlanta and was living with me, had gone back to Mississippi after our disagreement. I had to begin training for the fight and would need to spend five days a week at my camp in Houston for a few months. With Sandy gone I needed somebody to stay with my kids while I was in camp. They would be in school and I couldn't take them with me without disrupting their studies.

It occurred to me that maybe Janice could take care of them for me. The more I thought about it, the more sense it made. The kids knew her and liked her, and she was exactly the kind of person I wanted them to be around. But when I floated it by her, she was hesitant. "I'd love to," she said, "but I've got a job and don't see how I could leave it for that long."

I offered her fifty thousand dollars so she wouldn't suffer financially. "I'm not paying you to do me a favor," I told her. "It's a real job and you should get paid like it. Plus, you can go home every weekend." She eventually agreed.

Every Fourth of July I throw a giant barbecue party on my property. A church helps me put it on and thousands of kids and their families attend. We have music and fireworks and truckloads of great food. A few days after the party I got back with Sandy, but I didn't want to ask her to stay with the kids because it might look like I was using her. Besides, I'd already made the arrangement with Janice so I stuck to it.

A week later I got one of the biggest honors of my life. When I got beaten by Riddick Bowe the year before, I said at the press conference that I had two goals at that point. One was to become world champ again, and the other was to carry the torch at the Olympics in Atlanta. The reporters laughed openly at both of those. HBO even did a show on why a fighter would never carry the torch. By the time the Olympics were getting ready to open, it looked like they were right.

But at midnight the night before the opening ceremonies, I got a call from Dr. Harvey Schiller, head of Turner Sports and executive director of the U.S. Olympic Committee. "Evander," he said, "we'd like you to carry the Olympic torch into the stadium during the opening ceremonies."

At first I thought he was playing a joke on me, but when I realized he was serious, the first thing I asked was who was going to light the Olympic flame. "Can't tell you that," Harvey said. "It's a surprise."

The next night, a runner handed me the torch in a tunnel below the Olympic stadium. I ran a few steps and emerged onto the middle of the stadium floor. In front of eighty-five thousand people in the stands and hundreds of millions more watching all over the world, I began running on the track and was soon joined by Greek hurdler Voula Patoulidou. I then handed the torch to the great Olympic swimmer Janet Evans, who ran the final leg and then handed it off to . . . Muhammad Ali!

When I saw him up there, my heart almost jumped out of my chest, it started pounding so hard. I didn't know until that very moment he was even going to be there, much less light the Olympic flame. The Games hadn't even started yet and already one of its most exciting moments was underway. It was doubly exciting for me personally. Not only were there *two* fighters carrying the torch to prove the sporting press wrong, but one of them had the high honor of lighting the Olympic flame.

It was one of the greatest nights of my life.

As soon as the Games left town and I started training for the Tyson fight, Janice flew out from Chicago and moved into the house. It worked out even better than I'd hoped. She got involved with the children's schoolwork and discovered something that I hadn't been aware of, that my kids weren't doing quite as well in school as I thought they were. They were getting high grades all right, but Janice thought that those grades were out of line with how hard they were working and how up on their subjects they were. So she went to the school to see what was going on, and figured out that the good grades had more to do with their last name than with their studies. She explained to the teachers how important it was to me for my kids to achieve their own successes and not ride through life on mine. I wasn't paying for private school so that they could get some useless piece of paper at the end and not be equipped to go out into the world. I wanted them to be pushed and tested, hard. They got the message, and so did my kids.

It was just another in a series of signs to me of Janice's worth. Despite all the attention I paid to the kids, I'd missed this one, and might have kept on missing it if it hadn't been for her. I spoke with her frequently by phone, and our conversations were still long and fulfilling. But it was the same old story: When I'd come home on the weekends and see her before she flew out, the deeper feelings just weren't there.

I was working as hard at training as I ever had. Aside from the fact that I wanted to win this fight, I was being paid a lot of money—$10 million—and I felt I owed it to the promoters and the fans to be as ready as humanly possible. I tried to stay focused, but this concern about the women in my life kept circling around and wouldn't go away. I knew I had to do something.

I thought about it and I prayed and I tried to look far into the future. Ten or twenty years down the road, how was I likely to feel about whatever decision I made? All these different scenarios whirled around in my head and ultimately it all boiled down to one thing: I simply couldn't envision ever thinking that giving Janice up was the right thing to do, not for me and not for my kids and, for all I knew, not for God, either. There's a great old story about a guy who drowns during a flood because he was so convinced God was going to save him he'd refused to get into a car, a boat, or a helicopter. When he gets to heaven he demands that God tell him why He'd allowed it to happen. God says, "What do you want from me? I sent you a car, a boat, a helicopter, and you refused them all!"

Is that what I was doing, waiting for God to give me a sign? He'd sent this woman who was steeped in the Word, provided counsel to my former girlfriend, was invaluable to my kids, and was living right there in my own house. Did I need the skies to open up and an angel to call down, "She's the one"?

I decided to quit running away and do what I thought was right regardless of how I felt about it. I said to God, "Lord, I'm going to step out on faith," and decided I'd learn to love Janice later. I called her on the phone, because I knew I wouldn't be able to do it in person, and told her that I was going to come home and marry her, right away. She agreed without hesitation, and that's just what happened. We got married on October 4, 1996, in a private courtroom ceremony. My firstborn, Evander Jr., was my best man.

I'd made a mistake, and I knew it almost instantly. I'd married a woman I didn't love, and in the process I'd given up someone I did love. Just as bad, Janice knew I didn't love her but married me anyway. "Give it time," she said, and I vowed that I would. But it was not to be.

I hadn't even told Sandy yet, and was planning to do that the next day, although I had no idea how. As it happened, she found out before I had a chance to tell her, and I was sick in my heart at how broken up she became. I knew she would be, but I'd felt that it was part of the price for doing what I thought God wanted. But when I saw how it affected her, it tore me up. It just wasn't possible that this was what God wanted.

I went back to camp feeling horrible. I couldn't do anything right in the gym. I was listless, distracted, my shoulder hurt and I was getting beaten up by my sparring partners. But I got on the phone with Janice and it was like old times. We prayed together and the next day my sparring partners thought they'd gotten into the ring with two guys instead of just one.

A perfect example of how back-and-forth my feelings toward Janice were came just two weeks later, on the day of my first fight against Mike Tyson. I was pacing around my suite at Caesars Palace, nervous and feeling bad. I rarely got tense before a fight, so this wasn't a good sign at all. Janice came in and saw right away that something was wrong. "I don't know what to do," I told her.

"You need to dance," she said.

I told her she was crazy, but she ignored me and put some gospel music on. Then she took hold of me and started waltzing me around. I resisted at first—I was supposed to be resting—but pretty soon I fell into the groove and we danced all around the place, and kept dancing until someone knocked and told me it was time to go. And then I went and whupped the Baddest Man on the Planet and was world champion again. It was one of the highest highs of my life, but as soon as the celebrating was over, I had to go back home to face one of the lowest lows.

As soon as we got back to Atlanta, we went to counseling. I just had to fall in love with Janice. Everything about her was right. When I was troubled in my mind she put me at peace, and I was starting to believe there had to be something wrong with me because I didn't love her.

I thought back to the time Janice told me God wanted me to marry her. I would never question anything that God said, but what I eventually came to realize is that I'd missed something important, and that is that God may have spoken to Janice, but He hadn't spoken to me. Not having heard from God myself, I chose to simply believe her when what I should have done is trust myself more. I'd convinced myself that God had planted all of these unmistakable signs. I'd been overwhelmed by how much Janice knew about the Bible and the interest she'd taken in my kids. I was completely honest in letting her know I didn't love her, but she was certain I eventually would and that God wanted us to be married.

All of those signs seemed so clear and yet I'd ignored the biggest, brightest sign of all, which was right there in my own heart telling me that marrying Janice was wrong, for the simple reason that I didn't love her. God may not have spoken directly to me, but He gave me enough common sense to know that without love nothing can grow, including a family. I tried to build a marriage based on what I thought was right for my kids but it was bound to fail, because love is the most important thing and we didn't have it.

My trust in God wasn't shaken one bit. I knew that when He lets you get hit on the head with a rock, it's to stop you from getting hit with a boulder. It's why mistakes don't bother me too much. At least I was out there trying, and somehow some good would come of it.

But that would be later. At the time, there was no doubt in my mind that our marriage would never work. I think Janice knew it, too, but she squelched any talk of separating. "We'll make it work," she insisted. I didn't think we could, and to be honest, I didn't want us to. It was just plain wrong.

I told Janice that I thought we should get a divorce, but she refused and begged me to give it a year. I still wanted to love her, because it would be so much better that way. Her good qualities hadn't changed, and I still believed that she was basically a good person. So I agreed, and we began counseling again, and I pleaded with God to let me love her.

The following June was my second fight against Mike Tyson, and five months after that I settled accounts with Michael Moorer, knocking him out in the eighth round and adding the IBF world championship belt to my growing collection. Three months later I beat Vaughn Bean, but there was more to that fight than just retaining my WBA and IBF world titles.

A reporter from the *Atlanta Journal-Constitution* interviewed me about the fight and mentioned my seven children. I corrected him and told him I had nine kids. He said he didn't need to print that, that he was writing only about the fight, but could I give him some details anyway. Of course I did, and every one of them was in the story that ran the next day, which wasn't about the fight at all. The wires picked it up and that was the end of any privacy I might have enjoyed about my personal life.

The following March I was going to fight Lennox Lewis to try to win the WBC belt and become undisputed heavyweight champ of the world for the second time. It was big news because that had only been done by two other fighters, Floyd Patterson and Muhammad Ali. (Ali did it a third time, too.) Not only that, it was the first time in seven years that the undisputed heavyweight crown was up for grabs, so this was a huge fight commercially. Publicity was spearheaded by undisputed heavy-weight hype champion of the world Don King.

In the packed press conference before the fight, Lewis surprised me by calling me a hypocrite and following it up with a vicious crack. "I'm not questioning Holyfield's faith," he said, "but he breaks a command-ment every other day."

It's a point of honor with me never to engage in the kind of empty bluster that some fighters go in for, and I try never to get mad at my opponents. To me it's an athletic competition and there's no need for anger, and I don't think that insulting the other guy has any place in the sport at all. So when I heard Lewis say that, I boiled up before I could stop myself and blurted out that I was going to knock him out in the third round. There was some stunned silence in the room, because everyone knew I never make predictions like that, and then reporters began firing questions at me all at once. There was no taking that rash statement back, but I tried not to make a big deal of it.

The fact is, I said it, so there was no reason for them not to write that I did. But one guy reported that I'd claimed God had told me I'd knock Lewis out in the third round. Given the nature of Lewis's nasty remark, that story got picked up and became the next day's headline. It was re-peated whenever anything was written about the fight, and still is.

You might be asking yourself, given the tormented year I'd just spent trying to understand whether God had spoken to Janice, how could I turn right around and say something like that myself?

I didn't say it. Not that or anything remotely like it. I admit to the knockout prediction, which was just foolishness in a moment of anger, but it would take a lot more than a careless and cruel remark by an opponent to get me to falsely claim I'd gotten a message from the Almighty. Again, though, I did nothing to correct the story. It would work itself out.

I didn't correct anything in the ring, either. The fight took place in Madison Square Garden, probably the single most prestigious boxing venue in the world. It went twelve tough rounds in which Lewis and I both fought as hard as we could. I thought I'd won, and when the decision was announced that we'd ended in a draw, I was disappointed. But I didn't react, and I didn't say anything about it. Anyone who's been in this business for any length of time knows that fight decisions are a lot like jury decisions: hard to predict, and even harder to know what was going through people's minds when they cast their votes. My thinking was that Lennox and I would just fight again to take care of unfinished business.

Lennox, on the other hand, started screaming and hollering about how unfair the decision was because he'd really won the fight. HBO, which had his contract, joined in and yelled foul at the decision, even taking the matter to court. There was talk that the judging was fixed to ensure a draw, because that would lead to an enormously lucrative rematch. (That last part would turn out to be true.) Sports reporters fell all over themselves trying to prove that the judge's decision had been the worst one since the Boston Red Sox decided to sell Babe Ruth to the Yankees. Charges were getting thrown around all over the place, and when testimony before a New York State Senate committee indicated that two of the judges had financial problems, implying that they might have been open to a bribe, things really started spinning out of control. I had to testify before the New York Senate Investigations Committee, which had already given evidence of possible criminal conduct to the Manhattan district attorney. He then convened a grand jury, which turned around and asked the Nevada Gaming Control Board to launch an investigation into betting patterns before the fight. Other reviews were undertaken by the New York State attorney general and the Athletic Commission. A federal grand jury in New Jersey was already investigating whether the IBF sold rankings and arranged fights in return for kickbacks, and now other law enforcement authorities decided to dive into it as well.

I've watched tapes of the fight a number of times, and you know what? I have to admit it was a bad decision. But it wasn't *that* bad. While there's a good case to be made that Lennox should have won, there's also a reasonable case to be made that I should have, especially if you take aggressiveness into account in the scoring. I think Lennox won six rounds for sure and I won three, with the other three up for grabs. So while it probably should have gone to him, it wasn't like it was the worst call in the history of Western civilization.

It simply shouldn't have been the big deal everyone was making it out to be. Questionable decisions happen all the time. Maybe the loser gets hot and blows off a little steam, which is only human, but at some point you let it go and take the next step, like fighting a rematch. I also thought that an overload of publicity like this fight was getting would only lead to more bad decisions in the future, because once you make judges fearful of public reaction, you compromise their objectivity. They start worrying too much about what people will say rather than what they themselves are being paid and trusted to think.

Through it all, I held my tongue. I've had my own share of bad-call disappointments, and not just the one at the Olympics. I fought Sherman Griffin at the Golden Gloves the year before the Olympic Trials. He was ranked number one in the world and I was an absolute nobody, but in the first round I knocked him down. The ref let the fight continue, and I decked Sherman again in the second. He was shocked and panting as he took an eight count, and in the last round I knocked him to the canvas yet again. I was all over him the entire fight and hadn't hit the floor once myself. When it was over there were only two people in that entire arena who thought Sherman had won. Unfortunately, they were both judges, and I lost the split decision. I stood there and I swallowed it, thinking, "I'll get him next time." I did, too, on my way to getting an Olympic slot.

I didn't think anything nasty had happened under the table to bring about the draw decision in my fight against Lennox. It was just poor judgment, and I thought the best way to settle it was in the ring, with a rematch. I'd congratulated Lennox on a great fight and hadn't told him that I thought I should have won, although he kept insisting that he was the real winner. When I wouldn't rise to the bait at a postfight press conference, Lennox looked at me and said, "What about your KO prediction in the third round?"

I said, "I was wrong. So what?" Lennox then told the reporters I wouldn't dare fight him again, to which I responded, "Let's fix a date right now."

Because of the draw, I retained the WBA and IBF titles and Lennox kept the WBC. We fought again in November, went the distance again, it was close again, and again I thought I'd won. But this time the decision went to Lewis, who became undisputed champ. I congratulated him, and that was the end of that fight, which still holds the record for the richest gate in Vegas history.

In the press conference the old song started up: "Evander, what are you going to do now?"

I said, "I'm going to get back in line. I want to be undisputed champ."

Meanwhile, as the millennium drew to a close, I was left without any world titles at all.

CHAPTER 18

Hard Lessons

All that counseling with Janice didn't work, and I finally decided to file for divorce after the Lennox Lewis fight. I'd made over $90 million in the short time we'd been married and, as things all too often do, it came down to money, because we didn't have a prenuptial agreement. I didn't believe in them, and I still don't. It never entered my mind that there would ever be a divorce, even though I'd already had one. When I look back on my first marriage and all the lessons that were there to be learned, I'm amazed at what a lousy student I was. Experience is a hard teacher—she gives you the test before she gives you the lesson—but even after I'd had one good lesson I still didn't pay attention, and now I was paying for it.

When we were in counseling and I told the counselor that I'd been thinking about a divorce, he said, "Do you realize that'd cost you about $35 million?" I told him I didn't care. I'd write out a check for $35 million on the spot if it would just make this situation go away. Some of my kids spent a lot of time around Janice and me, and I didn't want my sons or my daughters growing up thinking that this was the way married people were supposed to behave, that there was no intimacy and all the

231

conversations were always about business. I also thought back to when I tried to pressure my sisters into marrying certain men because they were very successful without giving enough thought to whether they were loving and would be good to them. Now that I'd seen the flip side, it really hit home how powerful and important love was, and I thanked God they hadn't listened to me. I was also able to get my kids to understand some things that they might find valuable later in their lives. If it cost me a lot of money to give them the benefit of the hard lessons I learned, it would be worth every penny.

The divorce became official in July of 2000. The details of the final settlement were sealed by the court and nobody who was involved is permitted to talk about it. I got on with my life, and it turned out Janice had been right about one thing: I did get better. There were to be no more kids out of wedlock.

I have a lot of friends, and a lot of friends I trust. But I have very few friends I trust with everything. There's this sort of modern philosophy that says trust is a good and wonderful thing, and that the more you trust, the better a person you are, and if you don't put great trust in people, there's something wrong with you.

I don't buy all of that. I do think that it's a wonderful thing to be able to trust people, but to trust them when it isn't deserved or earned is just plain crazy. Of course, if you don't have anything to lose, you can be trusting as all get out and think you're pretty swell. But if you have a lot to lose, one of the quickest ways to lose it is by trusting people before you get a chance to figure out if that's a smart thing to do. And trust me on this: The more you have to lose, the harder you better work at figuring out who to trust.

Having grown up poor, I learned early on the importance of managing money. We were even on welfare at one point, but everyone in the family still worked hard, at whatever kind of jobs we could get. When those nickels and dimes came in, every one of us knew just how valuable they were because of how hard we'd worked to get them. So we were careful not to fritter them away or allow ourselves to get scammed out of them.

I've made more money in the ring than any other fighter ever, and I'm proud to say that I managed my finances carefully. I learned a lot along the way, not just from my own experiences but from watching what happened to others. You know who some of them are, because you've read the news stories. Maybe you wondered, How can a guy who made $50 or $60 million as a professional athlete end up dead broke at the age of forty? Worse than broke, sometimes, because when you lose sums like that, you're probably in debt, too. How is a thing like that possible? How is it that somebody with that kind of money doesn't take a million or two and stick it in a personal bank account or under a mattress so no matter what happens, there's something to fall back on?

Too many talented young athletes today are being thrown into big-league sports and major-league money without enough education. I'm not talking about college education—I only graduated high school, and where I went to school, that was about a ninth-grade education at best—but about how to behave, how to react to and deal with adversity, how not to be an obnoxious, whiny brat when things don't go your way and how to show a little grace and humility when they do. Money is an especially bad problem, because some of these kids see a few million dollars and think they have it made for life. They rush out and buy closets full of fancy and expensive clothes, exotic cars, a lot of jewelry . . . just to show off, as if to say to the world, "Look how great I am, because I have all this great stuff."

Kids who grow up in middle- or upper-class environments have a huge advantage when it comes to money. Not just because they have it, but because they know how to manage it, or at least know that it needs to be managed. They watched their parents buy stocks, put money into retirement accounts and college funds, set up things like living wills.

They've heard them on the phone with brokers or accountants or friends talking about the best places to invest. Planning for the future becomes second nature to them, and even if they don't understand all the details, they know that there are people out there who are experts and can help.

But take a kid who had to run around the neighborhood collecting bottles for a month in order to buy himself a pair of sneakers. He's lucky if he had two parents in the house and there was food on the table. He's never been inside a bank, the only savings he knows about is a tin can in the cupboard and the scariest days were when the rent collector came around because he never knew if there was going to be enough money to pay him. But the kid is a tremendous athlete and he gets drafted by the NBA right out of high school and some team sticks $10 million in his hand.

Kids like that think that $10 million is all the money in the world and there's no way they could possibly spend it fast enough to make it run out. They don't stop to consider that the first thing that's going to happen is that the government is going to slice off a whopping percentage of everything they think they're earning. They don't stop to consider that people supposedly on their side—managers, agents, publicists, accountants, lawyers, promoters, coaches, trainers—can work that huge pile of money down in less time than they'd think possible. And that's if everybody's honest. If they're not, if the kid hasn't learned how not to get taken advantage of, he's not only going to wind up with nothing, he's going to have a mountain of debt he can't possibly pay off.

Money isn't everything. I know that. But in this world it's more important than we like to admit. For me it's not about being able to buy stuff; it's about being able to live the life I want and to be in control of that life. Whether you're a boxer or a doctor or a steelworker or just about anything else, the more money you have, the less people can push you around. When I was negotiating to try to get the right fights to move my career along, my financial situation played a big part in what kind of bargaining position I was in. If I needed money, like I did in the beginning, I had to take what promoters were willing to give me, even if I thought I was fighting the wrong guys or the percentages were unfair. What else was I going to do? If I walked away I might never get a fight.

But once I had money I could be tougher. I could tell a promoter that the fight he was offering wasn't right, and that I had plenty of time to find another one with another promoter because I wasn't hurting financially and had enough in reserve to tide me over.

The other good thing about having money is that you can give it away. One of the things I care most about is trying to give as many kids as possible the same kind of opportunities I had. I obviously can't do that one-on-one but because I have money I can fund people and organizations that are good at doing things like that, like the Boys Club that was so important in my life. I also started my own organization, the Evander Holyfield Foundation, to make sure that the money I was donating got where it was supposed to go and was being used effectively.

Even when these fresh-out-of-school superstars read about an athlete who ended up deep in debt after making millions, it doesn't register, because nobody sat them down and explained, in a way that they would hear, that a giant wad of money comes with a giant wad of responsibilities and it has to be *managed.* It's easy to get expert help, but you have to know to ask. And what's the biggest reason they don't ask? Either nobody taught them to or they were too full of themselves to think it was necessary.

Which brings us back to trust. I've had an awful lot of different people working for me over the years. You wouldn't believe how much support it takes to be a world champion professional athlete in an individual sport like boxing. If you're a member of a large organization, such as a Major-League Baseball or an NBA basketball team, much of that support is provided for you. You don't have to worry about airline arrangements, hotel bookings, transportation, uniforms, equipment or laundry. The team determines when and where you're going to play, how you're going to get there, where you're going to stay and a ton of other such matters. They also provide coaches and trainers, massage therapists, workout facilities, even physicians and accountants.

But if you're a professional fighter, you're on your own for everything. There's no organization in place to arrange your fights or negotiate the deals. Nobody provides trainers or transportation or medical services. In order to get all of those things done, you have to create your own organization, and you have to pay for it all out of your own pocket. That costs a lot of money, especially if you're fighting at the championship level. You're going to have a couple of full-time employees, mostly to manage the other resources, and a whole lot of part-timers or "as needed" specialists on call. If a fighter does everything right and has good people, he can devote most of his time to doing what he's supposed to do, which is to train for the next bout.

There's a lot that can go wrong in this type of setup. There are few guidelines and no professional organizations to set the rules, like lawyers and doctors and accountants have. The trick is to have smart, competent and reputable people. You have to be as specific as possible about what you expect and what the boundaries are, what people can do on their own and what you need to be consulted about. If you have great people working for you, you find yourself delegating more and more as time goes by. It's nice when that happens, and much of the burden is lifted from your shoulders, but there's risk as well.

I know very few world champion athletes who haven't been bitterly disappointed at least a time or two in their careers by people they thought they could trust. You read about these kinds of things all the time: agents get fired, managers get sued, financial managers get indicted. Most painful of all is when the athlete gets into a tiff with a family member who was part of the staff. Talk about problems with trust. You only have to get burned once by a brother or a sister or a parent or an in-law to really have your whole perspective about people change.

Hard to believe, isn't it, that a parent and a child or a brother and a sister could sue each other? But it happens all the time among celebrities. Money can make people do some pretty crazy things.

The temptation to take advantage of someone you're supposed to be helping must be pretty powerful, because I've seen it overwhelm people I wouldn't have thought in a million years would ever go over to the "dark side." First of all, the dollar amounts involved can be dizzying. Second, some of the people making all that money aren't always equipped to pay attention. A crafty and unscrupulous accountant or lawyer or manager can siphon off millions without the athlete ever realizing what's going on until he's left penniless and in debt and everyone around him disappears.

It's not necessarily out-and-out theft, either. It can just be taking unfair advantage. "My cut is 25 percent. Trust me that's standard." Or, "Sacrifice some up-front money and you'll make a fortune on the back end. Trust me. I've been doing this a long time." Or, "Put everything in this pork belly tax shelter. You can't lose." Things like that.

I've learned a few things over the years that have helped me manage my affairs. Even if you're not a professional prizefighter, some of these lessons might be useful to you, too.

First, I'm careful about who I trust, and I don't trust everything to one person. I divvy up the pie and try never to put more of it in one place than I can stand to lose.

Second, I never assume that someone working for me or on my behalf is incorruptible. Even if you believe deep in your heart that someone has a good soul, there are times when things like drugs, gambling or insurmountable family problems can bring the best of us to our knees.

Third, I break the second rule whenever I can. There are a couple of people I trust with my very life, like my wife and Tim Hallmark and a few others. If they ever turned on me, I'd be so disappointed I wouldn't care what I lost.

Fourth, I try to have people stick to what they're good at. I lost a lot of money when I let one lawyer negotiate some deals for me. He was one of the best litigators in the business. In the courtroom, it was like he owned the place and could do no wrong. But when he started getting into things he was less good at, all of that self-confidence betrayed him. He wouldn't go to his colleagues for help when he needed it, because he saw that as a sign of weakness. So he muddled through things as best he could, and a couple of times, it just wasn't good enough. The sad thing is, once you go down that path, it's very hard to pull back. I couldn't just say to this guy, "You're not so hot at this stuff, so let's get someone else in here." Why? Because he should have recognized it himself, just like Ken Sanders did when he brought Shelly Finkel on as my co-manager. It was my lawyer's job to watch out for me. If he wasn't willing to yell for help when he needed it, then I couldn't trust him to do it in the future.

That last one is a special problem for celebrities in particular. There are so many people trying to get close to you and be seen with you, it's hard to know who really has your best interests at heart and who's just blowing smoke. This is the part where I'm supposed to say that's why I value my family and my old friends so dearly, the ones who knew me when. But real life isn't that simple. In real life, money changes everything. Coming into a lot of money doesn't mean you find yourself relying on your true friends. Rather, it's when you find out who your true friends are. At least for the time being. Things change over time, and you have to stay alert.

One of the things I've learned is to be wary of people who try to protect me too much and make a big show of it. Too many times, it's turned out that the reason they were so tuned in to people trying to take advantage of me is that *they* were trying to take advantage of me. Takes one to know one, I guess.

I don't have any of those cute little tricks some people like to play to test loyalty. I also don't expect people I deal with to be saintly or to make sacrifices for the privilege of being in my corner. What I do expect is for people to be honest about their self-interest. If someone says to me, "Oh, I want to come work for you because you're so great and I want to devote my whole life to you!" I turn and run the other way. There's nothing in all of that for me to rely on. Once they figure out I'm just human, their motivation is gone.

But if someone says to me something like, "There's a service I can provide for you, and I'm very good at it, and if you give me the chance, I'll make a bunch of dough for both of us," now I have something I can hang my hat on. This guy is offering a fair business deal, and there's something in it for him as well as me. As long as he does what he says he's going to do, and does it well, I hope he gets rich and has a great time doing it. If he winds up getting more business for himself because of his association with me, more power to him. I'm all for it and happy to help him out, as long as the job I'm paying him to do is getting done.

In the end, I tend to put my faith in God and rely on my own feelings about people, because I rarely have five or ten years to really test how things are going to turn out. I've often been a little too trusting and have been disappointed more often than I would have liked, but you know what? Usually all it's cost me is money, and there are far worse things to lose than that. I figure if I can come out of a bad situation with nothing more than a monetary loss, I'm still way ahead of the game.

As it happens, I have very few complaints about how my life has gone.

PART IV

It's How You End

CHAPTER 19

———

"Holyfield V: The Final Chapter"

Despite losing to Lennox Lewis, I wasn't done. I still had plenty of gas in the tank, so on August 12, 2000, I fought John Ruiz, who'd won the WBA title from Lennox. When the ref raised my hand in victory, a place was set for me in boxing history: I was the only heavyweight to become world champion four times, a distinction I still hold.

It's funny how life works out. If I'd gotten all three belts after the Moorer fight, there's a good chance I would have retired, having accomplished what I'd set out to accomplish. Same thing with Lennox Lewis. Had I beaten him, I would have retired as the undisputed champ. But, as so often happens in life, something good came out of something bad. I've always said that setbacks pave the way for comebacks, and this was a great example. Because of those two disappointments, I was able to achieve something with greater historical significance than retiring as the undisputed champ.

But Lennox wasn't through giving me a hard time. While the rest of the world was congratulating me on an unprecedented achievement, he started complaining about the unfairness of it all. Back when Lennox beat me, he became the undisputed champion, and John Ruiz was next in line to fight him. But Lennox refused the fight, saying Ruiz wasn't good enough for a title shot. The WBA insisted that Lennox follow the rules, and when he continued to refuse, they took his belt away and gave it to Ruiz. When I fought Ruiz and beat him, it became mine.

Lennox was unimpressed with my unprecedented fourth world title. "That ain't no real belt!" he howled. "Holyfield got that belt out of the trash can!" He felt that Ruiz hadn't earned it, and as a matter of fact he was right, because Ruiz hadn't done anything to earn it except be in the right place at the right time. To me it didn't matter that Ruiz hadn't fought for it. Lennox hadn't fought to keep it, either, as he was required to do.

But there was something Lennox seemed to have forgotten about. He'd gotten his own WBC belt "out of the trash," because that's where Riddick Bowe had literally thrown it. I was painfully aware of that because when I beat Bowe, he had only the WBA and IBF titles. Lennox got the trashed WBC belt by fighting Tony Tucker for the vacant title.

And Lennox's second belt? It had been stripped from Mike Tyson and given to Lennox. He never fought for it, just as Ruiz hadn't fought for his. When I reminded him of that, he got quiet, and I asked him why he wanted to change the rules only when they didn't suit him. Anybody who refuses to fight a mandatory fight gets stripped. That's it. Those are the rules we all agreed to going in.

It was all great theater, and the fact is, I like Lennox Lewis a lot. He was a truly gifted fighter and a great showman, and at least in part because of his antics following our draw, our second fight in 1999 became the largest-grossing gate in Nevada history and hasn't been topped since. (Numbers two and three were my two fights against Mike Tyson.) There are also some sides to Lennox that most people aren't aware of. For one thing he's a dedicated supporter of educational opportunities for disadvantaged kids. In 1995 he started Lennox Lewis College as a pilot program to keep troubled British kids in school, and right after our second fight in 1999 he was awarded an honorary doctorate by the University of North London for his efforts. He's an avid chess player, too, and sponsors the Oakhaven Lennox Lewis Chess Team, made up of kids from disadvantaged families. In 2003 they won the U.S. Chess Federation's National Elementary Championships.

John Ruiz and I fought again. This time he beat me and got the WBA belt back. Our bout had a funny side, which is rare in boxing. John kept banging his head into my leg and tried to get the ref to rule that I was hitting him with my knee. It didn't work. Then I hit him a good one in the solar plexus and he went down. His corner men started yelling that I'd hit him with a low blow. Except . . . John was down on his stomach. That's the last thing you do if you get hit in the chops. When John heard his guys yelling "Low blow! Low blow!" he quickly rolled over onto his back, but then he grabbed his chest, which is where I'd actually hit him. As soon as he realized what he was doing, he finally dropped his hands down to his crotch. It was really great showmanship, like when an NBA player gets brushed by an opponent and then hits the floor like he'd been struck with a mortar shell. Meanwhile, John's corner is yelling for him to stay down and claim the foul. It was an Oscar-caliber acting job because the ref dinged me for a low blow even though he'd never seen it. Then, as soon as we got going again, John hit *me* with a low blow, a real one this time.

The third time we fought it was a draw and John retained the title. When reporters asked me what I was going to do now, I told them the same thing I'd said the last three times I'd lost the world title: "I'm going to get back in line."

My shoulders were acting up again, and instead of following my doctor's advice and giving them a chance to heal, I kept fighting. In June of 2002 I beat Hasim Rahman, but it took its toll, and I had to have surgery on both shoulders. Too impatient to let them heal, I took a bout against Chris Byrd and lost a twelve-round decision. For somebody who'd started his pro career by rarely going past the sixth round, I sure seemed to be fighting a lot of long bouts. Before the Rahman fight I'd gone the full distance six times in a row.

A few weeks after 9/11 I was in an airport in Arkansas on my way back home after a meeting. The air traffic system was still a mess and the terminal was crowded with people trying to get on flights or waiting around during long delays, and I was signing a lot of autographs. One young lady caught my eye, and it happened that we were on the same flight. Once on board I beckoned to her and she came over. Her name was Candi Calvana Smith. "I apologize for doing that," I told her, and explained that everybody was watching me so I couldn't just go over to her and say hello. She laughed and said it was all right. We talked for a few minutes and then she had to go back to her seat.

I got off the plane first and went to the bathroom. When I came out she was standing nearby and I heard her humming to herself. Even in that noisy space I could tell she had a beautiful voice. When she began walking off, I caught up with her and asked her if she did a lot of singing. When she said she did, I said, "I have a record label." She rolled her eyes, and said, "You don't have to have a record company to talk to me," and I said, "I'm not kidding. I really do."

She was on her way to Miami to visit some friends, and I convinced her to come to the studio for an audition on her way back through Atlanta. Everyone in the studio was blown away by her singing. I had a chance to find out a little about her: She was born in the Cayman Islands, went to college in Wales and was now in nursing school in Arkansas. We started seeing each other, and she began visiting the studio occasionally to lay down some tracks with an eye toward cutting an album. The following summer I invited her to stay in my house in Atlanta so she could work on the album seriously and arranged for her to transfer to Emory to continue her studies.

One time when her guardians from the Cayman Islands came to

visit, they saw how well she got on with my kids, especially Evette, and thought she was working for me as a nanny. They told her—and me—that they didn't approve of this arrangement, and that it wasn't right that she was living in my house. I thought they were right, and said so, because if my daughter was in that situation, I'd think the same thing. So I said, "We should get married," and she said, "You mean, now?" That's exactly what I meant, and that's what we did. She was still wearing her nursing scrubs when we took our vows on her birthday, July 1, 2003.

We had Eli Ethan a year later and Eve Elizabeth a year after that, so Candi never did go to work as a nurse. But she's getting ready to go back into the studio so she can use the gifts that God gave her and finish off that album she started.

My next fight was against James Toney. Frankly, I never should have stepped into the ring. But I was over forty years old and didn't think I could afford to take the time to let my shoulders heal properly, so I ignored what my doctors and my body were telling me and went for it anyway. After James TKO'd me in the ninth, I still didn't wise up. My original contract with Don King had expired, but I signed another one because I thought he was in the best position to get me more fights. He set up a bout against Larry Donald, and I went the full twelve rounds, but it wasn't pretty. One of my shoulders was on fire and I essentially fought the guy with one hand. This time any decisions about further fights were taken out of my hands. After the judges awarded the fight to Larry, the New York State Boxing Commission lifted my license owing to "diminished skills and poor performance."

Although I wasn't happy about that, one good thing came out of it. My shoulders finally got the time they needed to heal completely. But even though I was getting healthier by the day and wanted to get my license back, Don King didn't seem interested in getting me another fight, and I had no other options because he wouldn't let me out of the contract. He figured I was washed up so what was the point of getting me a bout? I said, if I'm so washed up, why do you want me under contract? As time passed, the boxing world pretty much wrote me off and assumed my career was now only about *Dancing with the Stars*. It took a bit of tussling to get myself out of a deal that wasn't doing either Don or me any good, but eventually he let me go. This time, rather than find a new promoter, I decided to become one myself. I started Real Deal Events and the first fighter in my stable was me.

The title of this chapter is what we decided to call my comeback, "Holyfield V: The Final Chapter," the "V" referring to a fifth world title, "chapter" meaning just that, the last chapter in the book that was my career as a boxer.

As soon as I was free of Don, I applied to the state of Texas for a boxing license and they granted it. When I announced that I would fight again, you would have thought I was planning to jump off the Eiffel Tower without a parachute. Sportswriters started burning up the wires, and I'll tell you without exaggeration, I don't think there was one single story supporting my decision and they were all singing the same song: Holyfield is too old, too burned out and too weak to step into a ring. This fight never should have been allowed to happen. If he's too addled to know he should retire, somebody should make that decision for him, for his own good.

For his own good . . .

I don't care if people criticize my skills. I don't care if they predict I'm going to go down in the first round. I don't care if they say I'm a broken-down palooka who couldn't beat their grandmother. I don't mind any of that because none of it matters. The fight will speak for itself.

What I do mind is people trying to make decisions for me. I mind when people think I'm not capable of directing my own life, so they feel obligated to step in and do it for me, "for my own good." One writer even went so far as to say in his syndicated column that if you love Evander Holyfield as much he does, don't attend this fight, don't even watch it on television. His argument was that, if I got my brains beat in, I'd no longer be able to do the kinds of charitable work I'd been doing, and I owed it to the community not to take that chance. And if I was determined to fight anyway, then the community should line up and boycott me. You know . . . to show how much they love me.

He calls that love?

I appreciated the sentiment, but it seems to me that, if you're going to claim you love somebody, the least you can do is try to get all the facts before you start urging people to interfere with his life. Didn't any of these guys think it might be a good idea to talk to me first?

That's what bothered me so much about the New York State Boxing Commission's decision to yank my license. They felt that my skills had deteriorated so badly that I needed to be protected from myself. Maybe they thought my brain had rotted and I didn't have the judgment to recognize my awful condition. Or maybe they thought I did know it but I was just too stubborn or glory-hungry to quit. Both of those were reasonable assumptions. I understood that.

Except . . . I never got a chance to present another side, because they were so busy halting my career "for my own good," they never got around to talking to me before pulling my ticket. That's how you treat a six-year-old, not a grown man. If they'd only asked me, I could have told them that my shoulders were shot, that I was in agony. I fought Larry Donald with only one hand from the second round on. Of course I looked awful. I should have been wearing a sling, not boxing gloves.

In other words, they were looking at an injured fighter, not a brain-damaged relic. Now, I'm ready and willing to acknowledge that I shouldn't have gone into the Larry Donald fight. That was bad judgment, me thinking I could take on a top-ranked heavyweight contender with one hand, literally. My bad and I admit it. And you know what? I got pummeled and learned my lesson. 'Nuff said, right?

Wrong. I never got a chance to make that case. I might not have won the argument, but I should have been given the opportunity.

And now, here it was all over again, all these experts telling me I had no business going back into the ring. They didn't come to see me in training camp. They didn't talk to me about why I felt this was the right thing for me to do and why I thought I had a reasonable shot at a comeback. They just said I shouldn't fight, "for my own good," because they loved me so much.

Man, if that's what they call love, give me respect instead.

In December of 2004, Dale Gentry, a prophet from Fort Worth, Texas, predicted that I would make a major comeback. Given everything that was going on, it seemed pretty ridiculous on its face. I'd lost three fights in a row, my shoulders were a mess, I'd looked so bad in the ring that my license had been suspended indefinitely. . . . I'd been written off by the boxing world and Gentry's prediction made no sense to anybody.

Except me. I took it as a prophecy, because Gentry was only confirming what I believed the Holy Spirit had already made known to me. Sure enough, it turned out to be a blessing that my license had been lifted because my shoulders got a much-needed twenty-one-month rest while I negotiated my way out of the contract with Don King. They were completely healed and I could throw every punch in the book again. I was fit and healthy top to bottom, and while some of my skills had gotten a bit rusty from nonuse, a little time in the gym and they were coming right back. Sure, I was forty-three, and that's old for a fighter, but George Foreman became heavyweight champion of the world when he was forty-five and was still champ when he was forty-seven. Age is just a number; what counts is the shape you're in. I know twenty-five-year-olds who can't make it up a flight of stairs, but on the day Jack LaLanne turned seventy he swam a mile and a half pulling seventy boats behind him while handcuffed and shackled.

Needless to say, I was as motivated as I'd ever been. I trained like I would for a title bout, and when fight week rolled around, I felt like I could go fifteen rounds against anybody.

The first opponent in my comeback was Jeremy Bates, a tough, hard-hitting journeyman with a record of 21-11-1. Eighteen of those wins were by knockout, and he'd lost only one of his last fifteen fights before retiring the year before. What I found especially interesting was that his only loss in that run wasn't his last fight but his next-to-last. After losing by decision, he came back, won one more fight and *then* retired, going out a winner.

We held a press conference at the Texas Motor Speedway. The place was packed and we had a lot of fun. There was none of that snarly, mean-spirited psyche-out stuff. Jeremy told the reporters how he'd gotten inspired to get into boxing when he saw me fight at the 1984 Olympics. Since then I'd been his hero, so when he got the call to come and fight me, he was out of the office and into the gym in a heartbeat. This was his *Rocky* moment, a day in the sun like he'd never gotten during his years as a professional. He'd been training his brains out for eight solid weeks and was ready to rock.

I may have been Jeremy's hero, but that didn't mean he planned to show me any mercy. He knew there was only one way to demonstrate his respect for me, and that was to try as hard as he could to knock me into the bleachers. He was much shorter than me but outweighed me by ten pounds and was built like a safe. People kept sidling up to me at the press conference saying things like, "Uh, Evander? This guy looks like a grenade wouldn't even hurt him. You sure you know what you're doing?"

Yeah, I knew what I was doing. If I was going to announce my return, I had to do it by fighting someone who wouldn't be seen as a human punching bag but would give me a true test. That wasn't just for the fans or the press, either, or for my trainer Ronnie Shields and Tim Hallmark and the people who were giving me their backing, including the Fox Sports Network. I had to know myself. Sure, I was confident, but I wasn't naïve. As Mike Tyson once put it so well, "You don't know anything until that first punch comes your way."

A lot of the training I did for this fight was much the same as it would have been for any other fight, but Ronnie made some adjustments based on his analysis of both my abilities and the strengths and weaknesses of my opponent.

Ronnie had been one of my trainers in the early 1990s. When he and I got back together in 2004 before the Larry Donald fight, I wasn't the same boxer he'd trained twelve years before, because of my shoulders. Before the surgeries they hurt all the time, and I found myself doing a lot of things to protect them, like not moving my head the way I used to. To compensate I had to twist around in funny ways to avoid punches. That made my back hurt, which made it hard to bend my legs, and so on and so on. It was a ripple effect that gradually threw my whole body out of whack. There were a lot of times that I had to call off sparring in the middle of a session because it was doing more harm than good, and neither of us was very happy about it.

Even after I finally had surgery to correct the shoulder problems, the effects of all that time I'd spent fighting "around" the injured muscles lingered. I unconsciously expected stabs of pain that never came, and it took a surprisingly long time to get over that and learn to trust my body again. But eventually I started getting back on track, and the more I did, the better I felt and the faster I improved. By the time we got the Bates fight lined up, I felt terrific. Sparring sessions became productive again, because I was able to concentrate on practicing the strategy Ronnie had devised for the fight instead of worrying about whether my next punch would hurt me worse than it would my sparring partner.

Ronnie's take on Jeremy was that he was more a brawler, like Tyson, than a boxer, like me. He felt that if I were twenty-five years old again I might be able to go toe-to-toe but, at forty-three, if I tried to outmuscle Jeremy I'd be giving him too many opportunities to land the big haymaker and put me down. In any event, there was no reason to fight like that. My strength was always in boxing, not brawling, and now that my shoulders had healed, I had a lot of my agility and speed back. I was dancing and moving again, and I had plenty of conditioning to keep that up for a long time. Ronnie's plan for the bout was to make sure that I fought my own way and not get drawn into Jeremy's. At least in the beginning.

"We're gonna fight him at some point," Ronnie said. All trainers talk like that, saying *we*, just like golf caddies do. "Just not in the early rounds. Why do that if we don't have to?"

Ronnie was nothing if not honest. "Jeremy thinks you're done," he told me straight out. "He thinks you're over the hill. So he's gonna come out and try to put a lot of pressure on you, try to make you fight instead of box. He loves to go toe-to-toe, and he can do it all day, so that's the last thing we want to do."

Ronnie and I both respected Jeremy. He was strong and had all the fundamentals down pat, along with a lot of savvy and guts in the ring. He could take a punch, too.

"We're gonna spend the first three or four rounds boxing," Ronnie said. "Dancing, moving all around the ring, throwing lots of jabs, avoiding punches."

The idea was for me to fight in the style I was most comfortable with, from the outside, reaching in with the jab and staying away from his punches at the same time. I'd throw a lot of combinations, too, since those are one of my best assets. Not only would this allow me to get a lot of good shots in, it would also wear Jeremy down. There's nothing like being taken out of your style to tire a fighter out. If I could keep dancing and moving, flicking out good jabs and throwing effective combinations, relying more on finesse than muscle, Jeremy would have to do more moving than he was used to and spend a lot of energy and concentration trying to keep out of the way of my punches.

"Three, four rounds of that," Ronnie said, "then we go in there and fight him."

If everything went according to plan, by Round Five or so I'd still be fresh and Jeremy would have used himself up trying to respond to me. He'd be vulnerable enough—worn down and taken well out of his comfort zone—for me to move inside and start finding opportunities to throw big power punches. Ronnie figured I'd knock him out in the seventh or eighth.

A good deal of Ronnie's training plan in support of that strategy was to get me to establish my jab. He felt that I'd been standing up too straight and just fighting. He was right. Because of all of the effects from my bad shoulders, I'd gotten away from the style that had brought me so much success back when Ronnie was training me from 1988 to 1992. Part of that style also included counterpunching, which means answering an opponent's shot with two or three better ones of your own. If he throws a jab, you might come back immediately with a right, a hook, and an uppercut or a double jab. If he throws two jabs, you come back with three. It's "offense plus," not just answering, but answering better. One of the reasons counterpunching is so effective is that the other guy is usually a little off balance after his own punch, so he can't defend himself as well as he normally might. Of course, counterpunching isn't easy, because it comes on the tail end of defending yourself from one of *his* shots. It takes a lot of skill and practice, and Ronnie had me working hard on it.

Tim Hallmark loved the whole concept, because counterpunching demands tremendous balance and he considers balance a critical part of any athletic endeavor. If you watch a lot of different boxers, you'll see that the best ones are like the best golfers. No matter how big and powerful a swing a great golfer makes, he always stays "within the shot." But look at a lousy golfer and you'll often see him sway to one side and then practically fall over on his follow through, because he comes "out of the shot." It's the same with boxers. No matter how big a punch you throw and how much body you put into it, you want to stay balanced throughout. If you start to fall over at the end, you leave yourself wide open for a counterpunch. Tim had me doing a lot of plyometrics to improve that part of my game.

My sparring partner for this fight was a big, strong twenty-five-year-old named Adam Richards, from Murfreesboro, Tennessee. Nicknamed "Swamp Donkey," Adam wasn't some washed-up club fighter we were paying to get beaten up, but a talented, up-and-coming heavyweight with a budding career of his own. A few years back he'd badly fractured the top rib on his left side during his third pro fight and made the wise decision to let it fully heal before resuming his career. That's when he'd come to Ronnie to train him. Since then he'd racked up eleven more fights and was sitting on an enviable record of 14-1, with eleven of those wins coming by knockout. He was strong as a bull, worked like one, too, and talk about being motivated? Adam had a fight of his own coming up the week after mine, so he was in intense training mode himself and never gave me a moment's rest.

Best of all, he absorbed ring knowledge like a sponge. After every sparring session he and I debriefed in the gym. I'd give him a detailed critique of his performance, and absolutely nothing got past him. If I pointed out that my jabs were getting through his defenses, I knew that I could pretty much kiss those jabs good-bye from then on. He was getting the kind of boxing education you couldn't buy and he wasn't squandering any of it. The more we sparred, the better he got, so the better I had to be. He wasn't intimidated in the ring with me, either, like a lot of guys are. I told him from the very start, "Forget who I am. Just get in there and fight like you know how." Boy, did he ever. On the Saturday two weeks before the fight, Ronnie had us go six hard rounds, and that kid didn't let up for a second. In the fourth round he slammed me into the ropes and almost knocked me out of the ring. It was the best session I'd had in years, and I doubted that fighting against Bates could be any harder than mixing it up with Adam.

Sparring was fun again, too. It had become a burden for me, a painful necessity that I didn't at all enjoy. It was round after round of agony in my shoulders and my back, and the frustration of fighting in a style that wasn't comfortable. But since my shoulders had healed, and under Ronnie's expert guidance, sparring became less and less of a chore and more and more enjoyable. By the time I began working out with Adam, I was back to my old form and primed to be tested by a young, aggressive pro.

That Saturday session was the toughest one Ronnie had planned for me. It was a simulation of the fight strategy, with a lot of dancing and jabbing in the first four rounds, close-in punching in the fifth, and back outside in the sixth just to make sure I could switch styles at the drop of a hat in case I needed to make that adjustment. I took a lot of hard shots but I gave a lot, too.

When it was over, Ronnie shot me a sly smile as he took off my gloves and I knew exactly what he was thinking: *We are ready!*

We made the right choice in putting the fight on in Dallas. Everyone told us that it was a lousy fight market, but the whole city seemed delighted to have us there, and I was greeted warmly wherever I went. That helped, because the press got even more merciless as the event approached.

Down in the locker room before the fight, we went through our usual routine. One of the last things I do before heading upstairs is hit the hand pads, practicing punches and getting the timing down. It's not much different from a basketball player shooting baskets before a game. You don't want the first shots you throw in the ring to be the first ones you've thrown all day.

I felt wonderful, snapping my punches and really slamming those pads. Even Ronnie was working up a sweat. I was throwing one-two combinations—a jab followed by a straight right—and following it up with another right. Ronnie looked a little surprised at how hard I was hitting, and a few minutes later as we were walking out, he said, "Follow the plan: jab, jab, jab," like he'd been doing all along, then he stepped closer to me and added, "but if you hurt him with that right, don't hold back. Go for it." I had to smile. It was like a fighter pilot being told to go ahead and light the afterburners or a baserunner getting the sign to steal if he felt like it.

Stepping out into the arena, it was like old times. We were in the American Airlines Center, where the Dallas Mavericks play, and the place was packed and jumping. When I came out of the tunnel and headed for the ring, the crowd erupted in cheers and tingles ran up and down my spine. Seven former world boxing champions were there, including Roberto Duran, and they came into the ring to be introduced to the crowd. Deion Sanders took the mike for a few words, as did former NBA star John Sally, who was one of the on-air commentators for Fox, which was broadcasting the fight live. I'd always fought on pay-per-view, which is a huge source of revenue, but I wanted to do this one for free so I wouldn't have to commit to a multifight deal before demonstrating my drawing power. I figured that once I proved myself in this fight, we could strike much better deals than if I jumped early.

The ring was full of people and it took a while to get through all the pomp and ceremony, but eventually there came that lonely moment when only three people are left in the ring, the fighters and the ref. Ronnie and I had talked about the opening moments of the bout and how they were likely to go. Jeremy would probably assume that I was a creaky old man and come at me like a freight train, unleashing everything he had in hopes of an early knockout before I got a chance to get my feet under me. And that's exactly what he tried to do, storming immediately to the center of the ring and throwing a big shot.

I was ready for it, and easily stayed out of the way of his punches while getting in a lot of my own. I wasn't being cagey, feeling him out and staying back or any of that stuff. I kept my hands going all the time, deflecting and counterpunching everything he threw. I could see the surprise in his eyes at how much and how hard he was getting hit while landing hardly any solid punches himself. I was following the plan, too, setting everything up with jabs.

It had been nearly two years since I'd been in the ring, and I hadn't felt that good in a lot more than that. I had everything going and it was all working. Toward the end of the first round I backed Jeremy into the ropes and was machine-gunning so many hard shots he was totally unable to respond. While most guys would have gone down under that kind of all-out attack, Jeremy stayed on his feet and took it. Despite that incredible display of guts and durability, he wasn't really defending himself adequately, so I thought the ref was going to stop the fight. But with less than a second left Jeremy dodged a bullet. I'd just driven a right hook into the side of his head and he started falling over. I stepped forward, all set up for a knockout punch, but Jeremy was so off balance that, when he grabbed the ropes to stop his fall, his momentum bounced him sideways and away from me. Just as I started to go after him, the bell rang to end the round.

In the corner, Ronnie was ecstatic. He'd had every confidence in me, and camp had been going really well, but you just never know, especially with someone who hasn't been fighting. Now, though, any uncertainty he might have been keeping to himself was gone, and he tried to keep his enthusiasm in check so I would stay focused and not get carried away.

"He's hurt," Ronnie said as he splashed some water on my face and Tim wiped me down, "but he's not done, so don't take any chances running into his right hand. Stick with the game plan, use the jab, and when he gets close, throw combinations, use a lot of hands. *A lot of hands!* You're hitting him with the right any time you want, so if you see an opening, go for it. But set it up with the jab. Always the jab."

That's exactly what I did. Jeremy was looking a little worried, but he didn't slow down a bit. As he'd promised before the fight, he kept coming at me, backing me up. I think he knew that he was in trouble and that if he didn't make something happen pretty soon, he was finished. He got a lot more aggressive about halfway through the round, and with a minute to go he launched a huge right at my chin. I saw it coming and managed to get a glove up so that it didn't catch me flush, but it rocked me pretty good anyway. Still, even while my head was snapping to the right, I threw a hard left that got him off balance just enough to make him take an extra step and give me time to cover up against his follow-up left. That shot didn't hurt me, and even though I was now vulnerable to a right, he was too out of position to throw it. Instead, he had no choice but to clinch to stop me from coming at him before he could set back up. Later, Tim would tell me that the left I threw even as Jeremy's right was coming off my chin was when he knew for certain I was back.

The clinch let me regain my footing, and as soon as the ref broke us apart I started peppering Jeremy with jabs again and following up with combinations. He was tiring visibly now, but showed a ton of heart and courage. Jeremy is one of those guys who prides himself on always moving forward, never backing away, and he kept on coming at me with whatever he had left. But I was overwhelming him, and with about half a minute to go in the round I had him up against the ropes and was raining blows down on him so fast and so hard he wasn't able to hit back at all. He was just covering up and trying not to go down. My footing wasn't as firm as it could have been, and I would like to have shifted my position just a touch to get a little more balanced so I could hit even harder, but I didn't want to risk easing up for even a fraction of a second and giving him a chance to escape. So I just kept on swinging. The ref let it go on for a few more seconds to give Jeremy an opportunity to get himself off the ropes and out of harm's way. But when it became obvious that he could no longer defend himself, much less go back on the offensive, the ref dove in between us and waved his hand in the air: Fight over. I'd won by TKO at 2:56 into the second round.

Jeremy was so disoriented I'm not sure he knew right away what had just happened. He had this stunned look on his face as the ref continued to hold him against the ropes and the crowd got more and more delirious. But then he shook it off and went back to his corner as the ring filled with people.

My heart was soaring. All that work, all that bad press, all those doubters . . . it wasn't just that I'd won. It was that I felt so good. I had barely broken a sweat and wasn't even breathing hard. I'd just thrown more quality punches in two rounds than I'd thrown in my last two fights and I felt like I could go twelve more against a world champ.

Jeremy pulled himself back together in a hurry and came back to give me a hug and some nice words. He also charmed the crowd as we were interviewed in the ring. When Sean O'Grady asked him what he thought when he'd hit me with that right in the second round, he said, "I thought, oh my God! I just hit Evander Holyfield!" It got a big laugh and Jeremy was a great sport about the whole thing.

I threw on some clothes and went to sit down with the Fox Sports guys for a live interview. Chris Byrd had been reporting the fight along with John Sally and Chris Rose. Byrd had won a decision against me in 2002 and was now the seventh-ranked heavyweight in the world. He was also a keen observer of the sport and a well-spoken commentator. Apparently he'd said earlier on the air that he thought I should fight one or two more times before taking on a top-ten contender, because when Rose brought it up with me sitting there ("I'm not gonna put you on the spot, Chris, but your answer was . . . ?"), Byrd got really flustered. I didn't have a problem with what he said—it was a perfectly sensible opinion—but everybody was getting such a kick out of how rattled he was, I just gave him a dirty look while he stammered his way out of it. It got a good laugh.

Later, at the postfight press conference, there were a lot of questions about what was next for me. It had been my plan to use the press conference to announce that I'd be fighting Sinan Samil Sam in November. Sinan was ranked fifth in the world, and if I beat him, it would vault me right up into contention for a title shot, but it wasn't clear we could make a deal with him. So we dropped some hints and then left it at that for the time being. Instead, I took the opportunity to introduce my father and my kids. They were all there except Evander Jr., who was getting ready to go on a trip.

Over the next few days I got a lot of questions about my next move, but I still hadn't announced anything. It didn't look like the Sam fight was going to happen. Ronnie and I were going to be in Mississippi for the weekend to watch Adam Richards fight, and we had a lot of time to talk about who my next opponent should be.

The sportswriters had kind of surprised me. I thought sure they were going to say that Jeremy was a bum and my beating him didn't prove anything. There was some talk like that but, for the most part, a lot of positive things were said, especially by people who really understood boxing and had watched the fight carefully. Was it possible I'd reached some kind of turning point with the press?

Nope. When we couldn't make a deal with Sam we decided to set up a fight with Fres Oquendo of Puerto Rico. He was a lot more dangerous than Sam, and had won the WBO Latino heavyweight title earlier in the year. When we announced the fight, it was the same old story all over again, a call for me to hang up the gloves. I'd come back, won one more fight, could retire as a winner and call it a career, but no way, no how, should I climb into the ring with a 23-3 heavyweight eleven years my junior who had sixteen knockouts to his credit and had just won a title. And if I didn't have enough sense to see that for myself, then the boxing authorities should make the call and not let me fight.

You know . . . for my own good.

CHAPTER 20

———

It's How You End

Ilove winning; I love being the best. I love it when my hard work pays off.

But when it doesn't, I don't go off and sulk and think I'm less of a person for it. I'm disappointed, and I wonder what I could have done different, but then I just go work a little harder and try again, because you only really lose when you quit.

I'm not tied up in myself about being a boxer. It's not who I am . . . it's what I do. And if I can't do it anymore, I'll do something else. I've done plenty of things to get ready for that already.

That's one of the reasons why I find it hard to deal with people who wonder why I want to fight again. My last few fights before the latest comeback were tough, and I lost. People think that if I fight again, I'm going to lose, and then I'll hate myself for having tried when I could have gone out on top.

They don't get it. There's a reason why I want to fight again, but if I lose, I'm not going to go to pieces. Far from it. I've been the heavyweight champion of the world four times and I don't have anything left to prove in the ring to anybody, least of all myself. I *want* to fight again, and if I win, I won't think I'm any better than I was before, and if I lose, I won't think I'm any worse.

There's a difference between quitting and stopping. Quitting is what you do when you can't handle a setback and leave a goal unfulfilled. Stopping is what you do after you've passed the test and are ready to move on to something else, or when circumstances beyond your control make it impossible to continue.

A popular fighter on the back end of a career can always expect people to start calling for his retirement. Every interview eventually gets around to when you're going to quit. Lose a couple of fights and everyone thinks you don't belong in the game anymore.

That's nothing new. Since the modern era of boxing began in 1892, fans and the general public have always clamored for champion fighters to retire, because they don't want to see them get hurt.

Let's be honest. People really don't get all that upset when athletes get hurt. Football players break bones all the time, pitchers ruin their shoulders, hockey players get concussions, and even when a career is ended by injury, we just think it's part of the game. Sad, sure, but they knew what they were getting into and it was their choice. Few people say, "See what happened? You shouldn't have played."

But when it comes to boxing, it's a different story, because the general public isn't worried about broken legs or missing teeth. What scares them is brain damage. The term "punch drunk" came from the boxing world, and now there's even a formal medical name for it: pugilistic dementia. Like I said, there's nothing new about fans and writers trying to get guys out of the ring before it's too late.

What *is* new is the intensity, and there's no mystery about why. It used to be, "You're going to wind up punch drunk."

Now, it's, "You're going to wind up like Ali."

Muhammad Ali was the most popular athlete of the last half of the twentieth century. As Yogi Berra himself might have put it, even people who didn't like him liked him. You couldn't help it, no matter what your politics were. Ali was an endless source of entertainment: brash, creative, quick-witted, good-looking and a better showman than P. T. Barnum. And unlike a lot of modern celebrities who are famous just for being famous, Ali had the real goods. He was one of the best heavyweight fighters ever. Even people who don't know a boxing glove from a baseball glove have heard of the "Thrilla in Manila" and the "Rumble in the Jungle" and saw him light the Olympic flame at the Atlanta Games of 1996.

His immense popularity added to the tragedy of his physical downfall, because we all got to see it played out in the media over a period of years. That's the thing about being so famous: You can't just switch it off when things turn sour. We watched as he began to shuffle, listened as his speech began to slur. The worse off he got, the more love we felt for him, and that made us even sadder as he continued to decline. We were still there watching when it got to the point where he could hardly walk or speak at all.

There were a lot of calls to ban the sport of boxing altogether, but those efforts were doomed from the start. There are several reasons, but most of them boil down to money. There's just too much of it to be made. That's why we'll never get rid of football, either, even though it's wildly violent and players get seriously injured all the time.

While efforts to ban boxing failed, it didn't stop people from trying to get boxers to quit. "You'll wind up like Ali," goes the standard song, and it's sung by a lot of well-meaning people. But one thing about well-meaning people is that they often don't stop to think before they try to influence events.

Life is about balance and trade-offs. For example, it's not hard to figure out how to prevent airline hijackings. Just don't let anybody on board, ever. That's ridiculous, so what we try to do is find some balance, a place in the middle. We figure out how to let people fly from here to there by balancing security against inconvenience. We don't always get it right, so we make adjustments, and we don't expect guarantees.

It's like that with boxing. One thing we can do is ban it altogether, and that would solve all the health problems. I don't think we should do that, because it's unfair to rob fighters and fans of a sport they love unless we also ban rodeo riding, parachute jumping and football, all of which are far more dangerous than boxing. On the other hand, we also don't want to go back to the old days, when two guys climbed into the ring with bare fists, few rules and no clock. The right way to do it is somewhere in the middle, with padded gloves, a thick book of rules and a skilled referee supervising the action.

"But what if they wind up like Ali?" you might ask.

To which I answer: That's their business. As long as a fighter has his wits about him and can pass the medical exams, he should be allowed to fight as long as he wants to. And I think other people, especially sports-writers with large followings, should be careful before starting campaigns to pressure someone into quitting.

A lot of people do a lot of things a lot dumber than boxing. They smoke cigarettes, they eat junk food until they blow up like blimps or become diabetic, they drink themselves into a stupor day after day. All of those things will kill you, and they're all legal. So if we really want to improve some lives, we should ban cigarettes, junk food and alcohol, which hundreds of millions of people abuse, before worrying about something like boxing, which has only a few thousand participants.

People have been telling me to retire almost since the day I won my first title. They say things like, "You already have plenty of money, so what's the point?" Or, "You're the world champion, so what more do you want?"

Those things are reflections of their own personal priorities, and they assume that mine must be the same. It's amazing how many people give me advice without first bothering to find out what's important to me. It's like me insisting that you drive this little tiny car because it gets forty miles to the gallon without bothering to find out that you've got six kids and two dogs. Maybe having a bunch of money is all some people need to feel they've had a great career. Maybe it sounds to some others like grabbing a world title is all any athlete could hope for. Or maybe they think that a professional fighter's life is all about trying to get a little something and then getting out before he gets hurt.

None of those things applies to me. It's not about the money or how many championships I've already won or what records I've set. My career goal from the very beginning was to retire as the undisputed heavyweight champion of the world. Mama told me over and over, you can't choose how you start, but you can choose how you finish. I've already chosen how I want to finish, and it's not something I made up last week. My mama didn't like the idea of me boxing, but what she didn't like even more was the idea of quitting. She had a lot of common sense and knew that there were times when you *had* to quit, because to do otherwise wouldn't make any sense, like the time I retired when I thought I had a bad heart. But she knew an excuse when she saw one and wouldn't tolerate it. She made me march right back and fight eleven-year-old Cecil Collins again and again until I finally beat him. Now it's my decision to retire as undisputed champion of the world and I'm still not looking for excuses. That's not the way I was brought up.

I've come close a few times. I was the undisputed champ at one point, but I'd only turned twenty-eight a few days before that and hadn't even reached my prime yet, so I kept fighting. I held on to that title for two years before losing it, then thought I had it again the following year when I beat Riddick Bowe, but by a crazy turn of events he had only two of the three belts. I won world titles two more times after that but never all three at the same time again. So as far as I'm concerned, I haven't yet finished what I started.

I should also mention something else, in case it isn't obvious by now. I love boxing. I love the training, the conditioning, the characters who populate the sport, and most of all I love the competition. "Yeah, but you might get hurt." Of course I might get hurt... it's *fighting*, not bowling. But as long as all my faculties are intact and I pass all the required medical tests, how much risk to take versus what personal satisfaction might be gained is my business.

Incidentally, everybody assumes that it was Ali's time in the ring that caused the Parkinson's he's suffering from now. It seems so obvious. But people get Parkinson's all the time. Thousands suffer from it and very few of them were prizefighters. And there are an awful lot of ex-fighters around who don't have Parkinson's. The simple fact is, nobody knows what brought on Ali's illness, including his doctors.

But even if it was fighting, you know what? That was his business. Just like smoking cigarettes, eating too much, getting drunk every day or bungee jumping are somebody else's.

I wonder sometimes why people think they know better than I do what's best for me. The Bible says I should love myself, and I do. I've always taken care of my body. I eat healthy, hardly ever drink any alcohol, I've never smoked or done illegal drugs or touched a steroid, and I stay fit with the help of a professional conditioning trainer. So why is it that so many people are ready to jump to the conclusion that I'm thoughtlessly risking serious injury or dementia by continuing to fight? Do they think I'm so obsessed or desperate or just plain crazy that I would throw a lifetime of healthy living down the drain?

I'm not obsessed. Having goals and working hard to fulfill them doesn't mean you're obsessive. And if I don't regain the world title it doesn't mean that I'm going to get depressed and slit my wrists. If it doesn't happen, it doesn't happen, and I'll find peace with that. But I won't find peace if I don't at least try while I'm able.

I'm not desperate, either. A lot of athletes who start out poor and suddenly find themselves wealthy think they're set for life but end up destitute because of bad financial management. I took great pains to protect my assets from the very beginning, and my family is well provided for even if I never make another nickel. I've got several thriving businesses going, including boxing promotion. I handle my own fights now and I'm starting to do it for other boxers as well.

Maybe I'm crazy for trying a comeback. It's a possibility, but I don't think so. I'm pretty sure I'll know when it's time to hang it up, which will happen when I feel I can no longer be competitive in the ring. I may have made a real mistake by not disclosing the injuries I had during my dismal fights in 2004. I didn't want to talk about my torn-up shoulders because it would have sounded like I was making excuses and it would have been disrespectful to the guys who beat me. I chose to fight hurt, they beat me fair and square, and they deserved to have the full benefit of their victories. My injuries weren't their responsibility.

Problem was, everybody thought that I was over the hill after those fights, my skills and power and speed all gone. I even lost my license because I looked so bad in the ring.

Then I had two shoulder surgeries and a lot of rest. I wanted to get back in line but the rest of the world wanted me to retire because they thought I was too old and too shot. I tried to explain that I wasn't old for real, I'd just been hurt, but nobody wanted to hear it. Or else they thought I was making it up so they'd let me fight again. Maybe they figured I was already too punch drunk to make rational decisions, so somebody else had to make them for me.

That's not fair. I surrounded myself with experts to be by my side as I trained, to observe me and test me and let me know if I was kidding myself about attempting a comeback. These are longtime friends who would lock me in a closet if they thought I was making a mistake or being reckless. They all started out skeptical but after watching me work, they decided that I still had what it takes to be a competitive fighter. I arranged a test fight against Jeremy Bates to show the boxing world that I deserved a comeback opportunity. All my skills were on display and I knocked him out. Even then, the editorials and the campaigns for me to retire didn't stop. No matter how rational I was and how good I looked in the ring and how many respected experts I had checking me out, sportswriters were still telling the world I was deluded and needed to be protected from myself.

For my own good. Because they loved me so much.

I've spent my entire career proving the critics wrong. They said I was too small to be a heavyweight, and I won the world championship four times. They said I couldn't go the distance, and I won my first world title in fifteen rounds of one of the most grueling matches ever fought, then did the same against the likes of George Foreman, Larry Holmes and Riddick Bowe. They said Mike Tyson was going to kill me, and I beat him twice. They said if I fought Bowe a second time, he'd put me in the hospital, but I beat him, too.

After a life of experiences like that, is it any wonder that I have this tendency to follow my own heart?

I've got the right to pursue my goal and I know what I'm doing. It's possible I might get hurt along the way, but that's always been a possibility, and you know what? That's my business. I've had a pretty good life minding it my own way. I've had a great life following my faith and my instincts, and that's what I plan to continue doing while I'm still in the process of "becoming Holyfield."

Evander Holyfield

Professional Fight Record as of March 17, 2007

WINS: 41 (27 BY KNOCKOUT)

LOSSES: 8

DRAWS: 2

KEY

KO X	WON BY KNOCKOUT IN ROUND X	L X	LOST BY DECISION IN X ROUNDS
KO'D	LOST BY KNOCKOUT IN ROUND X	D X	DRAW AFTER X ROUNDS
TKO X	WON BY TECHNICAL KO IN ROUND X	WDQ X	WINNER BY DISQUAL. IN ROUND X
TKO'D X	LOST BY TECHNICAL KO IN ROUND X	(X)	WON WORLD TITLE FOR XTH TIME
W X	WON BY DECISION IN X ROUNDS		

LIGHT HEAVYWEIGHT

1984

NOV 15	LIONEL BYARM	W 6	MAD. SQ. GDN.

1985

JAN 20	ERIC WINBUSH	W 6	ATLANTIC CITY
MAR 13	FRED BROWN	KO 1	NORFOLK
APR 20	MARK RIVERA	KO 2	CORPUS CHRISTI

CRUISERWEIGHT

JUL 20	TYRONE BOOZE	W 8	NORFOLK
AUG 29	RICK MYERS	KO 1	ATLANTA
OCT 30	JEFF MEACHEM	KO 5	ATLANTIC CITY
DEC 21	ANTHONY DAVIS	KO 4	VIRGINIA BEACH

APPENDIX

1986

MAR 1	CHISANDA MUTTI	KO 3	LANCASTER	
APR 6	JESSE SHELBY	KO 3	CORPUS CHRISTI	
MAY 28	TERRY MIMS	KO 5	METAIRIE, LA	
JUL 12	MUHAMMAD QAWI (I)	W 15	ATLANTA	WON WBA
DEC 8	MIKE BROTHERS	KO 3	PARIS, FRANCE	

1987

FEB 14	HENRY TILLMAN	KO 7	RENO	RETAINED WBA
MAY 15	RICKY PARKER	KO 3	LAS VEGAS	WON IBF
AUG 15	OSSIE OCASIO	KO 11	ST. TROPEZ	RETAINED IBF AND WBA
DEC 5	MUHAMMAD QAWI (II)	KO 4	ATLANTIC CITY	RETAINED IBF AND WBA

1988

APR 9	CARLOS DE LEON	KO 8	LAS VEGAS	WON WBC

—Undisputed world cruiserweight champion—

HEAVYWEIGHT

JUL 16	JAMES TILLIS	KO 5	LAKE TAHOE
DEC 9	PINKLON THOMAS	KO 7	ATLANTIC CITY

1989

MAR 11	MICHAEL DOKES	KO 10	LAS VEGAS
AUG 15	ADILSON RODRIGUES	KO 2	LAKE TAHOE
NOV 4	ALEX STEWART	KO 8	ATLANTIC CITY

1990

JUN 1	SEAMUS MCDONAGH	KO 4	ATLANTIC CITY	
OCT 25	BUSTER DOUGLAS	KO 3	LAS VEGAS	WON IBF, WBC, WBA (1)

—Undisputed world heavyweight champion—

1991

APR 19	GEORGE FOREMAN	W 12	ATLANTIC CITY
NOV 23	BERT COOPER	TKO 7	ATLANTA

1992

JUN 19	LARRY HOLMES	W 12	LAS VEGAS	
NOV 13	RIDDICK BOWE (I)	L 12	LAS VEGAS	LOST IBF, WBC, WBA

APPENDIX

1993

| JUN 26 | ALEX STEWART | W 12 | ATLANTIC CITY | |
| NOV 6 | RIDDICK BOWE (II) | W 12 | LAS VEGAS | WON WBA AND IBF (2) |

1994

| APR 22 | MICHAEL MOORER (I) | L 12 | LAS VEGAS | LOST WBA AND IBF |

1995

| MAY 20 | RAY MERCER | W 10 | ATLANTIC CITY | |
| NOV 4 | RIDDICK BOWE (III) | TKO'D 8 | LAS VEGAS | |

1996

| MAY 10 | BOBBY CZYZ | TKO 6 | MAD. SQ. GDN. | |
| NOV 9 | MIKE TYSON (I) | TKO 11 | LAS VEGAS | WON WBA (3) |

1997

| JUN 28 | MIKE TYSON (II) | WDQ 3 | LAS VEGAS | RETAINED WBA |
| NOV 8 | MICHAEL MOORER (II) | KO 8 | LAS VEGAS | WON IBF |

1998

| SEP 19 | VAUGHN BEAN | W 12 | ATLANTA | RETAINED WBA AND IBF |

1999

| MAR 13 | LENNOX LEWIS (I) | D 12 | MAD. SQ. GDN. | FOR WBC |
| NOV 13 | LENNOX LEWIS (II) | L 12 | LAS VEGAS | LOST WBA AND IBF |

2000

| AUG 12 | JOHN RUIZ (I) | W 12 | LAS VEGAS | WON WBA (4) |

2001

| MAR 3 | JOHN RUIZ (II) | L 12 | LAS VEGAS | LOST WBA TITLE |
| DEC 15 | JOHN RUIZ (III) | D 12 | LEDYARD, CT | FOR WBA TITLE |

2002

| JUN 1 | HASIM RAHMAN | TKO 8 | ATLANTIC CITY | |
| DEC 14 | CHRIS BYRD | L 12 | ATLANTIC CITY | |

2003

| OCT 4 | JAMES TONEY | TKO'D 9 | LAS VEGAS | |

272

APPENDIX

2004

| NOV 13 | LARRY DONALD | L 12 | MAD. SQ. GDN. |

2006

| AUG 18 | JEREMY BATES | TKO 2 | DALLAS |
| NOV 10 | FRES OQUENDO | W 12 | SAN ANTONIO |

2007

| MAR 17 | VINNIE MADDALONE | TKO 3 | CORPUS CHRISTI |

Acknowledgments

We are indebted to many people for their invaluable assistance, including Teddy Atlas, David Brenner, Bo and Buddy Davis, Tom Casino, Rick Dressler, Jim Fox, Dale Gentry, Dr. David S. Greenfield, Cherie Gruenfeld, Tim Hallmark, Graham Higgins, Eloise Holyfield, Candi Holyfield, Bernard Holyfield, Laurie Liss, Ronnie Shields, Lisa Smith-Putnam, Adam "Swamp Donkey" Richards, Neal Tabachnik, and Mike Weaver. Sincere apologies to those we might have inadvertently omitted.